Lucy de Bruyn

Woman and the Devil in sixteenth-century literature

A Bear Book

To my Mother
with happy memories

© Lucy de Bruyn 1979
This Bear Book has been designed, printed and published by
The Compton Press Ltd, The Old Brewery, Tisbury, Wiltshire
ISBN 0 900193 72 7

Contents

vi

Acknowledgements

My grateful thanks in the preparation of this book are due to the following:
Prof Geoffrey Bullough, Prof G. M. Meredith Owens, Janet Kalvin, Dr David Rogers, Dr D. E. Rhodes, Dr Norman Tanner, Pamela Baker, Luke Verhees, the Rev Prof J. M. Redford, Dr L. Velthuis, and Margaret Garman.
London University Library has kindly provided some of the illustrations.

LUCY DE BRUYN

Kew, Surrey
May 1979

Author's Notes and Abbreviations

All Shakespeare texts quoted are from *A New Variorum* edition except where *First Folio* is referred to. For the convenience of the reader, references to Peter Alexander's edition have been added in parentheses in each case.

With regard to other authors, I have generally quoted from sixteenth-century texts. Reference to some later editions of these have been added to footnotes where appropriate and these editions are listed in the BIBLIOGRAPHY. When citing foreign works, page and line references are given in English.

The transcript shows certain peculiarities and inconsistences in spelling and punctuation common to the age.

DNB	*Dictionary of National Biography*
EETS	Early English Text Society
MLN	*Modern Language Notes*
MDR	*Modern Language Review*
MP	*Modern Philology*
PL	*Patrologiae cursus completus series Latina*, ed. J. P. Migne
PMLA	*Publications of the Modern Language Association of America*
PQ	*Philological Quarterly*
RES	*Review of English Studies*
SP	*Studies in Philology*
SPDS	*State Papers Domestic Series*
STC	*Short-Title Catalogue*, ed. Pollard and Redgrave
STS	Scottish Text Society
YAS	York Archaeological Society
e.s.	extra series
n.s.	new series
o.s.	original series

Introduction

Sur les femmes pourrait dire tout ce
qu'on voudra; tout sera également vrai[1]

There was perhaps no other period in English literature which presented so many different aspects of womanhood as the sixteenth century. Never was woman praised more highly or so bitterly abused. The same literature also displayed an extraordinarily rich variety of devils. They were of mixed stock; Jewish, Christian, heathen, monstrous; elfin and spectral elements in them mingled with human villainy, foreign hostility and Machiavellian deceit. The century itself, manifesting all the qualities of a great transitional era, was of a no less complex nature than either Woman or the Devil. Although the old traditional beliefs were shaken, yet religion remained one of the elemental forces in human life. The 'Ego sum alpha et O', so familiar in the mystery plays, was by no means dead, neither was the people's love for the Virgin Mary and the Saints. Trust in the heavenly forces and fear of the evil ones intermingled, whilst aspiration to holiness vied with a strong attraction to what the bartering fiend had to offer. Worldly progress and the new learning lay at the Devil's disposal, in full measure, and the *nouvelle richesse* of the Renaissance made 'the apple' look more tempting than ever. As of old, woman was seen to play an important part in the Devil's transactions either by assisting or by thwarting his plans. As a result, a great deal of man's happiness, or misery, depended upon this mediator.

Amid the vast mass of literature enveloping this peculiar relationship between Woman and the Devil, two works in particular stand out as representing the spirit and ideas of the age. In them are concentrated a mass of material which we meet elsewhere in a more dilute form. They are the anonymous *Mariken van Nieumeghen*[2] which depicts the Virgin Mary as the highest embodiment of the contemporary ideal of womanhood, routing the Devil and saving the human race; and Marlowe's *Dr Faustus* with Helena, the woman in league with the Devil, working for man's damnation. Between these extremes stretches woman's range of influence. It was after witnessing these plays, the one in the Market Square at Nijmegen, the other, soon after, in the Oxford Playhouse, that I decided to investigate the matter further which resulted in writing this book.

The sixteenth century tried to explain the forces of evil in terms of a personal Devil, and this Devil in collusion with human beings who act as his agents willingly or unwillingly. The twentieth century apparently has

---

[1] Jules Lemaître; quoted in *De Vrouw*, F. J. J. Buitendijk (Utrecht-Antwerpen, 1951), p. 55.

[2] *cf.* notes on p. 4.

strayed a long way from this world view. Today we tend to explain the presence of evil in terms of economic, political and other impersonal powers. Yet it could also be argued that we are faced with a growing interest in the occult so apparent in film, drama and other literature. Is this because, in spite of our 'scientific modernity', in fact deep down we wonder if this world is in reality a conflict on the ultimate level of person and spirit?

As in sixteenth-century literature, the role of woman has become a much debated subject. It will be discussed here in its various aspects. Starting with the Virgin and the Good Woman, we shall eventually meet the Wanton, the Witch and the Shrew.

In the Christian tradition the Virgin, and after her the good woman, save man from the Devil's clutches. In chivalric literature the woman inspires her knight to conquer the Dragon. In the quasi-romantic tradition it is woman who breaks the spell of the Fairy and emerges victorious from contact with the dark powers of a pagan past. Although the Virgin Mary herself was suppressed in post-reformation literature, her qualities were attributed to the reigning queens and to their literary counterparts as well as to other dramatic heroines. The gradual secularisation, characteristic of this age of transition, is reflected in the literary presentation of both the Woman and the Devil.

The Good Woman proving too strong for the Devil, the latter turns to the weaker members of the sex with whom he establishes various relations. He wins the Wanton through the new luxuries and freedom of the sixteenth century and uses her to lure man to his fall. He enters into a close physical relationship with the Witch from which she draws her much feared powers. But he cannot cope with the sharp tongue and waspish disposition of the Shrew. In short – he played with the Wanton, he lay with the Witch, and he humoured the Shrew. In all cases woman was rewarded with power either to seduce, revenge, or have her own will. But in bartering the strength of true womanhood, she became the menial of a devilish spirit, a caricature disappointing man's expectations.

Man's ideal of the female sex was that of a creature 'Faire, kinde and true',[3] an ideal fully realized in the Good Woman. It was, however, refuted in the Wanton who proved false to her own nature; in the Witch whose blear-eyed and wrinkled appearance, obscure habits and revengeful attitude of mind, could hardly be named fair; and in the Shrew whose hostile and envious disposition lacked all kindness.

[3] Shakespeare, *Sonnets*, 105.

1

Mary of Nemmegen and Doctor Faustus

1 *The bartering fiend*

1   Mary of Nemmegen and Doctor Faustus

nam mulier damnauit,
& mulier saluauit[1]

Mary of Nemmegen written at the beginning of the century, and Marlowe's
Doctor Faustus towards the end, embrace ideas as widely apart as Catholicism and Lutheranism; extreme worldliness and profound spirituality; traditional medievalism and renaissance secularism. Both masculine and
feminine instincts of humanity are here represented. Moreover, nowhere
perhaps in sixteenth-century literature has *das Ewig-Weibliche* as well as
the Demon's infernal quality been portrayed more forcibly, beautifully and
terribly than in these two works. The main reason for their success may be
attributed to the authors' strong belief both in Woman and in the Devil.
Furthermore, various aspects of womanhood which are more fully dealt
with in the following chapters, are here introduced, as are also a variety of
devils of different rank and standing including an important functionary,
Masscheroen, the Advocate of Lucifer.

It was, undoubtedly, a revolutionary period. For the last hundred years

forces had been at work which, with much else, tended to uproot, or at least
re-orient many of the intellectual signposts of the Middle Ages. There was the
break with traditional ways of thinking; the renewed interest in secular learning; the establishment of the northern universities; the rise of individualism; a
general widening of the horizon. But the older Church and the new Protestant
group both viewed this development with consternation and something resem-
bling fear.[2]

The new learning, however, had not succeeded in abolishing the occult art
of necromancy which had now begun to take a powerful position side by
side with the so-called liberal sciences. The 'widening of the horizon' had
taken people's minds further away from heaven, but not from the underworld, and the general decline in religious fervour and stability gave rise to
greater fear and superstition which, at times, took on alarming proportions.
It was a disease difficult to combat. Religious and temporal authorities had
openly declared war against 'Witchcraft', but by doing so had only streng-
thened the belief in a possible compact with the Devil. In 1484 Innocent
VIII had published the bull *Summis Desiderantes affectibus* by which wes-

---

[1] Bartolus de Saxoferrato, *Tractatus Quaestionis*; in *Opera omnia* (Basileae, v libri,
1588-89), v, 349, col. i, l. 8.
[2] P. Mason Palmer and R. Pattison-More, *The Sources of the Faust Tradition* (New
York, OUP, 1936), p. 4.

tern Europe was declared to be teeming with devils, witches and sorcerers. The *Malleorum Quorundam Maleficarum* by Jacob Sprenger and Hendrik Kramer followed in 1487. Thus it was that at the beginning of the sixteenth century people's interest was focused on the subject.

MARY OF NEMMEGEN

About this time there appeared from the press of Jan van Doesborch at Antwerp

a lyttel story that was of a trwethe done in the lande of Gelders of a mayde that was named Mary of Nēmegen y^t was the dyuels paramoure by the space of .vij.yere longe.[3]

The story tells us how Mary, when shopping at Nijmegen, is overtaken by darkness and seeks hospitality with her aunt. The aunt is in a bad humour, refusing to let her in, and pouring one accusation after the other upon Mary's innocent head. In despair and loaded with her heavy shopping, Mary cries out

nowe care I nat whether that I kyll my selfe or whether that I goo to drowne me and I care nat whether ye dyuell or god come to me and helpe me I kare nat whether of them two itbe.[4]

[3] *Mary of Nēmegen* (Antwerp, J. van Doesborch, c. 1518); facs. edn. H. Morgan Ayres and A. J. Barnouw, *Mary of Nimmegen* (Harvard, 1932), A. i. [hereafter referred to as *Mary of Nemmegen*]

G. W. Wolthuis, *Duivelskunsten en Sprookjesgestalten* (Amsterdam, 1952), pp. 55 and 86. 'In 1920 the famous Christie-Miller collection was put up for auction and the unique copy of *Mary of Nemmegen* passed into the hands of the firm of Quaritch, who quoted it in their catalogue No. 369 at £900. In 1924 it passed into the possession of the Henry E. Huntington Library, San Marino, California (p. 55). The writer is unknown, but there is a marginal note in the *Quaritch Catalogue*, no. 384, April 1924, Lot no. 682, which mentions: "Laurence Andrewe . . . who is known to have worked in . . . [that] capacity for J. van Doesborch." ' (p. 86)

The year of van Doesborch's publication, a Dutch dramatic version was printed, *Marikē van nieumeghen* (Antwerpen, Willem Vorsterman, c. 1518); facs. edn. A. L. Verhofstede (Antwerpen, 1951). [hereafter referred to as *Mariken van Nieumeghen*] The original edition is at the Bayerische Staatsbibliothek at Munich. The editor (p. xxxv) refers to the opinions of P. Leendertz, Jr and J. van Mierlo regarding an older version of c. 1500, from which both the English and the Dutch may have taken their inspiration.

Which of these two, the Dutch or English version, can claim priority is a point of controversy which has been discussed at length by Miss M. E. Kronenberg, 'Het mirakel-spel van Mariken van Nieumeghen en het Engelsche volksboek', *De Nieuwe Taalgids*, xxiii (Groningen, 1929), pp. 24-43; and Professor A. J. Barnouw, 'Mary of Nimmegen', *The Germanic Review*, vi. (Columbia Univ., 1931), pp. 69-84.

One point of internal evidence at least makes me side with Prof. Barnouw in favour of the Dutch text: the inset play of Masscheroen, *inf.* p. 7, which is obviously the climax of the story and is barely touched upon in the English version.

Although the authorship of *Mariken van Nieumeghen* has not been established, J. van Mierlo provides some convincing evidence in favour of Anna Bijns, particularly so in *Anna Bijns en Mariken van Nieumeghen* in *Sprokkelingen op het gebied der Mnl. poëzie*, 2^e reeks, Gent, N. V. Drukkerij Erasmus, 1950 [Koninklijke Vlaamse Academie voor Taal en Letterkunde].

[4] *Mary of Nemmegen*, A. iii^v.

4

The Devil, in the guise of a young man, offers his services, introducing himself as 'a master of many scyances', and promises 'if that ye wyll be my paramoure I shall teche to you all the forsayde scyances'. He promises to give her gold and pleasures, and love her above all women. All he asks in return is that Mary will give up her name;

for by one mary I & all my felashyp fare the worse . . . Thā sayd Mary to kepe your coūsayll I am content but for to chaunge my name I wyll neuer whyle I lyue for maria is all my cumforde and helpe in all my nede[5]

They compromise; she is allowed to keep the first letter of her name and is henceforth called 'Emmekyn'. Together they visit 'Shertegebossche' and 'Antwarpe'[6] where they put up at 'yᵉ Gylde Tre'. Here Emmekyn displays her newly acquired knowledge by which she draws admiration from all the visitors. Soon they are jealously striving with each other for her favour. Murders are committed daily on her account. Yet Emmekyn, despite all dissipations, never quite loses sight of eternity. After seven years she grows tired of life at Antwerp; at her insistence they take their leave and travel to Nijmegen[7] arriving on the day of Our Lady's procession when it was customary to perform pageants in her honour.

than sayd Emmekyn to yᵉ dyuell what do all yender folkes yᵗ be yender gathered than sayde the dyuell the play a play yᵗ is wont euery yere to be played/ than sayde Emmekyn good loue let vs goo here it for I haue harde my vnkyll

[5] *Ibid.*, A. v ʳ⁻ᵛ.
[6] Big cities were often referred to by moralists as the seats of Satan.
Adam's wife, in T. Lodge and R. Greene, *A looking glasse for London and England* (1594); in *The Plays and Poems of R. Greene*, ed. J. Churton Collins, vol. i, IV, iv, 1594-5, has obviously taken it to heart. 'Oh but, Adam, I am afraid to walke so late because of the spirits that appeare in the Cittie.'
Cf. also T. Nashe, *Pierce Penilesse* (1592); *Works* ed. R. B. McKerrow, i, 161, l. 28, where Hell itself is described as 'a huge Cittie'.
[7] In the Dutch version *Mariken van Nieumeghen*, D. iii., the Devil (named Moenen) allows Mariken to settle the account at the inn and tip generously, which shows her to be a fully emancipated woman.

EMMEKEN	Ick gae bescheet halen
	Weten watter noch achter staet
	int briefken
	Ende al betalen
MOENEN	So doet mijn liefken
	Betaelt vri opelijc en siet op een
	oneffen mite niet

The emancipation of Dutch women attracted the attention of foreigners.
Albrecht Dürers Niederländische Reise von J. Veth und S. Muller (Berlin und Utrecht, 1918) Band ii, p. 31, mentions the freedom women at Antwerp enjoyed and that much of their time was spent in dancing, singing, the playing of musical instruments, in addition to their complete management of domestic affairs without their husbands' control. 'Schon 1506 hatte der venetianische Gesandte Quirini von den niederländischen Frauen geschrieben: "Le donne hanno costumi tutti allegri, ed il tempo, che lor sopravvanza, tutto lo spendono dopo sue faccende in balli, canti, suoni, ne altro fanno che darsi a piacere; governano poi le case e tutte le faccende familiari senza cura del marito." '

say often tymes that a play were better than a sermant to some folke/ ... than went Emmekyn and harde the playe and the playe was of synfull lyuynge and there she sawe hyr lyuyng played before hyr face than she began to be sory and take repentance/[8]

The Devil, seeing that all is lost, carries her high up in the air and casts her down hoping to break her neck, but God would not allow it and she falls in the street in sight of all the people, among them her uncle the priest to whom she confesses her sin. The old man counsels her that 'there is no body loste without the fall in despayer'.[9] To obtain absolution for such a grievous sin, she goes to the Pope himself who gives her a heavy penance.

2 *The most terrible medieval fury*

She is to wear three iron rings round her neck and arms. After two years the rings miraculously fall away, a positive sign of God's forgiveness.

Mary of Nemmegen is not a traditional morality merely composed of ideas and abstractions. It is a story of living beings taken from contemporary daily life. There is no apparently pre-conceived plot and its natural sequence of events grows out of the psychology of the characters. These are excellently portrayed, particularly in the Dutch dramatic version, *Mariken van Nieumeghen*; Satan the gentleman-seducer plays upon Mary's femi-

[8] *Mary of Nemmegen*, B. v[v]. Cf. *inf.* p. 8. In the Dutch version this is the inset play of Masscheroen.
[9] *Ibid.,* C. i[v].

6

nine weakness and vanity flattering her in every way,[10] but once his case is lost, he turns into the most terrible medieval fury imaginable. The aunt is a typical village shrew, without any self-control. Soon after Mary's departure, in a fit of temper and instigated by the Devil, she cuts her own throat. Since she had been the cause of Mary's despair, it was necessary for the writer to emphasize her wickedness. For all his saintliness, the learned uncle could not resist dabbling in the forbidden art of necromancy, which makes him very human. But especially Mary herself, guided more by feelings than by intelligence, has been depicted throughout the story with the utmost care for detail. She appears to be boastful yet shy. Under a show of self-confidence need of help is often apparent. Lighthearted but with a deeply religious core, she is sympathetic and affectionate; a determined and attractive personality.

THE INSET PLAY OF MASSCHEROEN

Woman Defeats the Devil

For the climax of the story we have to follow the Dutch dramatic version where the inset play of Masscheroen is fully developed. This is a fraction of the medieval pageant of Masscheroen[11] which was frequently produced at Antwerp and other cities, and forms a link in the long chain of the traditional mercy-justice theme, the contest between the Devil's procurator and the Virgin Mary, as it is portrayed in the various medieval versions of the *Processus Sathane.*[12] Under the pretence of a plea for justice, the Devil's advocate, named Masscheroen, demands of God that the sinfulness of Mankind may be judged by the same measure as that of the Fallen Angels. With great noise and ostentation he appears before the judgement seat.

> Bre hierioh masscheroen advocaet van luciferre
> Wilgaen appelleren mijn ghedinghe
> Teghen den oppersten iuge gheringhe
> Waer om dat hi dmēschelijke geslachte misdadich
> Meer ontfermt eñ es ghenadich
> Dan ons arme gheesten eewich versmaet[13]

---

[10] That the Devil was an adept in the art of wooing is well illustrated in *Mariken van Nieumeghen* where Moenen addresses her as 'schoon kind', 'aanschijn blank', 'scoon edel blomme', 'beelde soet', 'lief', 'mijn schoone minne', 'troost', and other terms of endearment. 'beautiful child, fair of face, fair noble flower, sweet image, darling, my fair love, consolation, etc.'

[11] In P. Rombouts and T. van Lerius, *De Liggeren en andere hist. archieven der Antwerpsche Sint Lucasgilde* (Antwerpen, 2 delen, 1872) i, p. 91, the following entry occurs in 1518: 'Item, dese Regerders deden in de vasten spelen 't spel van de Messcharon, daer grote cost om ghedaen was.' [During Lent the masters of this Guild produced the Play of Messcharoen which involved them in great expense]

[12] *Inf.* p. 157 *et seq.*

[13] *Mariken van Nieumeghen*, D. iv[v]. 1048-53. 'Bre! hieroh! I Masscheroen, advocate of Lucifer, will call upon the highest judge: and demand why more mercy and grace is given to man than to us poor spirits who are for ever rejected.'

7

He complains that God is too lenient with Mankind and is no longer a just God as in the days of Abraham, Moses and David; whereupon God asks him what he considers to have been the purpose of His death upon the cross. But Masscheroen maintains:

> Dies hoordi te wesen te stranger eñ te quadre
> Dan te voren aengesien dat ghi naect hebt
> Sulcken scandelijckē doot ghesmaect hebt[14]

People are far worse than they have ever been before, he alleges, and pleads his cause so well that God has to admit the truth of the argument and considers that it may be necessary to have recourse to punishment. At this the Devil takes heart and claims the right of acting as God's avenger. But at this point, the Virgin Mary who has watched the procedure with growing anxiety, intervenes. No creature has easier access to the heart of the God-Christ than his mother, and since 'mercy is aboue this sceptred sway,' and 'is enthroned in the hearts of Kings,'[15] it is the Virgin who averts the disaster by a compassionate appeal.

> O sone die mēschen sullen hem beteren van als
> En wilt niet te haeste u punicie toogen
> Denckt om die borstkens die ghi hebt ghesoghen
> Denckt om dat buixken daer ghi inne gelegē hebt
> Dinckt om die passie die ghi geleden hebt
> Dinckt om alle dbloet dat ghi stortet in ghescille
> Waert niet al om smenschen wille[16]

Now Masscheroen knows that the case is lost. His voice is heard no more in the pageant and he is seen to make an ignominious retreat. To Mariken, the scene is better than a sermon. Her tears begin to flow which means that the satanic spell is broken and she is once more herself.[17]

[14] *Ibid* ll. 1094-6. 'For this thy severity and anger should be the greater since nakedly thou didst suffer such shameful death.'

[15] *The Merchant of Venice*, IV, i, 203-4; (188-9).

[16] *Mariken van Nieumeghen*, E. i. 1176-11. 'O son, the people will repent themselves of their evil ways; do not punish them too hastily. Remember the breasts that gave thee suck. Think of the womb in which thou didst lie. Recall thy suffering. Think of all the blood which thou hast shed in the process. Was it not all for man's sake?' *Cf.* Bartolus de Saxoferrato, *Opera omnia*, v, 354, col. i, l. 45. 'Ego bene dixi S̄. quòd durum mihi erat habere matrem iudicis aduocaram contra me:' 'I was right in saying that it was hard on me to have the judge's mother as advocate against me,' Satan said. *Cf. inf.* p. 160.

[17] The strongest evidence against Witches and their intercourse with the Devil, was that they were unable to shed tears at the trial. See J. Sprenger and H. Kramer, *Malleorum Quorundam Maleficarum* (Francofurti, 1582), Par. III, Q.xv, p. 557. 'Hoc ipsum enim pro certissimo signo ex fide dignorum antique relatione, ac propria experientia docente, adeò cōpertum est, quòd etiamsi ad lachrimandum coniurationibus aliqua hortetur, & compellatur si Malefica existit, hoc ipsum, scilicet lachrimas emittere non potest: . . .' p. 558: 'Experientia docuit, quantò amplius coniurabātur, tantò minus flere poterant, . . . Quòd si causa impedimenti fletus in Maleficis quaeritur, potest dici, quòd quia gratia

8

The inset-play of Masscheroen forms the climax of the entire drama. All action flows towards and proceeds from it. Its powerful realism is combined with an absolute expression of happy idealism. The Devil's role is not important for its own sake, but only to glorify the Virgin's victory. The idea of *advocata nostra* whose persuasions never failed to soften the heart of the Almighty, had developed strongly since the Council of Ephesus in AD 430 when Cyrillus stated that Mary

should not only be known as Christ-bearer but far more as the Virgin-Mother of God.[18]

Already in AD 325 a meeting of bishops had been called to declare the God-head of Christ against certain heretical principles then prevalent. And with such emphasis laid on the idea of Christ as God, people felt the need for a new mediator between God and Man. It was natural for the mother to be considered as having the first rights. This is one reason why the cult of the Virgin spread throughout Europe. For the Devil in literature this was unfortunate.[19] More than ever he lived under the threat of being vanquished by a woman, and whenever he asserted his plea for 'justice' he was invariably shown to be in the wrong.[20]

MARY OF NEMMEGEN—A FEMALE FAUSTUS

Mary of Nemmegen is generally looked upon as a female Faustus. K. F. Rinne in *Speculation und Glauben*[21] takes it for granted that in her we are dealing simply with a version of the German Faust legend which has been weakened and adapted to foreign taste.

---

lachrimarum in poenitentibus praecipuis donis ascribitur, cùm coelum penetrare, & inuincibilem vincere, humilis lachrima à Bernardo asseritur:' Tr. by M. Summers in *Malleus Maleficarum* (*inf.* 250) p. 227: 'For we are taught by the words of worthy men of old and by our own experience that this is a most certain sign, and it has been found that even if she be urged and exhorted by solemn conjurations to shed tears, if she be a witch she will not be able to weep: . . .' 'And it is found by experience that the more they are conjured the less they are able to weep, . . . And as for the reason for a witch's inability to weep, it can be said that the grace of tears is one of the chief gifts allowed to the penitent; for S. Bernard tells us that tears of the humble can penetrate to heaven and conquer the unconquerable.' *Cf.* C. Marlowe, *Dr Faustus*, ed. W. W. Greg, Parallel texts, 1604-1616 (text A, 1604) (OCP 1950), p. 282, ll. 1416-17 [hereafter referred to as *Dr Faustus*] 'ah my God, I woulde weepe, but the diuel drawes in my teares,'. *Inf.* p. 15. On reasonable evidence, Greg, in his introduction, suggests that the play dates several years earlier.
[18] L. Etmüller, *Theophilus, der Faust des Mittelalters* (Leipzig, 1849), p. ix. 'daß Maria nicht nur, wie Nestorius wollte, . . . "Christgebärerin", sondern vielmehr . . . "immer jungfräuliche Gottgebärerin" genannt ward.'
[19] *Cf. inf.* p. 28 *et seq.*
[20] *Cf.* F. Bacon, *Essayes* (1597), in *A Harmony of the Essays of Francis Bacon*, ed. E. Arber (1871), p. 502. '*Reuenge* is a kinde of Wilde Iustice; which the more Mans Nature runs to, the more ought Law to weed it out. For as for the first Wrong, it doth but offend the Law; but the *Reuenge* of that wrong, putteth the Law out of Office.'
[21] K. F. Rinne, *Speculation und Glauben* (Zeitz, 1859).

9

Faust's keen endeavour to probe beyond all human knowledge, has here developed into a desire for the cultural refinement and knowledge of the age. In fact, the Dutch showed a more rational approach to scholarship. Moreover, the hero changed into a heroine, which points to the eager participation of the sixteenth-century Dutch woman in intellectual life. The gruesome catastrophe also gave way to a happier ending, more in keeping with the ancient Theophilus legend[22]

Rinne's remark supports the opinion of many Dutch scholars, especially J. van Mierlo's,[23] that a member of the *Rederijckers* and a woman, possibly Anna Byns who was a Catholic, was the author of *Mariken van Nieumeghen*. This would account for its peculiarly feminine character and Catholic logic contrasting strongly with the masculine and Lutheran Faust. Whether we accept this view or not, it remains true that among the host of stories on devil-compacts only *Mary of Nemmegen* and *Dr Faustus* show that the bargain is made through the desire for learning for its own sake.

than sayde marye to the dyuyl for that ye lye w^t me ye shall teche to me the forsayde scyāces[24]

Faustus goes a step further. He will not stop at the liberal sciences.

yet faine would I haue/ a booke wherein I might beholde al spels and incantations/ that I might raise vp spirits when I please.[25]

This had also been Mary's desire but she had given it up on the advice of Satan.[26] The yearning for secular learning, together with the freedom and pleasures which the sixteenth century afforded, made them representative of their age. For, although learning was the first instalment of the Devil's contribution towards the contract in either case, there is no doubt that soon after he turned both Mary and Faustus from learning to lewd pleasures so

[22] *Ibid.*, p. 138. 'Aus dem kühnen speculativen Streben ist ein der holländischen Gelehrsamkeit und verstandesmäßigen Kunstbestrebsamkeit entsprechendes Verlangen nach polyhistorischem Wissen geworden und der Held hat sich in eine Heldin verwandelt, – wie ja damals dort verzüglich auch Frauenzimmer großen Anteil an der Gelehrsamkeit nahmen. Aus der schauerlichen Katastrophe dort ist aber hier ein in die Theophilussagen zurückfallender legendenartiger Ausgang geworden.'

G. W. Wolthuis, *op. cit.*, pp. 173-176, mentions the scholars who regard Mary of Nemmegen as a female Faustus: K. Engel, *Zusammenstellung der Faust-schriften* (Oldenburgh, 1885); L. v. Plönnies, *Reise-Erinnerungen* (Berlin, 1845); F. A. Snellaert *Schets eener Geschiedenis der Ned. Letterk.* (Gent, 1855); A. Kühne, *Ueber die Faustsage* (Zerbst, 1860), etc.

[23] Cf. *sup.* p. 4, note [3].

[24] *Mary of Nemmegen*, A. v.

[25] *Dr Faustus*, p. 196, ll. 614-16.

M. Rudwin, *The Devil in Legend and Literature* (Chicago, 1931), p. 189. '. . . in the Faust legend the devil-compact is not the *root* but the *fruit* of Faust's sin, which consists in the abandonment of sacred for secular learning. The Faust legend is the creation of orthodox Protestantism, which, through it, expresses disapproval of the humanistic movement of its day. [It is said of Faust in the oldest Faust-book that he sold his soul "to search into all the deep things of heaven and of earth"]'.

[26] *Mary of Nemmegen*, A. v.

that learning appears of little substance or value. Mary was satisfied with the ability to do paltry tricks which flattered her vanity; Faustus' aspirations deteriorated into mere voluptuousness, Helena being 'the ripest fruit of all'.[27] It is curious that Mary when confessing her sins to the Pope, omits the desire for learning altogether and merely emphasizes more material matters.

O holy fader the great gyftes that he gaue vnto me bothe of syluer and of gold and also the pleasure y^t that I had with hym dayly bothe in daunsyng and playinge and had all that I desyred for that cause dyd I agree vnto hym ...[28]

Mary and Faustus sinned against the intellect as well as the senses, but in either case, as the story develops, the emphasis is shifted from the first to the second.

It may be noticed also that their tastes adapt themselves to those of the Devil. After giving Emmekyn a description of all the different wines they will enjoy: 'muskeadell/bastard/romney, & all maner of other wynes at your owne wyll', Satan pictures before her the kind of companions they will meet at the 'gylde tre' and the sinful life they lead.

Thā sayde Emmekyn good Satan let vs goo thyder and see that pastyme for that is the thynge that I reioyce moste in and loue beste to see[29]

Faustus, after the apparition of the seven deadly sins, calls out: 'O this feedes my soule'.[30] It shows how much both Faustus and Mary lived completely under the spell of the Devil.

DOCTOR FAUSTUS

A Descendant of The Virgin Mary Legends

The tradition of a compact with the Devil had taken deep roots in religious belief as well as in popular fancy.

In the form of the Theophilus-legend, which, in the sixteenth century, merged into the Faust-myth, it entered the literatures of all European countries and formed the subject of poem and play, novel and short story, throughout the civilized world for full thousand years.[31]

The Devil looked upon this written pact as a last resource. By it he hoped to lay claim to the soul despite repentance and penances. L. Radermacher in 'Griechische Quellen zur Faustsage' illustrates the fact that this custom

[27] C. Marlowe, *Tamburlaine the Great*; in *The Works* ed. A. Dyce, (3 vols.) i; II, vii, 27.
[28] *Mary of Nemmegen*, C. iv^v.
[29] *Mary of Nemmegen*, B. ii.
[30] *Dr Faustus*, p. 208, l. 797.
[31] M. Rudwin, *op. cit.*, p. 181.

3 *The devil's last resource – the pact*

became popular on account of the unreliability of the Christians.[32] In Helladius (Besantinus)' story the Devil blames them for turning to him when in need whilst they desert him after their wishes have been granted. For this reason he demands a written denial of the Christian Faith and promise that the young man will side with him on the Day of Judgement.[33]

P. Leendertz, Jr,[34] regards this mention of a pact in the *Historia von D. Johan Fausten*[35] as part of the evidence that originally it was a story in which the sinner was saved by the Virgin Mary. This would explain the reason for the Devil's anxiety and precautions. There is further evidence in the *Faustbuch* pointing to that origin, for instance the 'O Homo fuge' ap-

[32] L. Radermacher, 'Griechische Quellen', *Akademie der Wissenschaften in Wien*, Sitzungsberichte Bd. 206, 4 Abh. (Wien und Leipzig, 1927), pp. 127-8.

[33] *Ibid.*, p. 50. The writer, comparing Helladius' story with that of Theophilus, draws attention to this 'Tadel des Teufels wegen der Unzuverlässigkeit der Christen, die zu ihm kommen, wenn sie ihn brauchen, und ihn verlassen, wenn sie ihre Wünsche erfüllt sehen. Er fordert eine schriftliche Ableugnung des Christenglaubens und Anerkennung seiner eigenen Majestät. Der Vertrag wird demgemäß aufgesetzt.'

It is interesting that Satan in *Mary of Nemmegen* decides on a less business-like and more feminine arrangement, that of oral promise. By this he ran a greater risk of course, but it is doubtful if Mary, as we know her from the story, would ever have agreed to signing a pact with her blood as was demanded of Faustus.

G. W. Wolthuis, *op. cit.*, p. 137, mentions a quite ancient distinction in demonology between a 'pactum implicitum', a 'pactum explicitum' and a 'pactum tacitum'.

[34] MS P. Leendertz Jr, 'Verzameling L 16-30. Doos xx B8' (Universiteits Bibliotheek, Amsterdam).

[35] *Historia von D. Johañ Fausten* (Frankfurt am Mayn, J. Spies, 1587), [hereafter referred to as the *Faustbuch*]

12

pearing in bloody letters on Faustus' hand when he is about to sign the pact (p. 20), the faint verbal traces in Faustus' wavering between good and evil, the warning of the old man, but particularly the agonizing cry at the point of death.

Ah wo is me, for there is no help for me, no shield, no defence no comfort. Where is my hold? knowledge dare I not trust: and for a soule to God wards that haue I not, for I shame to speake vnto him:[36]

Theophilus, at this point, had found a solution.

> I will to his mother, nearste of alye,
> make meanys, if shee maye optayn mee m'cye[37]

There was the ambiguity in the account of Faustus' end

I dye both a good and bad Christian; a good Christian, for that I am heartely sorry, and in my heart alwayes praye for mercy, that my soule may be de- liuered : a bad Christian, for that I know the Diuell will haue my bodie, and that would I willingly giue him so that he would leaue my soule in quiet: . . .[38]

As E. M. Butler suggests, this glimmer of a doubt may have been a verbal survival or reminiscence of the more merciful tradition according to which another famous pact-maker, Pope Sylvester II (his actual name was Ger- bert), who was suspected to have dabbled in black magic, drew down grace from heaven.[39] One may reasonably infer therefore that *Mary of Nemmegen* and *Dr Faustus* are branches of the same tree.

THE DEVIL GETS HIS DUE

Christianity had always been a strong opponent to tragedy. The belief in an ultimate resurrection had deprived death of its sting; and the belief in the Virgin who had crushed the serpent's head had given rise to an uncon- ditional faith that she would continue to do so until the end of time. Tra- gedy in European literature was practically dead when Lutheranism

---

[36] P. F. *Gent., The historie of the damnable life, and deserued death of Doctor Iohn Faustus,* (1592), p. 77. [This is a translation by P. F. of *Spies's Faustbuch* and will here- after be referred to as the *Faust Book*]
The title page of this edition states: 'newly imprinted, and in conuenient places im- perfect matter amended :' which suggests an earlier edition.
[37] William Forrest, 'MS Harley 1703' (Brit. Mus.) f. 139ᵛ, ll. 18-9. See *inf.* p. 32, note 46.
[38] The *Faust Book*, p. 80.
[39] E. M. Butler, *The Myth of the Magus* (Cambridge, 1948), p. 137. '[Gerbert] com- manded that his body should be mutilated before and after death, and that his burial should take place wherever the horses dragging the bier should halt. As they drew up outside the Lateran Church, it would seem that he had been forgiven, and that his soul was saved. Faust's last night on earth followed the precedent set by Gerbert.'

opened the way to despair and to the prospect of eternal damnation.[40] In the *Faust Book* we read how Faustus was 'neuer falling to repentance truly' but 'in all his opinions doubtfull, without faith or hope'.[41]

Luther, followed by such English theologians as Richard Hooker, in his revolt against Catholicism had made contrition so difficult that at times it seemed virtually unattainable.[42]

To Faustus, knowledge of sin, without hope for forgiveness, is sheer agony and his lamentations bring no relief.

What meane I then to complaine where no helpe is? No, I know no hope resteth in my gronings. I haue desired that it should be so, and God hath sayd Amen to my misdoings:[43]

How different sounds the advice of Mary of Nemmegen's uncle, 'say nat so good cosen for there is nobody loste with out the fall in despayer'.[44] Mary, though she professes to have been 'yᵉ dyuels paramoure by the space of vij yere', was saved in the end, as were the Bishop of Adana, Theophilus, and Gerbert, Frau Jutte or Pope Joan,[45] Twardowski,[46] all of whom succeed through the intervention of the Blessed Virgin in escaping the punishment for dealing with the Devil.

But the wizard of Wittenberg was duly carried off to Hell by way of payment at the expiration of the bond. The Church, which forfeited its power at the Reformation, could not aid the man who had mortgaged his soul to Mephistopheles. Faust had to meet with the traditional doom. He was irrevocably damned, lost and fallen into the power of the Devil. The friend of the Fiend belonged to Hell.[47]

To the Elizabethan dramatist, Christopher Marlowe, the Lutheran Faust Book afforded scope for an unrelieved tragedy which became the basis of the dramatic development of the Faust material.

> Christ cannot saue thy soule, for he is iust,
> Theres none but I haue intrest in the same.[48]

[40] E. M. Butler, *Fortunes of Faust* (Cambridge, 1952), p. 11. 'Overwhelmed, overpowered, overridden by the Lutheran belief in the malignant might of the devil and in the numberless hosts of the damned, the salvation of an arch-sinner such as Faust had no chance to prevail, . . .'

[41] *Faust Book*, p. 14.

[42] H. Levin, *The Overreacher* (1953), p. 156.

[43] *Faust Book*, p. 77.

[44] *Mary of Nemmegen*, C. iᵛ.

[45] *Inf.* pp. 153 *et seq.*

[46] Generally regarded as the sixteenth-century Polish Faust. He also sold his soul to the Devil but was rescued by a prayer to the Virgin Mary.

[47] M. Rudwin, *op. cit.*, p. 188.

[48] *Dr Faustus*, p. 204, ll. 714-15.

Lucifer's words echo those of Masscheroen, his advocate, except that here there is no question of a plea, it is a settled statement. There is no merciful God, nor an interceding intermediary for Faustus. 'Hell calls for right'.[49] Mary of Nemmegen's tears had broken the satanic spell, but Faustus' bond is unbreakable; 'ah my God, I woulde weepe, but the diuel drawes in my teares'.[50] Nothing can reclaim Faustus.

The theme of *Mary of Nemmegen* is one of perpetual mercy whereas that of *Dr Faustus* is irrevocable justice. If we accept the opinion of P. Leendertz and of other scholars that the origin of the Faust legend is rooted in an ancient Catholic tradition, Marlowe's statement at the end of the play takes on a far wider meaning. 'Cut is the branch . . .'. The Compact with the Devil remained, but a possible source of salvation had been put out of bounds.

POETIC JUSTICE DONE TO MARY AND FAUSTUS

The poets who gave a lasting form to these legends did not lose sight of poetic justice. They created their characters according to the doom awaiting them. Mary, destined by her author to enjoy a happy ending, had to retain the sympathy of the reader or audience throughout. Faustus had to give just cause for his damnation. And here, although the points of difference between the two characters are many, I shall only touch upon those which tend to have a direct effect upon the final issue.

Faustus invites Mephostophilis into his presence, asks him to appear; Satan forces himself upon Mary at a moment when she is distressed and miserable and seeking protection. Mary is seduced by the Devil; Faustus welcomes his ruin almost despite Mephostophilis. He bolts the door from the inside, as all 'spirits' do, against the grace of heaven, and when his last hour approaches he lacks the strength to unbar. Mary leaves it ajar, symbolically represented by the preservation of the letter 'M', and the Virgin hastens to her rescue. Justice is foremost in the mind of Faustus.

> I and Faustus wil turne to God againe.
> To God? he loues thee not,[51]

Mary never quite loses her trust in God, and, when watching the play of Masscheroen, her imagination is immediately arrested by the Virgin's plea for mercy. There is a marked deterioration in the character of Faustus towards the end of the play which, apart from 'a swinish and Epicurish life',[52] is manifested in weakness and cruelty. He is cowed by Mephostophilis and

---

[49] *Ibid.*, p. 276, l. 1316.
[50] *Ibid.*, p. 282, ll. 1416-17. *Cf. sup.* p. 8, note 17.
[51] *Dr Faustus*, pp. 186-88, ll. 446-7.
[52] *Faust Book*, p. 72.

begs him to torment the good old man. Mary, keeping her eyes upon the Virgin in the pageant, is brave enough to defy Satan's threats.

than arose the dyuyll fro the growne and sayde holde your peace and be styll or elles I shall bere the with me to euerlastynge payne/ Than sayd Emmekyn O good Lorde haue mercy on me/ and defende me from the handes of the dyuyll that he do to me no harme.[53]

Mary, despite the companions surrounding her, remains childlike, believing and trustful. She never suspects that her ugly, one-eyed companion[54] will play her false. She is still concerned for her relatives. There is no trace of revenge towards her aunt and when hearing of her death, she expresses her sorrow. Faustus is wholly egocentric. His only interest lies in himself and his own passions. He seems cut off from the rest of humanity. There is a malignant, twisted strain in Faustus' character; Mary is simply led astray. Faustus signs a pact for twenty-four years, during which period at least he is safe. Mary has no written pact, she makes only a verbal agreement; she is at the mercy of Moenen who watches anxiously for the first opportunity to break her neck. Consequently, she is in need of continuous protection, which is obtained by the prayers of her uncle, the priest, and particularly by the slender contact with the Virgin whom she had refused to reject. Unlike Faustus, Mary feels a deep contrition for her sins. Watching the pageant, she is moved at seeing God's love for mankind and wishes to return to Him at any cost. Faustus merely fears the bitter consequences. To the very end his mind is fixed on hell. 'oh spare me *Lucifer!*' . . . 'come not *Lucifer,* . . . ah *Mephastophilis.*'[55]

Yet despite Faustus' fiendish disposition, a strong narcotic is needed to bring him to his deserved end. He himself begs for it in the person of Helena of Troy:

> Whose sweete imbracings may extinguish cleane
> These thoughts that do disswade me from my vow,
> And keepe mine oath I made to *Lucifer.*[56]

She is brought to him 'in twinckling of an eie'.[57] And here Marlowe's inspiration reaches a climax, as did the Dutch poet's in the pageant of Mass-

---

[53] *Mary of Nemmegen,* B. vi.

[54] It was not possible for the Devil to take on a perfect form of man, he always had to show some marked defect, in this case he was deprived of one eye.

[55] *Dr Faustus,* pp. 288, 290, ll. 1466, 1507-8.

[56] *Dr Faustus,* p. 278, ll. 1352-54.

A. W. Ward, ed., *Marlowe's Doctor Faustus; Greene's Friar Bacon and Friar Bungay* (OCP, 1901), pp. 122-23, sees 'nothing improbable in the assumption that the story of Helena, the companion of Simon Magus, helps to account for the introduction of the figure of Helen of Troy into the Faust-Legend. Simon Magus, it was said, was accompanied in his journeys by a Tyrian courtesan named Helen, whom he raised to the position of his ἔννοια or divine intelligence.'

[57] *Dr Faustus,* p. 278, l. 1356.

cheroen. In either case feminine influence plays a concluding part and the plot is determined by the relationship between a Woman and the Devil.

THE MASQUE OF HELENA

The Devil uses Woman to Draw Faustus to Hell

When, after witnessing the Virgin scene in *Mariken van Nieumeghen* we turn to the scene of Helena in *Dr Faustus*, we enter a different atmosphere. The scene of Helena forms the climax of the play. Faustus' wish to 'liue in al voluptuousnesse,'[58] has gradually been fulfilled but here he has reached the summit of his passionate desires. He can go no further and leaves his body and soul with Helena.

> Her lips suckes forth my soule, . . .
> . . . . . .
>
> Brighter art thou then flaming *Iupiter*,
> When he appeard to haplesse *Semele*,[59]

sufficiently explain the situation. They are the truth, for

With Faustus' union with Helen the nice balance between possible salvation and imminent damnation is upset.[60]

Marlowe is unsparing of dramatic irony. Throughout the drama Faustus shows a twisted mind, his values are false; here confusion is at its height. To him and to his students Helena is 'the admirablest Lady that euer liued'; 'heauen be in these lips / And all is drosse that is not *Helena*'.[61] He is the prey of devilish enchantment.

The apostrophe to Helen stands out from its context, . . . Characteristically, it does not offer any physical description of the heroine. It estimates, as Homer did, her impact.[62]

To please her, Faustus will do anything; but the feats he promises are destructive and dishonourable: he will sack Wirtemberg, combat and wound men for no other reason than to satisfy his 'paramour'. He will wear the crest of hell, 'all for love'. The lines are uttered in a delirium. They express Faustus' subconscious self, his 'owne appetite, / wherein is fixt the loue of Belsabub.'[63] This destructive and voluptuous beauty is the personifica-

---

[58] *Dr Faustus*, p. 180, l. 337.
[59] *Dr Faustus*, p. 278, ll. 1360, 1372-3. Note, p. 388. 'l. 1360 text A 1604 reads 'suckes', text B. 1616 reads 'sucke'. Little as one can rely on A, it seems just possible that the false concord is original and was corrected by the editor in B.'
[60] W. W. Greg, 'The Damnation of Faustus', *MLR.*, XLI (1946), p. 107.
[61] *Dr Faustus*, p. 278, ll. 1362-3.
[62] H. Levin, *op. cit.*, pp. 147-8.
[63] *Dr Faustus*, p. 188, ll. 448-9.

tion of Faustus' passionate and evil desires. The first condition laid down in the Devil-compact had been, *'that Faustus may be a spirit in forme and substance'*.[64] It is the apparition of a woman that completes the metamorphosis.[65] The calling up of Helena is different from the paltry Howleglass tricks and other toys sent to him by Mephostophilis. She is seduction personified.

he (Marlowe) did not shrink from depicting, beside Faustus' spiritual sin of bartering his soul to the powers of evil, what is in effect its physical complement and counterpart, however he may have disguised it in immortal verse.[66]

It was Marlowe's peculiar contribution to augment the tragic significance of Helena.

In the Faust books she was merely a devil in disguise who put the crowning touch to Faustus's 'swinish and epicurean life'; in the drama love and beauty played an organic part in banishing thoughts of remorse and despair.[67]

To Faustus she is the culmination of all his achievements; but 'culmination' here means destruction and death. The tragedy lies in the pathos of a gigantic illusion. It is *'die antlitzlose Maske des Weiblichen'*[68] that he mistakes for reality. He turns to Helena for comfort, and finds only a seducer, the enslaver of his passions.

The imagery used for Helena is in sharp contrast to that used for the Virgin in the play of Masscheroen in the Dutch version *Mariken van Nieumeghen*. For the Virgin, we find images of loving care: 'borstekens', 'hertelyck', 'ontfermen,' 'openen armen';[69] for Helena, 'suck forth', 'sacked', 'combat', 'wound'. It is the antithesis of Give and Take. The virgin has the power to save; Helena can only destroy.[70]

Faustus has paid dearly for this passing intoxication. He has drunk deeply of the opiate, and the awakening comes too late. The *noctis equi* who carry their victim to hell, have already galloped past the cross-ways. Now only one road lies before them.

> Ah Faustus,
> Now hast thou but one bare hower to liue,
> And then thou must be damnd perpetually:[71]

[64] *Ibid.*, p. 192, l. 541.
[65] W. W. Greg, *op. cit.*, p. 103, remarks upon the significance of how very consistently the devils in *Dr Faustus* are called 'spirits', even in stage directions.
[66] *Ibid.*, p. 107.
[67] E. M. Butler, *Fortunes of Faust*, p. 50.
[68] G. von le Fort, *Die Ewige Frau* (München, 1955), p. 25. 'The empty mask of womanhood.'
[69] 'breasts, lovingly, compassion, open arms';
[70] Like the brazen virgin at Breslaw visited by Faustus in his travels. *Faust Book*, p. 42. 'they [the naughty town-children] are brought to kisse this virgin, which openeth her armes, the person then to bee executed, kisseth her, then doth she close her armes together with such violence, that she crusheth out the breath of the person, breaketh his bulke, and so dieth :'
[71] *Dr Faustus*, p. 288, ll. 1450-3.

Faustus has chosen Helena. He has adapted his choice to hers as Adam once did to Eve's. In the arms of Helena he has become 'a thing', dead and barren. It was she who cut 'the branch that might haue growne full straight'. Justice is done to Faustus.

CONCLUSION

The contrast between the Virgin's influence and that of Helena stretches from heaven to hell. The entire history and scope of womanhood lies between these poles: woman can be a curse or a blessing. She can aspire to *das Ewig Weibliche* in the noblest sense or degrade herself to merely *die Antlitzlose Maske des Weiblichen*. From the two plays under discussion we may conclude that her task is by no means a merely passive one.

It is active and creative: it not only sustains activity, but calls it forth. That is indeed the most obvious fact about woman throughout the course of history: it is her fate to bring out either what is best or what is worst in men. They will perform herculean feats of bravery to win her, or they will cheat and lie and do crimes of violence; they will fight among themselves for her; for her sake they will become wise and strong and gentle, or they will sink into a servility and a degradation which in the end empty them of their manhood.[72]

Between the pageant of Masscheroen, and the masque of Helena there is almost a century of literature in which women are seen to fluctuate between good and evil, siding either with the Devil, or with the Virgin; pleading for man's destruction on the side of Masscheroen, with Helena enticing him to perdition, or with the Virgin guiding him to the *Lucem eternam*. The interplay of these two themes, together with the relevant historical and literary background, will be discussed in the following chapters.

[72] G. Vann, *Eve and the Gryphon* (1952), p. 56.

2

The Good Woman and The Devil

4 *She was held in high esteem*

2 The Good Woman and The Devil

If God thy Center be and thy defence
Be Hell, be Deuil thy Circumference.[1]

GENERAL CLIMATE OF OPINION

The ideal picture of woman as it had existed in the Middle Ages and which was still prevalent in the sixteenth-century mind was of an *Il Penseroso* quality, 'Sober, steadfast, and demure'.[2] Peace, retirement, the veil, these belonged to the 'femynyn gendere'. Even outside the cloister the veil has generally been regarded in Christian tradition as a symbol of womanliness. It not only meant withdrawal from the world or outside influences, it was a sign of submissiveness. For the Bride or Wife to cover her own head meant the recognition of the head of the family. This may have been the reason why married women in sixteenth-century England usually wore a hat indoors, as is mentioned by van Meteren, the Dutch consul, in his *Commentarien*, 1587: 'eenlick de ghemeyne ghehoude Vrouwen / gaen met eenen hoet / so wel op strate als in huys/'[3]

No doubt the startling stress laid upon the cultivation of obedience (as well as insistence on simplicity of dress and food, and self-repression generally) is to be traced to the long persistence of the one great ideal of the single profession of the Middle Ages for women, the seclusion of the nun's life. This had the effect of greatly enhancing the respect and reverence paid to the good woman outside the nunnery as well as the one in it, so long as she preserved the characteristics of the 'religious,' although she lived in the world as maid, wife, or widow.[4]

Woman's sobriety and reticence in dress and behaviour, her surrender to her husband's wishes, her perfect self-control in difficult situations, all these were only the visible counterparts of her inward state of mind. The God-directed steadfast mind of the good medieval nun or housewife had been focused

> Vpon the pillours of Eternity,
> That is contrayr to *Mutability*:[5]

[1] A. Copley, *A Fig for Fortune* (1596); printed for the Spenser Society (Manchester, 1883), p. 40, verse 2.

[2] *Cf.* F. Bacon, *op. cit.*, p. 209. 'Vertue is like a Rich Stone, best plaine set.'

[3] Emanuel van Meteren, *Commentarien . . . ende Gheschiedenissen van onsen tyden* (Schotland/buyten Danswijk, 1608), BK. xiii, f. xviij, col. 1, AD 1587. 'Married women only wear a hat both in the street and in the house.'
See W. B. Rye, *England as seen by Foreigners in the Days of Elizabeth and James I* (1865), p. 73. [Rye translates 'ghemeyne ghehoude' as 'married'. The phrase is ambiguous but historical and pictorial evidence give support to Rye's belief.]

[4] *Vives and the Renascence Education of Women*, ed. Foster Watson (1912), p. 24.

[5] E. Spenser *The Faerie Queene*, Variorum edn. Cantos of Mutabilitie, VII, viii, 2.

and by doing so, she had kept herself out of harm's way. She was safe, could be relied upon. Not living for this world, she saw things in their right proportions, objectively as it were, and it was to her that man turned with his troubles. When angry, she soothed him;[6] when disheartened, she gave him new hope; it was she who listened sharing his suffering or good fortune, she who nourished, clothed and inspired him. As the Scots poet sang,

> Scho wait my wo/ þat is ago/
> Scho wait my weilfair and remeid
> Scho wait also/ I lufe no mo/
> bot hir the well of womanheid
> Scho wait wᵗ outtin faill/ I am hir luvar laill
> Scho hes my hairt alhaill/ till I be deid[7]

This was the kind of woman to whom man aspired and for whom he undertook his feats of bravery, 'for her price is farre aboue Rubies',[8] 'And many *Jasons* come in quest of her'.[9] Sinners and the unfortunate took refuge under her protection. 'True gentles should be lightes and guides.'[10] This was what man expected of them. Woman's power was recognized and her sobriety, retirement and obedience did not lessen her 'leadership of love' but only heightened man's respect, at the same time enabling her to be active and creative.

Throughout the ages the good woman had been held in high esteem by pagans and Christians alike, among barbarian tribes as well as nations of the highest civilization. The degree and manner of deference, however, varied according to social and economic conditions, traditional customs and the religious background of a nation. It is a rather surprising fact in history that the Goths had a far greater regard for woman, allowing her more freedom, than, for instance the Greeks and Romans, for

No sooner was the Roman empire overthrown, and the Goths had overpowered Europe, than we find the female character assuming an unusual importance and authority, and distinguished with new privileges, in all the European governments established by the northern conquerors. [Even in savage war violence to woman was forbidden.][11]

[6] *Cf.* S. Brant, *The Shyp of Folys*, tr. A. Barclay (1509), ed. T. H. Jamieson (1874), ii, 3.

> A woman iust and to goodnes inclyned
> If wrath and yre hir husbonde do inflame
> With hir good counsell shall mytigate his mynde
> And peas his wrath

[7] A. Scott, *Quha is perfyte*; in *The Bannatyne MS* (1568), ed. W. T. Ritchie (4 vols.) iii STS, n.s. 23 (1928), p. 317, ll. 13-18.

[8] *Prouerbes*, authorised version (1611), xxxi, 10.

[9] *The Merchant of Venice*, I, i, 182; (172).

[10] Stephen Gosson, *Pleasant quippes for vpstart newfangled Gentlewomen* (1596), in *Remains of the Early Popular Poetry of England*, ed. W. C. Hazlitt, iv, p. 260, l. 235.

[11] Thomas Warton, *The History of English Poetry*, revised edn. H. Carew Hazlitt (1871), i, 144.

24

Many ancient tribes were strongly influenced by the matriarchal-agrarian culture in which woman, the earth, and food wrested from the earth by woman, were looked upon as the great life-giving sources. It is mother earth, the *terra mater*, the *bona dea*, who is well-disposed towards man and sustains him despite the dark forces of evil surrounding him. Woman had skill in studying 'simples', she understood the art of healing. Birth-giving and healing were arts reputed mysterious and divine. They meant power over the evil one who produced sickness, wounds and famine. Moreover,

The Goths believed some divine and prophetic quality to be inherent in their women; they admitted them into their councils, and consulted them on the public business of the state.[12]

Tacitus tells us that in the latter half of the first century of the Christian era, when the chieftain of the Gauls, at the head of his army, marched against the Roman legions,

matrem suam sororesᵭ, simul omnium coniuges paruosᵭ, liberos consistere à tergo iubet, hortamenta victoriae, vel pulsis pudorem.[13]

In Anglo-Saxon literature we often meet her on equal footing with man. It even happened at times that a woman took charge of a monastery of hundreds of monks. We meet with such an abbess in Bede's account of the poet Caedmon who, on reporting himself to the alderman, was soon led 'tō þǣre abbudyssan' that she might judge what should be done in such an extraordinary case.[14]

From these instances it can be seen that a good woman was taken at her proper value. It was rude instinct which instigated these early tribes to honour her as an indispensable being and to recognize her peculiar strength. Deference for the female sex was not merely grounded on superstitious beliefs, it was based on facts; woman had given evidence of her qualities. Agrippa von Nettesheim in *De Foeminei sexus praecellentia* mentions how woman has contributed to the well-being of both mind and body of mankind. 'Moreouer, in the Inuention of thynges, Ifis, Minerua, Nicostrata, be examples.'[15] Thomas Elyot in *The defence of good women* also mentions woman's power of invention:

And perdy, many artes and necessarie occupacions haue ben inuented by women, ... Latine letters were first founden by Nicostrata, called also Carmentis. The .vii. liberal artes and poetry by the .ix. maidens called the Musis.

[12] *Ibid.*, p. 145.
[13] Tacitus, *Historiarum et Annalium Libri* (Antverpiae, 1574), Hist., Lib. iv, p. 161, ll. 27-9. 'he ordered his mother and sisters, together with all the wives and children to stand by to encourage them to victory or make them feel ahamed to flee.'
[14] *Bede's Account of the Poet Caedmon*; in *Sweet's Anglo-Saxon Reader* (Oxford, 1950), p. 44.
[15] Agrippa von Nettesheim, *A Treatise of the Nobilitie and excellencye of Woman Kynde*, tr. D. Clapam (1542), E. viiiᵛ.

Why was Minerua honored for a goddesse? but because she founde firste in Grecia, plantyng or settynge of trees: ...[16]

By quoting from various sources, Agrippa assures us that woman is, in no way, held inferior to man.

but both of them naturally haue equall libertie of dignitie and worthynesse. But all other thynges, the which be in man, besydes the dyuyne substance of the sowle, in those thynges the excellente and noble womanheed in a maner infynytely dothe excell the rude grosse kynd of men.[17]

It is a mistake therefore to think that 'the excellente and noble womanheed' was always looked upon as the weaker sex. She is the gently-strong, and where she is dispraised it is because men fear the abuse of her strength.

We hear of mighty Amazons in the past, who by mere strength of arms have overthrown their enemies. Yet despite their marvellous feats of warfare, they were not allowed to wear their laurels in sixteenth-century literature. For instance, Hippolita, when coming on to the stage is not referred to as a conqueror; she speaks of love; she is 'faire Hippolita' whose nuptial hour is approaching.[18] The Knight of the Sun is not overthrown by his warlike Empress Claridiana when she competes with him in a duel, but one word of reproach from her lips pierces his heart and makes him tumble off his steed in a dead swoon.[19] In order to discover what man looked for in woman and what it was in her that put the Devil to flight, we must turn to Shakespeare's converted 'Amazon', Katharina, explaining the physiognomy of her sex.

> Why are our bodies soft, and weake, and smooth,
> Vnapt to toyle and trouble in the world,
> But that our soft conditions, and our harts,
> Should well agree with our externall parts?[20]

Jessica, on being asked her opinion on the lord Bassanio, replies:

> It is very meete
> The Lord *Bassanio* liue an vpright life
> For, hauing such a blessing in his Lady,
> He findes the ioyes of heauen heere on earth,[21]

---

[16] Sir T. Elyot, *The defence of good women* (1545), C. vi.

[17] Agrippa, *op. cit.* tr. D. Clapam, A. ii^v.

[18] Shakespeare, *A Midsommer Nights Dreame*, I, i, 1-19.
Cf. Henry VI, Pt. 3, 1st Folio, Histories, p. 151; (I, iv, 114), where Queen Margaret is referred to as 'an Amazonian Trull'.
Also the derogatory remarks about Joan la Pucelle, 'A Woman clad in armour', in *Henry VI*, Pt. 1, 1st Folio, p. 100; (I, v. 3 *et seq.*).
Only when making a direct attack on the Devil, was woman admired as virgin-Knight or Amazon. See *inf.* pp. 37-38.

[19] Diego Ortuñez de Calahorra, *The third part of the first booke of the mirrour of princely deedes and Knighthood*, tr. R. P. [1598-99?] f. 47.

[20] *The Taming of the Shrew*, 1st Folio, Comedies, p. 229; (V, ii, 165-8).

[21] *The Merchant of Venice*, III. v. 69-72; (64-7).

These then are the two requirements man looked for in a woman: she should answer to her outward form, and she was expected to be his guide and inspiration. Shakespeare epitomized the idea in one of his sonnets:

> Faire, kinde, and true is all my argument,
> Faire, kinde, and true' varrying to other words,
> And in this change is my inuention spent,
> Three theams in one, which wondrous scope affords.[22]

Finally, the Virgin-cult which had begun its spread through Europe in the early Middle Ages played a considerable part towards the enhancement of womanhood in literature, for as Agrippa von Nettesheim observed:

This is a stronge argumente of Aristotle: Of what kynde the beste is nobler thanne the beste of an other kynde, that kynde muste needes be nobler thanne the other. In the Femynyne kynde, the best is the vyrgyn Marye,[23]

It now remains to investigate the relationship of good women with the Devil. In the literature available on the subject, whether the material is based on Christian belief, chivalric tradition, or romantic superstition, certain characteristics prevail throughout: woman has power over the Devil; she succeeds in saving man from his clutches; and she is counsel for the defence against the Devil's advocate. All three of these characteristics were fully realised in the Virgin Mary who can be regarded as both the origin and centre of the Christian tradition of the 'Woman and the Devil' theme in literature.

I THE CHRISTIAN TRADITION

The Virgin Mary and the Devil

Numerous songs, ballads, stories and plays grew up around the Virgin whose power with God was unlimited and whose pity and mercy for mankind knew no bounds. How much the Virgin Mary was feared by the Devil was manifest in the fact that soon after her conception

> All the deuylles of the erthe/ of ye ayre and of hell
> Helde theyr parlyament of that mayde mylde[24]

The gravity of the occasion is emphasized by the fullness of their council in which not only the *Lucifugi*[25] took part, but a combined operation was called into action. Their attention was directed to *Genesis* 15:

[22] Shakespeare, *Sonnets*, 105.
[23] Agrippa von Nettesheim, *op. cit.*, tr. D. Clapam, D. iii^v – iiij.
[24] *The Plyament of deuylles* (Wynkyn de Worde, 1509), A. i^v. Reprinted for the Roxburghe Club [1820?].
[25] The spirits of the nether regions. See *inf.* p. 154.

... I will put enmitie betweene thee and the woman, and betweene thy seed and her seed: it shal bruise thy head, ...[26]

Not a consoling conclusion to arrive at. It meant fighting a losing battle. Consequently it went hard with the Devil in literature. For centuries he became utterly powerless, all his efforts being foiled by the Virgin. Openly disgraced, he soon became the butt of mockery and object of derision. *The Harrowing of Hell* in the Mystery Plays proved one of the most popular entertainments. Man could afford to be merry; there was no need for him to fear the Devil if he had the Virgin Mary on his side, whose cloak served as shelter against the attacks of the evil one. Even supposing a man did fall into the Devil's clutches, he was soon rescued by the Virgin, and could confidently assume that

> All shall be pardonyd that we haue done amys
> Syns thou art in eternall ioy and blys
> Our mediatryce:[27]

We have seen in *Mary of Nemmegen* how this idea was prevalent at the beginning of the century. The different forms in which belief in the Virgin was manifest are collected in Wynkyn de Worde's *The myracles of our lady*.[28] This selection forms, as it were, the epitome of most of the representative medieval stories extant in the sixteenth century. Among them we find

How a knyght felle to pouerte/ and by the deuyl was made ryche/ & by the merytes of his wyfe was by oure lady restored agayne to good and vertuouse lyuynge.[29]

The writer tells us what 'a full honest woman' can do to render the Devil's power ineffective. The knight, her husband, who had been used to live in luxury and entertain liberally, found that his resources had come to an end. With Christmas approaching he felt ashamed at not being able to display his accustomed generosity. The Devil, finding him in a disconsolate mood, provided him with 'golde and syluer & precyous stones', on condition that, on a certain day, he would deliver up his wife to him. When the appointed time arrived, he called his wife and said: 'Take your horse/for ye must go a good was [*sic*] hens'. Feeling uneasy, not knowing what this meant, she nevertheless obeyed her husband; but on passing a wayside chapel, she entered in to commend their safety to Our Lady, the knight waiting for her outside.

... and as she prayed deuoutely to our lady/ sodaynly she fell a slepe. Thenne a none the gloryous vyrgyn mary came out of the chappell in rayment and

---

[26] *Genesis*, iii, 15.
[27] S. Brant, *op. cit.*, ii, 335.
[28] *The myracles of our lady* (Wynkyn de Worde, 1514).
[29] *The myracles of our lady*, A. vii.

28

shap lyke the knyghtes wyfe in all thynges & lyghted vpon her horse she bydynge styll in ye same chapell. This knyght knewe not but she that came out of ye chappell had ben his wyfe and so wente forth his way. And whan he was come to ye place that was assygned to hym anone the prynce of derkenesse the deuyll with grete fyersnes hasted hym to that place. And whan he was nye it/ he began anone to rore and sayd. O y^u moost falsest of men/ . . . for the grete wronges that thy wyfe dothe to me. I wolde haue be auēged on her. And thou hast brought this woman that she myght punysshe me and commaunde me to helle. And whan this knyght herde this gretely he meruayled/ and for drede and wōder myght not speke one worde. Thenne sayd the blessyd vyrgyn Mary. By what boldenesse hast thou presumed wycked spyryte to noye or trouble my seruanut [*sic*] this mannes wyfe. This shall not be vnpunyshed. . . .[30]

There is a metrical version of the same story in the Porkington MS. Here the fear of the Devil for the good woman is emphasized.

> This fend saw this knyȝt sorry,
> And to his wyfe he had envye,
> But he myȝt not come here nyere
> For holly lyve and good prayere;
> But to here lord he come in haste,[31]

In the Dutch text the knight is afraid to barter his own soul but he does not mind giving up that of his wife, an exchange to which the Devil agrees.[32] Wynkyn de Worde also relates the story of *a certayne nonne called Beatryce*. This beautiful sacristan and portress, unable to withstand the temptation of the flesh, elopes with a lover. On her way out of the convent, she passes the statue of the Virgin Mary and says :

O good Lady I haue serued the as deuoutly as I coude/ & lo I resynge my keys to the for I may no lenger bere ye temptacions of my flessche. . .[33]

After fifteen years of sinful life, disillusioned in every respect, she returns to her convent to find that Our Lady has appointed someone to replace her in her absence thus saving her from dishonour. In the oldest Dutch version it is the fiend who tempts her to elope and who persuades her not to confess after she has returned.

[30] *Ibid.*, A. vii^v – viii. There is a Latin version similar to the English one in *A Selection of Latin Stories* ed. Th. Wright; in *Early English Poetry*, Percy Society (1842) xxix, 31 : 'De milite qui pactum fecit cum diabolo'.

[31] *The Tale of the Knight and His Wife*, in *The Life of St. Katharine*, etc., ed. J. Orchard Halliwell (Brixton Hill, 1848), pp. 20-21. [known as the Porkington MS.]

[32] C. G. N. de Vooys, *Middelnederlandsche Marialegenden* (Leiden, 2 delen, 1903) i, p. 22.

[33] *The myracles of our lady*, D. ii^v. In the Dutch as well as in the text of Caesarius von Heisterbach, *The Dialogue on Miracles*, tr. H. von E. Scott and C. C. Swinton Bland (1929), i, 502-3, the Blessed Virgin herself fulfills the office of sacristan.

Beatrys; uitg. D. C. Tinbergen (Groningen, 1938), p. 33. That some of the Protestants were taking a serious view of the matter is shown by Rauscher who in 1562 ranks the story under the 'papistische Lügen'.

Die duvel becorese metter scame,
Dat sie haer sondelike blame
Vore den abt niet en soude bringhen.[34]

Most of these miracles are adorned with the conventional imagery. Wynkyn de Worde tells us 'How a conuers of the charter house was delyuered by Our blessyd lady fro the fere of deuylles.' A monk resting on his bed at night and thinking upon holy things, was visited by a company of devils,

in lykenesse of hogges/ the whiche wente all aboute in the celle with a gastefull noyse/ & gronynge as they were woode/ ... his fere encreased and sawe also a certayne mā of an horryble gretenesse come in to his celle: & after his demenynge he was the prynce of deuylles . . .[35]

Despite Lucifer's endeavours to make the hogs seize the monk, they seemed unable to do so, nor could he do it himself, for when

he straught forthe to this good holy man with a gastfull coūtenaunce/ a ferefull Instrument of Yron with croked hokes to take hym/ & all to tere hym . . . . . Anone yᵉ gloryous moder of god/ and truely the moder of mercy/ in whome nexte after god he put all his hope vysybly came to hym/ and with a lyght yerde that she helde in her hande sayd to yᵉ wycked spyrytes. How durst ye wycked spyrytes come hyther this man is not yours ne agaynst hym in ony thynge ye shall preuayle/ and whan she had sayd/ that all that company vanysshed awaye as a smoke dooth.[36]

'How this holy name Maria put the deuyll a waye' is illustrated by many instances.

In Spayne there were certayn monkes that sawe vysyly the deuyll at a certayne wyndowe of yᵉ abbaye in a gastfull lykenesse. And yᵉ forsayd monkes coniured hym in ye name of yᵉ trinyte to go thens/ and he wolde not. Also they coniured hym by crystes passyon/ and he wolde not go They redde there our lordes passyon/ and the .vii. psalmes with the letanyes/ and he wolde not obeye. Afterwarde came thyder a preest in holy vestymentes and cast holy water on hym/ and yet he wolde in no maner wyse auoyde. For our lorde Jhesu wolde shewe the vertue of his moders holy name Maria/ and atte the laste they coniured hym by the holy name of the blessyd moder of god. And than anone he wente his way/ for that name is full gastfull to all Deuylles.[37]

The 'specyall Joys of oure Lady' was another popular theme.[38] These joys had been enumerated by John Mirk in one of his festival sermons, 'De Annunciatione marie'.[39] There were five in all, beginning with Mary's con-

---

[34] *Beatrijs*, facs. uitg. 'MS. 76 E 5', 's Gravenhage, door A. L. Verhofstede (Antwerpen, 1948), p. 13, ll. 929-31. 'The Devil tempted her with shame, that she might not lay her sinful life before the abbot.'
[35] *The myracles of our lady*, C. iiij.ᵛ – C. v.
[36] *Ibid.*, C. v.
[37] *Ibid.*, C. viii.
[38] *Ibid.*, D. iiijᵛ.
[39] J. Myrc [Mirk], *Liber Festiualis et Quatuor Sermones* (1502) M. v.

ception and ending with her entry into heaven. They might well be called the Devil's sorrows, especially the last one, for by Mary's assumption mankind gained a most powerful ally in heaven. People loved to think how on that day,

Helle full of malyce houleth/ and yᵉ cursed deuylles crye vnto her & drede her.[40]

The ostlers at York, more than any preacher, succeeded, by their simplicity of language and presentation, to bring the scene within human understanding. Christ speaks

> Ressayue þis croune, my dere darlyng,
> Þer I am kyng, þou schalte be quene.[41]

In the prayers of the Church. 'At tyerce Antempne' of the Monday Service, we read:

O Victrix, O moste mighty ouercomer. in whose syghte the wycked enmy of mankynde ys broughte to noughte. by the oure herytage ys restored agayne to vs.[42]

Flemish Miracle Plays presented 'Seuen Bliscappen' which were put on in yearly succession on the Procession Day, or *Groten Ommegang* at Brussels. This custom was decided upon by the town council at the centenary celebration of the *Ommegang*, in 1448, and continued until 1566, the year of iconoclasm. In the play of the Assumption, which is here the *Sevenste Bliscap*, stress is laid on the efforts to prevent the Virgin's glorification. A double attack is made, first by the Devils *in propriis personis* and afterwards by the Jews.[43] Michael, meeting the Devil's representative party at the entrance of Our Lady's house, asks them if they do not know what is written in the Canticle, that she is

> 'Terribilis ut castrorum acies',
> Dats verveerlic, diet wel merke,
> Ghelijc den casteele of bollewerke.[44]

---

[40] Jacobus de Voragine, *The Golden Legende* (W. de Worde, 1512), f. ccxviiiᵛ.
F. S. Ellis in his preface to Caxton's edn. (1483), i, p. vii, suggests that 'probably no other book was more frequently reprinted between the years 1470 and 1530 than the compilation of Jacobus de Voragine'.
[41] *The assumption and Coronation of the Virgin*, York Plays, ed. L. Toulmin Smith (Oxford 1885), p. 496, ll. 155-6.
[42] *The Myrroure of Oure Lady*; (1530) ed. J. H. Blunt, EETS, e.s. xix (1873), p. 186.
[43] *Die sevenste Bliscap van Onser Vrouwen*, (1447); bewerkt door W. Smulders('s Hertogenbosch, 1913), pp. xvii-xix.
Often these productions were attended by the ruling monarch, the Duke of Brabant. In 1549 they were played before Charles V who at that time resided at Brussels.
[44] *Ibid.*, iii. 1086-1088.
> Fearsome like an army in battle array,
> Awe inspiring like the keep of a castle.

The Jews, Michael resumes, hate her as the Devils do, because they do not believe that she is the Mother of God. They are in league with hell. And indeed, the Devils having failed to obtain the Virgin's soul, now incite the Jews to get the mastery of her body after death, but the Jews meet with the same defeat as the Devils.[45] Nothing was more pleasing to an early sixteenth-century audience than the Virgin's triumph especially where man's benefit was concerned. The fiend was made responsible for the sin of man and was often obliged to bear the brunt of the penalty. He was lashed and laughed at, beaten and put in the stocks. Moreover he was invariably cheated of his pact, his bond. It cannot be denied, therefore, that Satan's part in literature is rather pitiable. The story of Theophilus, Bishop of Adana who, in order to rise to a higher position in the Church, sold his soul to the Devil, is one of the many examples in which the Virgin Mary deprives the Devil of his pact. The only extant sixteenth-century English version is in the Harleian MS. 1703, in the British Museum, dated '27 Octobris 1572 per me Guilelmus Forrestum'.[46] It is a dignified, reformation rendering of a popular medieval legend and portrays a change of expression in sentiment brought about by the more reserved attitude of a recusant who defends the ancient devotion of the Mother of God against the view of some of his Lutheran contemporaries. These regarded praying before a statue as a

desperate synne of ydolatrye, agaynst the immaculate, and fearefull commandement of god. . . . soche dampnable allusyones of the deuylle to use theme [the images] as goddes contrary to the immaculate scripture of gode, . . .[47]

After Theophilus has abjured 'the crucyfyed Christe/ with what ells he promysed in his Baptysme' the Devil demands:

[45] Cf. The Golden Legende, f. ccxxvi^v-vii^r. 'Lo here the tabernacle of hym that hath troubled vs and our lygnage/ beholde what glorye he now receyueth. And in the sayenge so he layde his hondes on ye bere wyllynge to tourne it & ouerthrowe it to the grounde. Than sodaynly both his hondes wexed drye and cleued to ye bere so that he henge by ye hondes on the bere and was sore tourmented and wepte & prayed . . .'

[46] To my knowledge, the MS. has not yet been printed. Cf. W. Heuser 'Eine Neue Mittelenglische version der Theophilus-sage', Englische Studien (Leipzig 1903), p. 1, who seems to have overlooked the contemporary value of this interesting work and does not consider it worth printing. ' "Guilelmus Forrestus" im Ms. Harl. 1703, ist noch ungedruckt, übrigens, wie ich nach einsicht des Ms. urteilen muss, eine späte und völlig ungeniessbare zusammenstoppelung, die es kaum verdient abgedruckt zu werden.'

William Forrest was made chaplain to Queen Mary Tudor soon after her accession. For bibliographical notes see Thomas Warton, op. cit., iv, 229, and DNB.

[47] D. Erasmus, A dialoge intituled ye pylgremage of pure devotyon [1540?], + iij; iv.

Cf. H. de Vocht, The Earliest English Translations of Erasmus' Colloquia 1536-1566 (Louvain, 1928), pp. xlii, et seq. mentions that in 1538 the 'cult of shrines and images', the so-called 'ypocrysy' was forbidden by authority. The translator took things far more seriously than Erasmus himself and introduced certain alterations suggesting that he was in the service of the English Church-reformers , or, at least an adulator, who for the sake of pleasing Henry VIII, or Cromwell, undertook this work.

Ferder yeate more, Sathanas Agayne
besyde that is sayde, thowe shalte eke denye
for that, myne owne, thowe shouldiste eaver remayne,
the mother of Christe, by name, called Marye,[48]

Satan still further requires a pact written with his blood.

Theophilus is now restored to his dignity as Bishop of Adana. But after a successful period he begins to feel sorrow for his sins and, lacking in courage to turn to Almighty God, he has recourse to the Virgin Mary throwing himself prostrate before her statue.

To thee I speake not, thowe Image present,
but vnto the Lyuelye Ladye soveraigne,
whiche highe in the heavins, ys theare reasident,
whom this saide Image representeth playne;
moving remembrance : in certayne kinde veyne,
none otherwise, myne Adoration,
but after hyperdulya fashion[49]

He tells the Virgin that he fears to call upon her son,

Yeat is hee my Lorde: he cannot denye
though I haue of caste his recognysance
over heaven, and hell : he hath the Seignorye,
to dooe, And vndooe: at his ordynance,[50]

The Virgin Mary obtains mercy for Theophilus who now publicly confesses his sin in presence of the former bishop and all the people. The characterization in this section of the poem is very effective. The good bishop tactfully protects him against the disappointment and horror of the parishioners.

And, what thoughe this man: hath roved astraye
him to abhorre: revyle, or deteste:
behoveth vs not, in Anye kinde waye
Sith with forgeuenes: god hathe him nowe bleste,
therefore, to him nowe: none his syn to keste,
who of you all, from syn is all cleare,
throwe stone at hym firste: yf he dare Appeare,[51]

Different as this poem may be from the medieval approach, yet the same confidence in the Virgin Mary is shown albeit in a more reserved style of writing.

[48] W. Forrest, MS. *cit.*, f. 135ᵛ. ll. 7-10.
[49] W. Forrest, MS. *cit.*, f. 140, ll. 1-7.
[50] *Ibid.*, f. 140ᵛ. ll. 8-11.
[51] *Ibid.*, f. 152ᵛ. ll. 1-7.

In comparison, I turn to a rather amusing Niederdeutsch dramatic version edited from a Helmstadt MS. by Hoffman von Fallersleben in which the medieval colouring is displayed in all its domesticity. The Virgin here has great difficulty in obtaining the written pact from the Devil. Satan pretends to have lost it. The Virgin tells him to go to hell and look for it. At his return he excuses himself,

> Vrouwe, ik segge ju ware:
> Ik hebbe alle de helle dorchvaren,
> By mijnen besten sinnen
> Des breves kan ik nicht vinden.
> Ik hebbe ene gevraget sere
> Mynen heren Lucifere, ...[52]

Our Lady now grows angry with the Devil, at which Satanas, full of fear, begs Lucifer to give up the pact, for

> Se is vrouwe unde wy syn Knechte
> Wy en mogen nicht wedder se vechten.[53]

There is a very long account in verse form in *Les Miracles de Nostre-Dame*.[54] Here Theophilus has to shed many tears before God will listen to his cries of repentance. On the third night Our Lady appears to him and says,

> Par mes preces, biaus douz amis,
> Cil qui en crois a tort fu mis
> Tes chaudes larmes a veües
> Et tes prïeres receües.
> Bien li soufist ta penitance,
> Ce saches tu tout sanz doutance.[55]

Abuse of Trust in the Virgin—The Change at the Reformation

There is no doubt that the best of this literature was born of a sincere trust in the power of the Blessed Virgin over the Devil, owing to her position as the mother of God and her love for mankind which had been placed under her protection. However, as all good things are at times abused, so did

[52] *Theophilus, Niederdeutsches Schauspiel*, ed. Hoffmann von Fallersleben Helmstädter MS. (Hannover, 1854), ll. 638-643. 'Lady, I tell thee truthfully: I have been all over Hell to look for the document but cannot find it and I have even asked my lord Lucifer about it.'

[53] *Ibid.*, ll. 654-55. 'She is the Lady and we are servants; we cannot oppose her.'

[54] Gautier de Coinci, *Les Miracles de Nostre-Dame*; éd. V. F. Koenig (Genève, Lille, 1955).

[55] *Ibid.*, i, p. 128, ll. 1291-96. The original version was in Greek by Eutychianos, translated into Latin by Paulus diacon. The oldest Latin poetic rendering was by Hrothwitha of Gandersheim. The difference in expression of one and the same idea, by poets of different nationality and period, is rather striking.

34

man's confidence grow blind and, overstepping the threshold of reason, it was degraded to a proud assurance that it was impossible for him to go astray whilst he had a mother in heaven who kept watch. Thus, many of the Virgin-Devil stories degenerated into mere absurdities and, according as man's personal endeavours slackened, so did his early love and devotion decline to mere presumption and a growing sense of irresponsibility.

The idea that all prayers should be answered and that no one who called upon the Virgin Mary, could go to perdition, had taken such firm root in the Middle Ages that it was not easily shaken in the sixteenth century. An incident which took place at Eisenach in 1322 is recorded in the *Chronicon Sanpetrinum*. When at Eastertime the play of the Wise and Foolish Virgins was performed before Count Friedrich of Misnia, and the Foolish ones, despite the Virgin's intercession, were damned, the Count grew angry and shouted:

'Was ist dann der Christen Glaube, wenn der Sünder durch die Fürbitte der Mutter Gottes und aller Heiligen nicht Gnade erlangen kann !'[56]

In this anger he continued for five days, and the learned found it hard to enlighten him.[57] The play of the wise and foolish virgins[58] was never popu-

---

[56] *Chronicon Sanpetrinum, Scriptt. rerum Germ.* hg. J. B. Mencke (1728-30), *iii.* p. 326, quoted in K. Hase, *Das geistliche Schauspiel* (Leipzig, 1858), p. 52. 'What then is Christianity, if the sinner, by the intercession of the mother of God and all the saints, cannot obtain grace from heaven !'

[57] *Ibid.* See also J. Rothe, *Chronik von Thüringen*, hg. E. Fritsche (Eisenach 1888) p. 173. 'zornig verließ er das Fest und begab sich nach seiner Wartburg zurück, wo er noch fünf Tage lang sich mit bangen Zweifeln abquälte und abmarterte.'

Harry Kemp, in *The Love-Rogue* (New York, 1923), p. 14, draws attention to the fact that the reason why Tirso de Molina [Gabriel Tellez], after writing *El Burlador de Seuilla*, abandoned dramatic composition for ten years, was that he packed his hero off to hell. Any triumph of the Devil in literature was attributed as a crime to its author or playwright.

DON GONZALO:	No importa, que ya pusiste Tu intento.
DON JUAN:	Deja que llame Quien me confiese y absuelva.
DON GONZALO:	No hay lugar, ya acuerdas tarde.
DON JUAN:	Que me quemo ! que me abraso ! Muerto soy.

Teatro español (Madrid, 1924). III, xxi, pp. 159-60.

Don G. It doesn't matter. You've had your chance.
Don. J. Let me confess to someone and be absolved.
Don G. There's no time, you've come to your senses too late.
Don J. Oh, I'm burning. I'm on fire. I'm dead.

[58] I have not seen an extant English version of the play. E. K. Chambers, *English literature at the Close of the Middle Ages* (Oxford, 1945), pp. 6-7 mentions 'two elaborate plays, which may be called eschatological, a *Sponsus* on the theme of the Wise and Foolish Virgins and an *Antichrist*'.

A. Harbage, *Annals of English Drama* (Philadelphia, 1940), p. 36, refers to an anonymous play, *The Wise and Foolish Virgins*, performed as a Court masque in 1561.

lar with the pre-Reformation Catholics, and as it was based on a gospel parable it was impossible to have its issue changed; the foolish must be damned. In a sixteenth-century Netherlands version *Het spel van de V vroede ende van de V dwaeze maegden*, Hoverdie, one of the foolish, seeing what sin has brought her to, cries:

> Och! hoe zwaer es my dit anschijn te anscauwen,
> Haddic toch ditte gheweten te voren!

at which Lucifer, gloatingly, responds:

> Dat ghi nu daeromme dinct, es al verlorei.
> . . . . . .
> Zonder cesseren zuldi branden vroech ende spade,
> Over hu en comt nemmer ghenade;
> Dus werpse daer binnen in de gloeijende colen.[59]

The Lutherans welcomed such moralities. They believed in giving the Devil his due. However, in trying to cut away the excess of confidence which they considered a disease, they performed their operation too thoroughly, leaving an empty void with no mediating saints and no merciful Mother of God to counteract demonic influences. As a result, the Devil installing himself in the vacated place, usurped all power; and under his regime there was serious reason for man to despair once he had got himself into trouble. Despite her excommunications and *anathema*, the early Church had always been referred to as 'our holy mother the church'. The Reformation bore in itself a more masculine character. Man was held fully responsible for his sins and he had to pay for them. Sanctuary was dispensed with and man had to face his adversary in the open field, with nothing to protect him.[60] Instead of appearing before the throne of a merciful God, with the *'advocata nostra'* at his side, he was led before another tribunal where

Lucifer princeps tenebrarum tristia profundi acherontis regens imperia: dux herebi: rex inferni: rectorq̢ iehenne:[61]

[59] P. Leendertz, Jr, *Middelnederlandsche Dramatische Poëzie* (Leiden, 1907). p. 419.
> Ah! woe to me to look upon this sight;
> had I but known this before!

at which Lucifer: 'It's useless now to look upon the past . . . . Thou shalt burn from morn to night, everlastingly, without mercy. Come, throw them into the glowing furnace.'

[60] Although Spenser in *The Faerie Queene* (II, viii, 2) introduced angels as intermediaries,
> They for vs fight, they watch and dewly ward,
> And their bright Squadrons round about vs plant,
> And all for loue, and nothing for reward:

Yet no legion of angels was able to replace the Virgin Mary in popular literature.

[61] *Epistola Luciferi ad regentes*; in *Controversial tracts, etc.* [1520?]. No. 2, A. ij. [Brit. Mus. 3907 aa 17.] 'Lucifer, prince of darkness, ruling the sad depths of Acheron, leader of Erebis, king of hell, ruler of Gehenna'.

was the Lord Chief Justice. Such was the doom of Dr Faustus. But if by the middle of the century the Mystery plays of the Virgin were suppressed,[62] the idea of a woman mediatrix who was both strong and merciful had been established, and we shall see later that it persisted, though in a different form, throughout the century.

Other Women in History and Legend who Fought The Devil

The Virgin Mary had always been looked upon as the Devil's most formidable opponent, but there were other women following in her footsteps, who

5 *She dealt with him effectively*

had acquired the art of dealing with him effectively. Thus Henry Constable, the recusant poet, addresses St Margaret as

> Fayre Amazon of Heaven: who took'st in hand
> St. Mychaell, & St. George to imitate:[63]

[62] In the *York Civic Records*, The House Books, ed. A. Raine, YAS Record Series CVIII (1945), iv, 176, the following entry occurs: 'Book xix. fo. 16b. 25 May 2 Edward VI, (1548). Agreyd that Corpus Cristy play shalbe playd this yere, certen pagyaunts excepte, that is to say, the deying of our Lady, assumpcon of our Lady and coronacon of our Lady.' See also CX (1946), v, 88: 'Book xxi. fo. H. 14 April 7 Edward VI (1553). Aggreed that for as much as the wollen weavers was woont to bryng forth a pagiant of the Assumption of Our Lady on Corpus Christi day yerely, which pagiant is nowe leaft of and soo the sayd weavers have nowe no pagiant to bryng forthe; [it is suggested that from now, the weavers shall produce the 'sledmens pagiant']'

In the *York Diocesan Registry*, Borthwick Institute, York, HC. AB. 9, f. 20, AD 1576, the entry occurs that the High Commission of York orders the Wakefield Corpus Christi Cycle of Plays to be suspended.

[63] L. I. Guiney, *Recusant poets* (1938), i. 322.

A short biography in the *Golden Legende* gives an illustration of how she rough-handled the Devil. When he appeared to her one day in the likeness of a man,

She caughte hym by the heed/ & threwe hym to the grounde. And sette her ryghte foot on his necke sayenge. Lye styll thou fende vnder ye fote of a woman. The deuyll then cryed O blessed Margarete I am ouercomen/ yf a yonge man hadde ouercomen me I had not retched, but alas I am ouercomen of a tender vyrgyn wherfore I make the more sorowe.[64]

Pieter Bruegel has left us pictorial evidence on how the Devil was rough-handled by woman in 'Flemish Proverbs' where he is tied to a mattress, a distaff lying nearby which indicates a thorough beating.[65] How virtue proved the woman's strength is also illustrated by Britomart in *The Faerie Queene*, whose 'noble prowess' was symbolic of her chastity. It made her 'The fairest woman wight, that euer eye did see'.[66] Her steadfast heart made her a virgin-knight. Having forced her way into the vile enchanter's secret cave,

> So mightily she smote him, that to ground
> He felle halfe dead; . . .[67]

She then breaks his spell by making him reverse his charms, standing over him all the time with her sword drawn. Thus she freed fair Amoret who had fallen into his evil power.

When we regard the variety of women in English literature who were at enmity with Satan, we begin to marvel at the wisdom of the words 'In my Fathers house are many mansions'.[68] They range from the Abbess Hilda whose life is related in the *Kalendre of the Newe Legende of Englande* and, for example, Mistress Stubbes whose husband's pen anatomized contemporary abuses.

The Abbess Hilda, the *Kalendre* tells us,

was of such great wisdome y^t not only pore men but also kyngys & pryncys wolde aske coūceyll of her/ by her prayers a great multytude of serpentys y^t feryd her susters soo y^t they durste scarcely come out of theyr cellys were turnyd into stonys/[69]

---

[64] *The Golden Legende*, f. Clxxvi.

R. Scot, *The discouerie of Witchcraft* (1584) Bk. XV, Cap. 36, p. 459, takes a very serious view of the situation, illustrating how 'The storie of Saint Margaret prooued to be both ridiculous and impious in euerie point'.

[65] Dahlem Galerie, Staatliches Museum, Berlin (1559), detail 104.

[66] *The Faerie Queene*, III, ix, 21.

[67] *Ibid.*, III, xii, 34.

[68] *S. Iohn*, XIIII, 2.

[69] T. Gascoigne, *Kalendre of the Newe Legende of Englande* (1506), f. lv.

Hilda was in charge of the Monastery of 'herthey' (Northumbria) which had been founded by Bega.

One is left in no doubt that these serpents were descendants of the paradisal one. For devils to be turned into stone was quite a usual procedure. The Lincoln Imp, the Stonegate Devil at York, and others are a lasting evidence. As long as Lincoln Cathedral stands, we shall have to suffer this stony image gloating over his own mischief, looking over the shoulder of a woman while keeping a firm grip on her.

The Abbess Hilda beat the Devil not once but on many occasions and her pupils were largely responsible for christianizing this country.

Wynkyn de Worde introduces to us 'Saynt Justyne' who conquered the Devil by the sign of the Cross. The story of Cyprian and Justina was well known. After Cyprian's efforts to gain Justina had been repeatedly rebuked,

he called a deuyll to hym to the ende that he by hym myght haue Justyne. And whan the deuyll came he sayd to hym/ wherefore hast thou called me. And Cypryan sayd to hym I loue a virgyne/ canst thou not so moche that I may haue my pleasure of her. And the deuyll answered I y^t myght caste man oute of paradyse/ and procured that Cayn slewe his broder/ and made the Jewes to slee cryste/ and haue troubled the men/ trowest thou I may not do that thou haue a mayde with the & vse her at thy pleasure.[70]

However, at his first attempt, Justina puts him to flight by the sign of the cross. Cyprian, disappointed, calls for another devil stronger than the first, but once again the Devil has to admit 'I am ouer comen and am rebouted'. After this Cyprian calls upon the prince of Devils himself. Lucifer, in order to save their reputation, considers that it might be easier to deceive Cyprian than Justina. He therefore takes upon himself the form of a maid and goes awooing. But as soon as Cyprian calls out 'Justina', Satan's power to disguise leaves him and he appears before Cyprian in his own person. This revelation of the Devil's impotence leads to Cyprian's conversion. There is an amusing incident when Cyprian and his friend Acladius, by their magic art, change themselves into various shapes in order to gain access to the maiden. Thus, on one occasion, Acladius was turned into a sparrow.

And whan he came to the wyndowe of Justyne/ & as soone as the virgyne behelde hym he was not a sparowe/ but he shewed hymselfe as Acladye/ & began to haue anguyshe and drede for he myght neyther flee ne lepe. And Justyne dredde lest he sholde falle and breke hymselfe/ and dyde do sette a ladder by the whiche he went downe/ warnynge hym to cesse of his wodenesse lest he sholde be punysshed as a malefactour by ye lawe.[71]

It would be an impossibility to mention all the good women who fought the Devil in the sixteenth century. A selection, therefore, will have to suffice. Among contemporaries of the period we meet with Mistress Katherine

[70] *The Golden Legende* f. CC. lxiiii^v.
[71] *Ibid.*, f. CC. lxv.

Stubbes, 'who departed this life in Burton upon Trent, in Staffordshire, the 14 day of December, 1590', and who had 'A most wonderfull conflict betwixt satan and her soule' which was 'set downe worde for worde as she spake it, as neere as could be gathered, by P. S. *Gent.*'

How now, Satan? what makes thou here? Art thou come to tempt the Lords seruant? I tell thee, thou hell-hound, thou hast no part nor portion in me, nor by the grace of God neuer shalt haue. I was, now am, and shalbe the Lords for euer. Yea, Satan, I was chosen and elected in Christ to euerlasting saluation, before the foundations of the world were laid: and therefore thou maist get the[e] packing, thou damned dog, & go shake thine eares, for in me hast thou nought.[72]

Although Philip Stubbes did not set down the Devil's replies, the following lines 'But what does thou lay to my charge, thou foule fiend? . . . what sayest thou more, Satan? . . .' clearly suggest a dialogue. The vocabulary shows how Katherine Stubbes, or else the recording Gentleman, must have been well acquainted with Devil literature. 'Thou hel-hound, . . . thou damned dog, . . . thou foule fiend, . . . thou firebrand of hell! . . . thou dastard, . . . thou cowardly souldier, . . .' It is surprising how the Devil could endure this long and by no means gentle speech, if, as we shall see in later chapters, he stood so much in fear of a woman's tongue. Finally, she threatens to call upon her 'grand-captaine Christ Iesus' at which the Devil vanishes.[73]

'Now is he gone, now is he gone! do you not see him flie like a cowarde, and runne away like a beaten cocke? He hath lost the fielde, and I haue wonne the victorie, euen the garland, and crowne of euerlasting life; and that, not by my owne power or strength, but by the power and might of Iesus Christ, who hath sent his holy Angels to keepe me.' And speaking to them that were by, she said, 'would God you saw but what I see! Do you not see infinite millions of most glorious Angels stand about me, with firie charets ready to defend me, as they did the good prophet *Elizeus.*'[74]

[72] P[hilip]. S[tubbes]. *Gent., A Christal Glasse* (1591); in *The Anatomie of Abuses* (1591), ed. F. J. Furnivall (New Shaksp. Soc., 1877-9), Pt. i, 205 *et seq.*

[73] *Cf. Los Libros de la Madre Teresa de Iesus*, (Al Salamanca, Por Guillelmo Foquel, 1588), 'Vida', Cap. XXV, p. 308, where Teresa de Cepeda, a Spanish contemporary, shows herself to be more practical in the matter and considers it waste of time and dignity to argue with the fiend.

> demonio, demonio: adonde podemos dezir,
> Dios, Dios, y hazerle temblar.

Oh, the devil, the devil! we say, when we might be saying o God! o God! thus making the devil tremble.

As Marcel Lépée remarks, 'c'est par le mépris qu'elle triomphe' (*Satan*, Les Études Carmélitaines', 1948, p. 103) This great woman and foundress of many convents, who had a habit of speaking with God quite familiarly, said that she was more afraid of people who were themselves terrified of the Devil – in particular some confessors – than of the Devil himself.

[74] P. S[tubbes]. *A Christal Glasse*, in *Anatomie* i, 207.

It was 'a most heauenly confession', no doubt. Whether it had a touch of realism is an open question. But at any rate, it emphasized the importance of the soul to this Puritan woman.

How the Devil dreaded these direct conflicts is shown by the many snares he set to catch a good woman. It is recorded in the life of Mary Ward, a Yorkshire girl who at the time (1598) was thirteen years of age and was staying with relatives in the country in order to prepare for her first Communion, how

. . . dans cette intervale, un soir environ l'heure du souper quil faisoit encor jour, un des serviteurs du logis luy vint dire quil y avoit en bas un gentilhome de la part de monsieur son pere, qui demandoit en grande haste de parler a elle. Elle, qui aimoit uniquement son pere surprise de la joye d'apprendre de ses nouvelles, s'oublia de sa civilité et retenue ordinaire, et sans mot de replique courut vittement a la porte: le gentilhome sans mettre pied a terre, ny passer la barrire, tire du sa poche une lettre, qu'il disoit avoir receue de m^r. son pere, avec ordre de la luy lire, mais deffense de la luy donner. Le contenu ettait que son pere luy commandoit sur peine dencourir sa malediction de remettre a un autre temps sa communion, parce quil traitoit un mariage pour elle fort avantageux, a scavoir avec un Seigneur Talbot de Grafton; ce que luy ayant dit il prit congé delle. Lon s'est depuis informé et lon a trouvé que son pere n'envoya jamais ny le messager ny la lettre.[75]

The mysterious visit caused much conflict in the young woman until she resolved to receive Communion at the first opportunity. It was afterwards generally believed that the nightly rider had been the fiend himself. It was no doubt a period in which the Devil was blamed for a great many things and it is hard for posterity to say for certain how far this blame was justified.

I end the Christian tradition with a woman saint who, perhaps in order of chronology should have been mentioned sooner, but has been reserved to the last because she, like the Virgin Mary, has inspired a literary interest which not only pervades the entire century, but forms also a link between the Christian and Chivalric traditions. It is Mary Magdalen 'out of whom went seuen deuils'.[76] This small legion provided capital entertainment in the mystery plays especially after Magdalen's conversion when they are cast out and driven, amid great thunder, to take refuge in hell.

Spiritus malignus hardly dares to face *Rex Diabolus* and cries

as flat as fox, I falle before your face.

[75] 'Vie de Mary Ward', Bar Convent *MS*. York, 1650-57. This is a translation of the English life 'Brief Relation' written in Paris soon after 1645 by Mary Poyntz, probably assisted by W. Wigmore, Mary Ward's companions.
Cf. M. C. E. Chambers, *The Life of Mary Ward* 1882) i, 34-35.
[76] *S. Luke*, viii, 2.
P. Viret, in *The worlde possessed* (1583), D. vi^v-viii. alleges that the Seven Devils in Mary Magdalene were indeed Devils and not deadly sins, as the Papists thought they were.

I^us Diabolus. thow theffe, wy hast þou don alle þis trespas,
to lett þen woman þi bondes breke?

mali[g]nus Spiritus. the speryt of grace sore ded hyr smyth,
& temptyd so sore þat Ipocryte.

I^us Diabolus. ȝa! thys hard balys on þi bottokkys xall byte!
In hast on þe I wol be wroke.
cum vp, ȝe horsons and skore a-wey þe yche!
& with thys panne ȝe do hym pycche![77]

Each one of them is served like the first. Yet for all that, matters cannot be altered. In vain do *Rex Diabolus* and his counsellors sit in state awaiting the grand spectacle of the judgement of a harlot; in vain are their piercing cries, so beloved by the early sixteenth-century audience. 'A, owt, owt, and harrow'! The judgement of Magdalen takes place elsewhere; 'thes betyll browyd bycheys' has escaped their clutches. The simple Gospel play was turned into a Morality by Lewis Wager. The Devils were transformed into vices, 'Infidelitie' being the leader of the band. They kept their victim enthralled until 'knowledge of sin', proving the stronger in the end, drives Magdalene to Christ who delivers her from her sinful passions.

Auoide out of this woman thou Infidelitie,
With the .vii. diuels which haue hir possessed,
I banish you hence by the power of my diuinitie,
For to saluation I haue hir dressed.[78]

From the stage directions: 'Cry all thus without the doore, and roare terribly', we know that at least part of the traditional entertainment had been kept intact.

The loyalty of this 'Blessed Offendour' and her perseverance are shown in later literature. Robert Southwell in *Marie Magdalens Funerall Teares* writes

She did not followe the tide of thy better Fortune, to shift saile when the streame did alter course. Shee beganne not to loue thee in thy life, to leaue thee after death : Neither was shee such a guest at thy table, that meant to bee a stranger in thy necessitie. She left thee not in thy lowest ebbe, shee reuolted not from thy last extremitie: In thy life shee serued thee with her goods: In thy death she departed not from the crosse: after death shee came to dwell with thee at thy graue.[79]

Returning to the beginning of the century, we come upon a similar idea of Magdalen's constancy expressed in ballad form, fusing the Christian and Chivalric traditions into one.

[77] *The Digby Plays*, ed. F. J. Furnivall, EETS, e.s. LXX (1896) pp. 82-3, ll. 730-8. *Cf. inf.* p. 156.
[78] Lewis Wager, *A new Enterlude*, (1567); ed. J. Farmer, Tudor Facs. Texts (1908), F. iii^v.
[79] R. Southwell, *M. Magdalens Funerall Teares*, (1594), f. 64, ^r-^v.

Lully, lulley, lully, lulley
The faucon hath borne my mak away

He bare hym up, he bare hym down,
He bare hym into an orchard brown.

In that orchard there was a hall,
That was hanged with purpill and pall.

And in that hall ther was a bede,
Hit was hanged with gold so rede.

And in that bed ther lythe a knyght,
His wounde bledyng day and nyght.

By that bedes side ther kneleth a may,
And she wepeth both night and day.

And by that beddes side ther stondeth a ston,
Corpus Christi wretyn theron.[80]

W. P. Ker considers it 'the frailest of all poetic creatures, of which no words can fitly express its beauty'.[81] The ideas hidden in this little frame are so rich that they can hardly be explained in a few lines. Here all that is most sacred in Christian tradition fuses with the highest chivalric expectations in the expression of woman's constancy and love once she has overcome the evil in her. The trust that her knight will recover never leaves her; hence the lullaby, which is so different from a funeral dirge. In these slender lines, the poet covers ground between Arimathea and Montsalvat where a virgin is guarding the vessel filled with the drops from 'His wounde bledyng day and nyght', the object of the quest which called into existence the noblest cycle of chivalric romance in literature.[82]

2 THE CHIVALRIC TRADITION

Woman's Function in The Chivalric Tradition

The Chivalric Tradition has three aspects: military, social and religious. In chivalry, religion and the profession of arms were reconciled. The change in attitude on the part of the Church dates from the Crusades when the

---

[80] M. J. C. Hodgart, *The Ballads*, Hutchinson's U. Libr. Eng. Lit., No. 38 (1950), p. 38.
[81] W. P. Ker, 'On the History of Ballads', *Proceedings Brit. Ac.* iv (1910), p. 200.
[82] E. K. Chambers, *English Literature at the close of the Middle-Ages* (OCP, 1945), p. 112, informs us – as we might expect – that the Corpus Christi carol first made its appearance not in oral tradition but with other carols in a sixteenth-century MS.

armies were devoted to a sacred purpose. Even prior to this, however, there was the 'Truce of God' when the knight vowed himself to the Church's service for the protection of the weak and innocent and of the churches. In return for this vow the Church ordained a special blessing for him *Benedictio novi militis.* The Knight, as we meet him in literature, had a sacred mission in which both Woman and the Devil played an important role. It was his task to overcome the Devil, symbol of all evil, and woman was to help him. Her function was threefold: she was often entrusted with the young squire's education and the formation of his character; she inspired the seasoned knight, and often found employment for him.

In the Christian legendary tradition, St Margaret had herself trampled the Devil under foot without the help of any knight. Chivalric literature expresses a joint operation in which woman features as the inspiration behind man's actions. Man performed his military feats in order to protect, honour and please the lady who, in her turn, made him aspire to great and difficult deeds.

> Fame si est de tel nature,
> Qu'ele fet les coars hardis.[83]

says a thirteenth-century poem.

Her Share in the Formation of the Young Squire

In the feudal days, and particularly at the time of the Crusades, the woman was left in charge of the castle and it was she who, to a large extent, directed the education of the young knight. By her example she ennobled and softened his manners teaching him courtesy and compassion. The ideal of a true knight, therefore, became, as it were, a fusion of masculine and feminine qualities. The idea is vividly portrayed in Wolfram von Eschenbach's *Parzival.*[84] Here the hero is brought up by his mother Herzloïde. Fear of losing her son in battle, prompts her to teach him only the feminine virtues. Nature, however, proves too strong and at his continual entreaties, she is obliged to let him go to his uncle Gurnemanz who will train him in knightly valour. Here Perceval receives an ultra-masculine education. He is taught to be independent, never to ask any question, to seek his own way and not to succumb to compassion. In consequence of this, the hero's first attempt in the quest of the Holy Grail becomes a failure. Perceval having arrived at Montsalvat and seeing Amfortas, the Fisher King sorely wounded, and the general sadness of the place, tries to be a man. He asks no questions and leaves the castle without any sign of compassion.

[83] M. Jubinal, *Jongleurs et Trouvères*, quoted in T. Wright, *Womankind in Western Europe* (1869), p. 162.
[84] Wolfram von Eschenbach, *Parzival und Titurel*; hg. K. Bartsch (Leipzig, 1875).

44

wol gemarcte Parzivâl
die rîcheit unt daz wunder grôz:
durch zuht in vrâgens doch verdrôz.
er dâhte 'mir riet Gurnamanz
mit grôzen triuwen âne schranz,
ich solte vil gevrâgen niht.[85]

As the bridge is drawn up behind him, he hears a page's voice shriek

'ir sît ein gans.
möht ir gerüeret hân den flans,
und het den wirt gevrâget!
vil prîss iuch hât betrâget.'[86]

But now it is too late. By lack of feminine virtue Perceval has failed to
break the spell of evil which hung around Montsalvat. He has failed the
Order of the Round Table. Cundri, the witch clairvoyant, comes to Arthur's
court to rebuke the King on account of his unworthy knight.

künc Artûs, du stüend' ze lobe
hôhe dînen gnôzen obe:
dîn stîgender prîs nu sinket,
dîn snelliu wirde hinket,
dîn hôhez lop sih neiget,
dîn prîs hât valsch erzeiget.[87]

Perceval's mistake is not rectified until he has learnt to combine with his
manly strength and valour the gentler virtues taught him by his mother
Herzloïde. Only then, being the perfect knight, is he given a second chance.
Thus in the chivalric tradition, it is woman and her knight together who
overcome the Devil.

St George—Type of the Chivalric Tradition

A knight was dubbed in the name of God and St George, the patron of
Chivalry. St George, whose warcry put the enemy to flight, is the oldest
champion of the chivalric tradition, and for centuries he was the hero in
folk-tradition. In 1415, on 23 April, 'St George's Day, was "made a major

[85] Wolfram von Eschenbach, op. cit., Buch v. ll. 458-63. 'Perceval was fully aware of
the riches and great marvel of the place, but did not consider it proper to ask questions,
remembering the advice given by Gurnemanz.'
[86] Ibid., Buch v, ll. 717-21. 'Fool! Why didst thou not open thy mouth and enquire
after thy host's misfortunes. It would have brought thee honour.'
[87] Ibid., Buch vi, ll. 1051-56. 'Thy rising fame and increasing honour have been
brought low. Thou hast fallen short of thy ideal; and thy value hath proved itself false.'

45

double feast and ordered to be observed the same as Christmas day, all labour ceasing" '.[88] From that day, the St George Play became 'the most popular and long-lived of English festival dramas'.[89] Numerous versions were performed all over England.[90] Pageants, dumb shows, May-games were held in his honour continuing as late as 1559.[91] Unfortunately, not much of this popular literature has survived. However, that he was born to fight the Dragon we know from the *Seuen Champions* to which I shall refer later.[92] The title of 'Red Cross Knight' was attributed to him after he was pressed into military service by the Normans as their patron saint, commanding the heavenly host that came to the aid of the Crusaders against the Turks, under the walls of Antioch, in 1098. On this occasion he was seen on a white horse bearing a white banner with a red cross.

The slaying of the Dragon is first credited to him in the latter part of the twelfth century and the belief became popular from its appearance in the thirteenth-century *Golden Legende*.[93]

The story probably spread during the Crusades when championship was much in vogue and the chivalric tradition came into being. Thus St George became the Christian hero of the Middle Ages. In oriental as well as in western pictorial art he is often shown in action with a crowned virgin by his side. In a fifteenth-century drawing in the British Museum it is the Virgin Mary who appears to St George. On behalf of her child who stretches his hand towards the champion, and supported by a heavenly choir of angels, she hands him a lance, demanding him to kill the anti-Christ or Dragon.[94] This symbolical representation of the Church or Christian Faith as a woman, and of the power of Evil as a Dragon was continued for many centuries. It inspired Edmund Spenser when writing *The Faerie Queene* for at the beginning of Book I

[88] M. C. Gayley, *Representative English Comedies* (New York, 1903), Vol. 1, p. xlii.
[89] *Ibid.*, p. xli. In the *York Civic Records*; Y. A. S. Record series, ed. A. Raine, CX (1946), v, 105, we find among many other items concerning the St. George celebrations: 'fo. 43, 20 April 1 Mary (1554). Aggreed that accordyng to the auncient custome of this Cite . . . . Saynt George that day to be brought forth and ryde as hath ben accustomed, at the Chambre costs.'
[90] Gayley, *op. cit.*, i, p. xlv. 'The St. George play is an example of how a legendary miracle, sacred in its origin, may pass into a folk drama of a national hero, and that again degenerate into a mumming or daunce;'
[91] *Ibid.*, p. xlii.
[92] *Inf.* pp. 48-9.
[93] *Oxford Dictionary of the Christian Church*, ed. S. L. Cross and E. A. Livingstone, 2nd edn. (OUP, 1974), p. 557.
The Golden Legende, f. cxviii[r]-[v].
[94] Brit. Mus. Prints and Drawings, Fawkener Coll. 5213-29. Flemish School XV century p. 6, Box 9, case 131.
In *The Booke of Reuelation*, xx, 2, Satan, the Devil and the Dragon are stated to be one and the same individual: 'And hee laid hold on the dragon that old serpent, which is the deuill and Satan, . . .'

46

>A Gentle Knight was pricking on the plaine,
>   Y cladd in mightie armes and siluer shielde,
>   . . . . . .
>
>A louely Ladie rode him faire beside,
>   Vpon a lowly Asse more white then snow,
>   Yet she much whiter, . . .[95]

The milk-white lamb by her side was a symbol of her own purity. She was of royal lineage,

>   Of ancient Kings and Queenes, that had of yore
>   Their scepters stretcht from East to Westerne shore,
>   And all the world in their subiection held;
>   Till that infernall feend with foule vprore
>   Forwasted all their land, and them expeld :
>   Whom to auenge, she had this Knight from far compeld.[96]

It was unmistakably St George for 'on his brest a bloodie crosse he bore'. The dragon 'horrible and stearne' proved a formidable opponent as all the dragons had been with which he had been confronted in the past, and during the combat the hero was much troubled.

>   His Lady sad to see his sore constraint,
>   Cride out, Now now, Sir knight, shew what ye bee,
>   Add faith vnto your force, and be not faint:
>   Strangle her, els she sure will strangle thee.[97]

Imbued with new courage by his lady's words, he 'struck his enemy with more than manly force, . . .' so that soon the dragon lay vanquished at his feet. The lady having watched the procedure from afar, now hastens to offer her congratulations.

>   Well worthie be you of that Armorie,
>   Wherein ye haue great glory wonne this day,
>   And proou'd your strength on a strong enimie,[98]

All is conducted according to tradition: a cry for help, the champion's readiness, the encouragement of the fair sex during the combat and praises after the deed has been successfully accomplished.

Woman Inspires the Seasoned Knight and Finds Employment for Him

It was, moreover, woman's peculiar contribution to chivalric literature that she was acutely aware of any lurking danger so that she was able to warn the knight to prepare for the attack, as the lady Una had done.

[95] *The Faerie Queene*, I, i, 4.
[96] *Ibid.*, I, i, 5.
[97] *Ibid.*, I, i, 19.
[98] *Ibid.*, I, i, 27.

> Be well aware, quoth then that Ladie milde,
>> Least suddaine mischiefe ye too rash prouoke:
>> The danger hid, the place vnknowne and wilde,
>> Breedes dreadful doubts: Oft fire is without smoke,
>> And perill without show:
>> . . . . . .
>>> the perill of this place
>> I better wot then you, . . .
>> . . . . . .
>
>> This is the wandring wood, this Errours den
>> A monster vile, whom God and man does hate :[99]

The examples of this womanly share in deeds of chivalry are numerous as for example further in the story where the lady Belge, after Arthur has vanquished the Giant, conducts him to another danger spot where she draws his attention to the hiding place of a monster 'Horrible, hideous, and of hellish race,' right beneath the altar of an idol in a heathen temple, where it fed on all the carcasses offered up as sacrifice.[100] Prince Arthur, at her request, exposes and attacks it.

> Vpon the Image with his naked blade
>> Three times, as in defiance, there he strooke;
>> And the third time out of an hidden shade,
>> There forth issewd, from vnder th' Altars smooke,
>> A dreadfull feend, with fowle deformed looke,
>> That stretcht it selfe, as it had long lyen still;
>> And her long taile and fethers strongly shooke,
>> That all the Temple did with terrour fill;[101]

There is yet another way in which Woman inspires the knight to conquer the Devil; the way of the fair Sabra. In *The most famous history of the seuen champions of Christendome* when St George arrives in Egypt, we read of

a dangerous and terrible Dragon nowe ranging vp and downe the Countrey, which if he be not euery day appeased with a pure and true virgin, which hee deuoureth downe his venimous bowels, but that day so neglected, will he breath such a stinch from his nostrels, whereof will grow a most grieuous

---

[99] *Ibid.*, I, i, 12-13.

[100] *Ibid.* V, xi, 19. It was a Christian theory that the Devils, after their fall from heaven, had taken upon them the form of heathen deities. St Paul writes to the Corinthians (I, x, 20): 'But I say that the things which the Gentiles sacrifice, they sacrifice to deuils, and not to God: and I would not that yee should haue fellowship with deuils.'
Cf. G. Gifford, *A Dialogue concerning Witches and Witchcraftes* (1593), ed. B. White, Shakesp. Ass. Facs. I (OUP., 1931), E. 4ᵛ. 'Dan[iel]. The deuils did make the heathen people beleeue that they were goddes, and so procured that they shoulde worship them with diuine worship . . . they conueied themselves into images, . . .'

[101] *The Faerie Queene*, V, xi, 20.

plague and mortalitie of all thinges, which vse hath beene obserued for these foure and twentie yeeres, but now there is not left one true virgin but the kings onely daughter throughout Egypt, which Damosell to morrow must be offered vp in sacrifice to the Dragon:[102]

Here it is not so much the liberation and protection of the fair lady that forms the central theme as the extinction of evil in the country. The woman appears as the victim whose willingness to be sacrificed has kept the Dragon

6 *She inspired the seasoned knight*

at bay until the hero can deliver the city, and it is she who inspires him when he comes. Her acceptance of her fate is stressed in a ballad version of the same story:

[102] R. Johnson, *The most famous history of the seuen champions of Christendome* (1608), pp. 13-14.

On the *Registers of the Company of Stationers*, the following entries occur in 1596.
'Vol. iii, f. 10ᵛ: 20 Aprilis: John Danter Entred for his copie vnder th[e h]andes of the Wardens. a booke Intituled *the famous history of the Seven Champions of Christiandom.*

'Vol. iii, f. 13ᵛ: 6 Septembris: Cuthbert Burby Entred for his copie by assignement from John Danter, Twoo bookes. *viz. the first parte and second parte of the vij champions of Christiandom.* Reservinge the Workmanship of the printing at all tymes to the said John Danter.'

W. Kemp, *Kemps Nine Daies Wonder* (for Nicholas Ling, 1600); ed. A. Dyce (1840), p. 22. Kemp refers to Richard Johnson as a kinsman of Jansonius, 'this beggarly lying busie-bodies name brought out the Ballad-maker'. He is obviously not in favour of the

Lo! here I am, I come, quoth she,
therefore do what you will with me.[103]

Steadfast and obedient in the face of danger and pain Sabra[104] stands as a mediatrix warding off the monstrous evil.[105] However, in *The Golden Legende*, the daughter of a Libyan King is presented in a more active role. One day St George rode

to a cyte which is sayd Sylene/ & by this cyte was a stagne or a ponde lyke a see/ wherin was a dragon whiche enuenymed all ye coūtree.

An order was issued that lots should be drawn who should next be sacrificed to this dragon. The lot fell upon the king's daughter. At this point our champion arrives. Throwing his spear into the dragon, he says to the maiden:

delyuer to me your gyrdell/ & bynde it aboute the necke of the dragon/ and be not aferde. Whan she had done soo/ the dragon folowed her as it had be a meke beest and debonayre. Than she ledde hym in to ye cyte/ . . .

where people were baptized and the dragon was slain by St George.[106]

These last examples are no imitation of the attack on evil by St Margaret 'Fayre Amazon of heaven', the Abbess Hilda and others (*sup.* p. 37 *et seq*). Woman here is simply the inspiration and strength of 'that *rough-hewn, boisterous* kind, the Male'[107] together with whom she achieves the conquest.

3 ROMANTIC STORIES BASED ON PAGAN SUPERSTITION

The Fairy Kind Explained

There is still another body of literature in which Woman confronts the Devil. These are the romantic stories based on pagan superstition. The Devil is no longer the terrifying fallen angel of Christian theology; nor is he the evil Dragon of Chivalry. James I, in his analysis of devils draws attention to this category:

---

profession as they are often to blame for unwanted publicity. He forgives Johnson but advises: 'Leaue writing thèsè beastly ballats, make not good wenches Prophetesses for litle or no profit, nor for a sixe-penny matter reuiue not a poore fellowes fault thats hanged for his offence; it may by thy owne destiny one day; prethee be good to them. Call vp thy olde Melpomene, whose straubery quil may write the bloody lines of the blew Lady, and the Prince of the burning crowne; a better subiect, I can tell ye, than your Knight of the Red Crosse.'

[103] T. Percy, *Reliques of ancient English Poetry*, (1794), iii,232, ll. 95-6.

[104] In Arabic, the word Sabra, صَبَرَ صُبَر means: the one who has patience.

[105] In Alexander Barclay, tr., *The Lyfe of Saynt George* by Baptist Mantuan (1515), ed. W. Nelson, EETS, o.s., No. 230 (1955), p. 42, ll. 834-5, the monster itself is impressed by the noble appearance of the maiden. 'Styll stode the monstre/ with iyen bryght as fyre/ Maruaylynge in maner . . .'

[106] *The Golden Legende*, f. Cxviii ʳ-ᵛ. Ucello's painting in the National Gallery shows in detail how the Dragon was yoked to the maiden.

[107] Agrippa von Nettesheim, *Female Pre-eminence*, tr. H. C[are], (1670), p. 2.

PHILOMATHES.

NOW I pray you come on to that fourth kinde of spirites.

Ep i. That fourth kinde of spirites, which by the Gentiles was called *Diana*, and her wandring court, and amongst vs was called the *Phairie* (as I

L   told

James here seems to refer to the minor local deities who were defeated by Christianity.[108]

The countless legions of earth-sprites and the army of giants that inhabited the countries of the North came under Satan's sway. Spirits such as elves, cobolds, fairies, hairy hobgoblins of the forest, waternymphs of the brookside, and dwarfs of the mountains were transformed by medieval Christianity into devils, or into hellish imps, a sort of assistant or apprentice devils.[109]

T. A. Spalding draws attention to the fact that the new converts of Great Britain may have fostered 'a certain lurking affection' for the gods they had deserted, perhaps under compulsion which

may have led them to look upon their ancient objects of veneration as less detestable in nature, and dangerous in act, than the devils imported as an integral portion of their adopted faith.[110]

At any rate, the power and range of these diminished deities were greatly limited by the Christian regime. They had to perform most of their work by night,[111] and they were restricted by the seasons:

[108] James I, *Daemonologie* (R. Walde-graue, 1597), Bk. III, Ch. v, p. 73.
[109] M. Rudwin, *op. cit.*, p. 22.
    R. Scot, *op. cit.* (1584), Cap. 21, pp. 521-2, mentions several names given to these Idols. Among them: '*Guteli* or *Trulli* are spirits (they saie) in the likenes of women, shewing great kindnesse to all men : & hereof it is that we call light women, truls.'
    Cf. T. A. Spalding, *Elizabethan Demonology* (1880), p. 25. 'The trolds obtained a character similar to that of the more modern succubus, and have left their impression upon Elizabethan English in the word "trull".'
    Autolycus, in *The Winters Tale*, IV, iii, 89; (84) speaks of 'Troll-my-dames'.
[110] Spalding, *op. cit.*, p. 24.
[111] *N.B.* The distinction made between the fairies and wandering ghosts in *A Midsommer Nights Dreame*, especially Oberon's boast in III, ii, 409 (388)
            'But we are spirits of another sort,'
Nevertheless, he hastens Puck,
                        'make no delay;
            We may effect this businesse, yet ere day.' 415-6 (394-5).

Some say that ever 'gainst that season comes
Wherein our Saviour's birth is celebrated,
The bird of dawning singeth all night long;
And then, they say, no spirit dare stir abroad,
The nights are wholesome, then no planets strike,
No fairy takes, nor witch hath power to charm,
So hallow'd and so gracious is the time.[112]

It was by no means easy to recognize this minor variety of Devil for they could take on any shape convenient for the occasion; 'all shapes that man goes vp and downe in, from fourscore to thirteen, this spirit walks in'.[113] It was not confined to human shape either.

'I am a man apo' de land,
I am a selkie i' de sea;[114]

Or he might transform into 'Some ayery Deuill',[115] but always in the end he would prove 'A Feind, a Fairie, pittilesse and ruffe':[116] They were malicious to the Christian and, no matter what their shape, not to be trusted, since

The Goblin-Bugs, and Faery Hiedegies
Are both the shades of hell, . . .[117]

Woman Breaks the Spell of the Fairy in its Different Guises

Most of the Fairy-literature has been expressed in ballad form. Its best representative is *The Tayl of the ȝong tamlene* told by the shepherd in *The Complaynt of Scotland*, and identified by Leyden with the later ballad of *the young Tamlane* in Scott's *Minstrelsy*.[118] It is the story in which a woman rescues her lover from the fairies who are about to sacrifice him as their seven-yearly tribute to hell.[119] In the ballad, Fair Janet is deeply concerned with the spiritual welfare of her lover:

[112] *Hamlet*, I, i, 158-64.

[113] *Tymon of Athens*, 1st Folio, Tragedies, p. 84; (II, ii,114).

[114] *The Play of de Lathie Odivere*; in *The Scottish Antiquary*, viii, (1894), p. 55, col. ii, verse 6.

[115] *King Iohn*, III, ii, 5.

[116] *The Comedie of Errors*, 1st Folio, Comedies, p. 94; (IV, ii, 35).

[117] A. Copley, *op. cit.*, p. 36, verse 2.

[118] *The Complaynt of Scotlande* (1549), ed. J. A. H. Murray (EETS, 1872), pp. lxxix and 63, ll. 30-31.

Cf. The English and Scottish Popular Ballads, ed. F. J. Child (5 vols. 1882-98), i, 335. [I shall refer to this edn. unless otherwise stated]

[119] M. J. C. Hodgart, *op. cit.*, pp. 126-7. 'The *motif* of the fairies' tribute to hell, paid at the end of every seven years, may also have some connection with the ritual murder of the divine kings made familiar to us by *the Golden Bough*. . . . This kind of human sacrifice is found elsewhere in folklore, and also in associations with fairies. In the witch trials of the sixteenth and seventeenth centuries, many of the accused testified to having

'The truth ye'll tell to me, Tamlane,
　　　A word ye mauna lie;
　　Gin eer ye was in haly chapel,
　　　Or sained in Christentie?'[120]

He then reveals his identity, confiding to her that Randolph, Earl Murray
was his sire, but that he was kidnapped by the Queen of Fairies. Life in
Fairy-land is very pleasant:

'But aye, at every seven years,
　　　They pay the teind to hell;
　　And I am sae fat and fair of flesh,
　　　I fear 't will be mysell.'[121]

He looks upon her as the only person who can save him and there is a ring
of hope in the lines:

'This night is Halloween,[122] Janet,
　　　The morn is Hallowday,
　　And gin ye dare your true love win,
　　　Ye hae nae time to stay.'[123]

He begs her to meet him at midnight, at Miles Cross, where the procession
of fairies will pass, and to seize on him, and not to let him go though he
may change into various shapes.

Gloomy, gloomy, was the night,
　　　And eiry was the way,
　　As fair Janet, in her green mantle,
　　　To Miles Cross she did gae.[124]

Fearlessly Janet waits for him at the appointed place. Her love proves
stronger than the power of the Fairy and she saves Tamlane by breaking its
spell.

---

relations with the fairies and to learning their arts from them, and the cyclical sacrifice
is mentioned. Sometimes it was at the end of seven years, but Alison Pearson, executed
in 1586, testified that the tribute was annual. She said that one William Sympson, who
had been taken away by the fairies, "bidd her sign herself that she be not taken away,
for the teind of them are taken away to hell everie year".'
　Cf. inf. p. 120.
[120] Child, i, 354, No. 39, I, verse 26.
[121] *Ibid.*, i, 354, verse 32.
[122] On the eve of All Saints the fairies had their greatest power, but this was weakened
on All Saints day for then there was a closer relationship between the heavenly inhabitants
and the earth-dwellers who then received greater protection.
[123] *Ibid.*, i, 354, verse 33.
[124] *Ibid.*, i, 355, verse 46.

> She pu'd him frae the milk-white steed,
> And loot the bridle fa,
> And up there raise an erlish cry,
> 'He's won amang us a'!'
>
> They shaped him in fair Janet's arms
> And esk but and an adder;
> She held him fast in every shape,
> . . . . . .[125]

Allegiance to hell is thwarted by a woman who proves loyal in the face of danger.

In a further group of ballads, classed together by Child under the title of *Lady Isabel and the Elf-Knight*,[126] woman is again the opponent of evil and the champion of good. Wickedness is represented either by a Daemon, a Nix, an Elf Knight, or even a human Bluebeard. In all these stories the woman is triumphant.

In *the Water o'Wearie's Well*[127] the opponent is a Nix or Merman, one of 'the woorser moitie of diuels',[128] who boasts of having killed seven ladies. Yet the maid is in no way daunted but gets a firm grip on him.

> 'Since seven king's daughters ye've drowned there,
> In the water o'Wearie's well,
> I'll make you bridegroom to them a',
> An ring the bell mysell.'
>
> And aye she warsled, and aye she swam,
> And she swam to dry lan;
> She thanked God most cheerfully
> The dangers she oercame.[129]

In *The Gowans sae gay* the lady uses different tactics.

> She stroakd him sae fast, the nearer he did creep,
> Aye as the gowans grow gay
> Wi a sma charm she lulled him fast asleep.
> The first morning in May.

[125] *Ibid.*, i, 355, verses 49-50.
[126] *Ibid.*, i, 22, No. 4.
[127] *Ibid.*, i, 55, No. 4B.
[128] *Inf.*, p. 154.
Spenser in *The Faerie Queene*, II, xii, 24-5, also mentions 'The griesly Wasserman', and continues
> For all that here on earth we dreadfull hold
> Be but as bugs to fearen babes withall,
> Compared to the creatures in the seas entrall.

[129] Child, i, 55-56, No. 4B, verses 13-14.

Wi his ain sword-belt sae fast as she ban him,
　　Aye as the gowans grow gay
Wi his ain dag-durk sair as she dang him.
　　The first morning in May.[130]

Woman had powerful weapons; mother earth and mother wit were on her side. Herbs discovered by her in the early matriarchal days and used to combat evil in guise of sickness, fever and disease, now formed a charm for her own protection.

　　　Parsley, sage, rosemary and thyme.[131]

In *The Elfin-Knicht* the conflict is waged by means of a dialogue in which the woman outwits the Elf's unreasonable requests.[132] The same feminine intuition which prompted Mariken van Nieumeghen to exclaim at her first encounter with the Devil: 'Ghi sijt die viant vander hellen',[133] identifies him in *The Unco Knicht's Wowing*.

　　　'Or what is greener nor the grass?
　　　Or what is waur nor a woman was?'
　　　. . . . . .

　　　'The pies are greener nor the grass,
　　　And Clootie's waur nor a woman was.'

　　　As sune as she the fiend did name,
　　　He flew awa in a blazing flame.[134]

One of the Danish Ballads, *The Water-King*, offers the simplest solution of all. The Lady who has been taken out to sea by the 'white chief' and is at the point of being drowned by him, calls out:

　　　Stop! stop! for God's sake, stop! for oh!
　　　The Waters o'er my bosom flow! –
　　　Scarce was the word pronounced, when knight
　　　and courser vanish'd from her sight.[135]

In the ballad universe where the demarcation line between fairies and human beings was so slight, the Daemon or Elf was easily replaced by a human villain when a historical incident gave occasion to do so.

[130] *Ibid.*, i, 55, No. 4A, verses 11-12.
[131] *Ibid.*, i, 18, No. 2G. verse 1. Considering the extensive herb-lore attributed to witches, woman here seems to be fighting the Devil with his own, rather than antithetical, weapons. *Cf. sup.* p. 25.
[132] *Ibid.*, i, 16, No. 2C.
[133] *Mariken van Nieumeghen*, B. ii, l. 310. 'Thou art the Fiend from hell'.
[134] Child, i, 4-5, No. 1C, verses 13, 18-19.
[135] M. G. Lewis, *Tales of Wonder* (1801), i, No. XI, p. 59. [The ballad is a translation from the Danish version in the Kiampe Viiser.]

This seems to have been the case with *The Historical Ballad of May Culzean*, or *May Colven*.[136] When Sir John, intending to drown the maid, asks her to take off her smock, she begs him

> 'O turn you about, O false Sir John,
>> And look to the leaf of the tree,
> For it never became a gentleman
>> A naked woman to see.'

> He turnd himself straight round about,
>> To look to the leaf of the tree;
> So swift as May Colven was
>> To throw him in the sea.[137]

The *naïveté* of the would-be murderer reminds one of the stupidity of the medieval Devil who was, on no account, to succeed.

Popularity of the Elfin Group and its Relationship with Continental Ballads

Child suggests that of all ballads, this Elfin group has perhaps obtained the widest circulation. It is known in most European languages.[138] Internal evidence, as W. J. Entwistle suggests,[139] points to a relationship with the medieval Dutch *Halewijn*[140] in which the woman returns home triumphantly, like Judith, with the head of her would-be seducer.[141]

In Scandinavia the ballad made contact with others which describe elfin malevolence, and so it appears in English in *Lady Isabel and the False Knight* and *May Collin*.[142]

[136] W. Motherwell, *Minstrelsy* (Glasgow, 1873), p. lxx, mentions ' "The Historical Ballad of May Culzean", to which is prefixed some local tradition that the lady there celebrated was of the family of Kennedy, and that her treacherous and murder-minting lover was an Ecclesiastick of the monastery of Maybole. In the parish of Ballantrae, on the sea coast, there is a frowning precipice pointed out to the traveller as "Fause Sir John's Loup".'

[137] Child, i, 56, No. 4C, verses 8-9.

[138] *Ibid.*, i, 22-54. There is sufficient evidence that this particular group of *Lady Isabel and the Elf-Knight* was in existence in the sixteenth century. Broadsheets appeared in Spain, Germany and the Scandinavian countries.
  Among the sixteenth-century versions Child mentions a Danish one in Grundtvig's Engelske Folkeviser (p. 233) printed from a fifteenth-century MS; a Spanish one dating from the middle of the century; and three German broadsheets dated 1555, 1560 and 1570.

[139] W. J. Entwistle, *European Balladry* (Oxford, 1939) p. 84.

[140] For the text see F. van Duyse, *Het oude Ned. Lied* ('s Gravenhage, 2 delen, 1903-8), i; for critical comments, G. P. M. Knuvelder, *Handboek tot de Geschiedenis der Nederlandse Letterkunde* ('s Hertogenbosch, 2 delen, 1970-1), i, pp. 280-1.

[141] Child, *op. cit.*, i, 51, summarizes Prof. Sophus Bugge's argumentation 'that the ballad we are dealing with is a wild shoot from the story of Judith and Holofernes'.

[142] W. J. Entwistle, *op. cit.*, p. 84.

It indicates the mingling of biblical with pagan ideas and contemporary events, the interchange of humans and fairies which was a frequent occurrence in this type of literature.

The ballads, though familiar in oral tradition, do not seem to have appeared as broadsheets in sixteenth-century England. There was a better sale for *A New Delightful Ballad, a godly Ballad, a very proper dittie,* or *Pleasant Quippes.* Certain Protestants and Puritans who objected to legendary stories of the Virgin Mary and the Devil, were also offended by this type of fairy lore. King James reckoned it among the sort of illusions 'that was rifest in the time of *Papistrie*'.[143] Moreover, Shakespeare has left us evidence that the simplicity of presentation in the ballads was jibed at by the sophisticated playwright and trained musician.[144] Yet the plentiful evidence of oral collections made at a later period, proves that the 'choice old ballads' continued to exist, and that the song of a woman conquering the Fairy was sung throughout the century.

4 PROCESS OF SECULARISATION OF THE CHRISTIAN TRADITION

Reigning Queens and the Concept of Mercy

As the century advanced, medievalism in drama and poetry underwent a gradual process of secularisation. Not only the Reformation and Renaissance learning, but also the long period of ruling Queens was responsible for this shift of interest in spiritual to that of temporal power. Poets, instead of directing their praises to the Queen of Heaven, considered it not unprofitable to dedicate their verse to 'our most vertuous Queene' of England. A unique broadsheet appeared, *An Ave Maria* in which the Queen was addressed as

> Marie, the mirrour of mercifulnesse,
> God of his goodnesse hath lent to this lande;
> Our iewell, our ioye, our Iudeth, doutlesse,
> The great Holofernes of hell to withstande.[145]

---

[143] James I, *op. cit.*, Bk. III, ch. v, p. 74.
Cf. Dr Richard Corbet, *The Faeryes Farewell*; in *The Poems* ed. J. A. W. Bennett and H. R. Trevor-Roper, (OCP, 1955) p. 49.

> But, since of late *Elizabeth*,
> And later *Iames* came in,
> They never daunc'd on any heath
> As *when the Time hath bin.*

> By which wee note the *Faries*
> Were of the old Profession;
> Theyre Songs were *Ave Maryes,*
> Theyre Daunces were *Procession.*

[144] *A Midsommer Nights Dreame*, IV, i, 233-4; (214). *Henry IV*, Pt. 1, II, ii, 41-5; (45-7). *The Winters Tale*, IV, iv, 212-31, 286 *et seq.*; (179-211, 279).
[145] Hyder E. Rollins, *Old English Ballads* (Cambridge, 1920) p. 14, verse 2.

With the succession of Elizabeth 'The cult of the Virgin Queen became a national variation of the cult of the Virgin Mother.'[146] Spenser in his invocation to 'The Faerie Queene' addresses her as 'Mirrour of grace and majestie divine'. In Book II, the fair Medina asks Guyon whence he came and whither he is bound, at which he describes the queen of his country for whom he fights and to whom he owes his homage.

> In widest Ocean she her throne does reare,
> That ouer all the earth it may be seene;
> As morning Sunne her beames dispredden cleare,
> And in her face faire peace, and mercy doth appeare.

> In her the richesse of all heauenly grace,
> In chiefe degree are heaped vp on hye :[147]

It was felt by poets and writers that no greater praise could be bestowed upon woman than that which had been conferred upon the Mother of God, and since mercy and intercession together with power and initiative in dealings with the Devil had been the most popular characteristics in the cult of the Virgin Mary, they were also reckoned among the necessary attributes of a good woman. Already earlier in the century Sir Thomas Elyot in *The Boke named The Governour* had devoted a chapter to mercy recounting how Octavius Augustus having been warned against Lucius Cinna as a mortal enemy who is conspiring against his life, finds himself in a fearful quandary whether to destroy Cinna and all his family or expose himself to this imminent danger.

To hym beinge thus perplexed came his wife Liuia, the empresse, who said unto him, Pleaseth it you, sir, to here a womans aduise. Do you as phisitians be wonte to do, where their accustumed remedies preue nat, they do assaye the contrarye. By seueritie ye haue hitherto nothing profited, proue therfore nowe what mercy may aduaile you. Forgiue Cinna; he is taken with the maynure, and may nat nowe indomage you, profite he may moche to the increase of your renome and perpetuell glorie. The emperour reioysed to hym selfe that Cinna had founde suche an aduocatrice, and gyuynge her thankes he caused his counsailours, whiche he had sente for, to be countermaunded, and callyng to hym Cinna only, he commaunded the chambre to be auoyded, and an other chaire to be sette for Cinna; ... neuer after was Augustus in daunger of any treason.[148]

Alois Brandl draws a comparison with Shakespeare.

Shakespeare hat manchen hervorstechenden Gedanken mit Elyot gemein. Der beredte Appell der Portia im 'Kaufmann von Venedig' an die Könige, sie

---

[146] *Concise Cambridge History*, ed. G. Sampson (Cambridge, 1941), p. 214.

[147] *The Faerie Queene*, II, ii, 40-41.

[148] Sir Thomas Elyot, *The Boke named the Gouernour* (1531); ed. E. Rhys, Everyman's Library (1907), pp. 142-44.

möchten in ihrem Herzen Gnade thronen lassen, hat ein Gegenstück im 'Governour' (II 79), wo es heißt, nichts knüpfe die Herzen der Untertanen so eng an ihren Fürsten wie *mercy*.[149]

Not only Shakespeare but other dramatists availed themselves of the idea. In Thomas Heywood's *Edward IV*, the Marquis of Dorset denounces Jane Shore to his mother who shows herself merciful, at which Mistress Shore is deeply moved.

> Most high and mightie Quéene, may I beléeue
> There can be found such mercie in a woman,
> And in a Quéene, more then in a wife,
> So déeply wrongd as I haue wronged you?
> In this bright christall myrror of your mercie,
> I sée the greatnesse of my sinne the more,
> And makes my fault more odious in mine eyes,
> Young princely pitie now doth wound me more,
> Then all your threatnings euer did before.[150]

In life as well as in literature mercy was the distinguishing mark of the good woman.[151] John Stow, in his *Chronicles* draws attention to the merciful initiative of the ladies of the Court. He describes how, after the May Day insurrection in 1517, when hundreds of rebels were taken prisoner and with 'the rope about their neckes' were waiting to be hanged,

there came a commandement from the King to respite the execution, and then were the prisoners sent againe to prison, and the armed men sent out of London. For it is to be noted that thrée Quéenes, to witte, Katherine Quéene of Englande, and by her meanes Marie the French Quéene, and Margaret Quéene of Scottes, the Kings sisters, (then resident in Englande) long time on their knees before the King had begged their pardon, . . .[152]

The examples of mercy set by women in history and literature were so potent that the idea grew to be a legend. The text of *The Notbroune Mayd*, C. S. Lewis informs us, was discovered among the curious miscellany of *Arnold's Chronicle* in 1502 'like a gold ring found in an old drawer full of odds and ends'. [153] To our twentieth-century ears, the lady's virtue transcends the confines of reality:

[149] A. Brandl, 'Thomas Elyot's Verteidigung guter Frauen' (1545), *Deutsche Shakesp. Gesellschap Jahrbuch*, 51 (Berlin 1915) p. 143.
'Shakespeare has some easily identifiable ideas in common with Elyot. Portia's eloquent appeal in *The Merchant of Venice* with reference to the power of clemency enthroned in the hearts of Kings has a comparable example in *the Governour* where Elyot states that there is nothing which binds the subjects's affection to their princes more closely than mercy.'
[150] Th. Heywood, *King Edward the fourth* (1600) H. 5.
[151] *Cf.* Agrippa, *op. cit.*, tr. Clapam, C. ii^v. 'It is well knowen, that for the more parte, a woman hath alway more pite and mercy than a man. whiche thynge Aristotle doth attribute to womākynd, as a thing appropried therevnto.'
[152] John Stow, *The Annales of England* (Ralfe Newbery, 1600), p. 851.
[153] C. S. Lewis, *Eng. Lit. in the 16th century*, p. 147.

Though in the wood
I undirstode
Ye had a paramour/   But that I wyl be your:
All this may nought   And she shal fynde
Remeue my thought/   Me softe and kynde
     And curteis euery our/[154]

A similar theme emerged from the pen of Erasmus, in *Coniugium*, one of his *Colloquies*. Here 'a certain gentilmā he as suche sort of men do, vsed much huntyng in the cuntre'[155] fell in love with a young girl, daughter of a poor old woman. For the sake of this maid he often spent the nights from home. His wife discovered the reason of his absence and, seeing how the cottage in which her husband spent his time lacked all comfort, she secretly provided him with the necessities and his accustomed fineries.

Not long after her husband stale thether againe, he sawe the howse otherwyse decked, and better fare then he was wounte to haue. He asked, frome whence commeth al this goodly gere? They sayde that an honeste matrone, a kynse-woman of hys hadde broughte it thyther and commaunded them that he should be well cherished when so euer he came, by and by his hart gaue him that it was hys wiues dede, . . .[156]

As a result he returned home never to leave her again. The story is based on the German folk legend of a Wildfrau who by her beautiful hair attracted and lay with an honest woman's husband.[157] The woman, dis-covering them, frees her husband from the power of this fairy who tells him that if his wife had shown any anger or hatred, he would have suffered. We may conclude therefore that mercy was considered to have greater power over evil than any other weapon. These few representative examples of a theme so widespread in sixteenth-century literature portray the one idea which was later so well expressed by the Countess in *All's Well*:

What angel shall
Blesse this vnworthy husband, he cannot thriue,
Vnlesse her prayers, whom heauen delights to heare
And loues to grant, repreeue him from the wrath
Of greatest Iustice.[158]

Literature Enriched by the Virgin Mary Ideal

It is evident that literature and particularly drama, were enriched by the concept of womanhood embodied in the Virgin Mary. In fact, the play of the Virgin itself paved the way towards the idea of mercy in secular

---

[154] W. C. Hazlitt, *Remains of the Early Popular Poetry* (1866), ii, 290.

[155] D. Erasmus, *A mery Dialogue* [tr. of *Coniugium*] (1557), B. iij.

[156] *Ibid.*, B. iiiᵛ-iiij.

[157] See V. B. Heltzel, 'Traces of a Wildfrau story in Erasmus', *PQ*, VIII (Iowa, 1929), pp. 348 *et seq.*

[158] *All's Well that Ends Well*, 1st Folio., p. 242. (III, iv, 25-29).

drama. C. M. Gayley in his introduction to the York Play *Joseph's Trouble about Mary*, remarks upon the significance of the character of the Virgin and her vindication.

In the Wakefield play she is somewhat curt in her replies; here she is the *ewig-weibliche*, worthy of adoration, winsome, mild. She is the first romantic woman in English drama, and the series of plays in which she figures is the forerunner of the modern comedy of love, – the drama of the maiden ideal victorious, and of woman adored.[159]

In this play, produced by 'The Pewtereres and Foundours' Our Lady appears as a mortal like ourselves, not as a mighty mediator but as a party personally concerned. The conflict here is of a homely kind and deeply human. Joseph is extremely worried because he has discovered that Mary is with child and by incessant questioning he tries to force her to tell him who is the father.

> Jos : Who had thy maydenhede Marie? has þou oght mynde.
>
> Mar: For suth, I am a mayden clene.
>
> Jos : Nay þou spekis now agayne kynde;
> Slike þing myght neuere naman of mene.
> A maiden to be with childe,
> þase werkis fra þe ar wilde,
> Sho is not borne I wene.
>
> Mar : Joseph, yhe ar begiled,
> With synne was I neuer filid,
> Goddis sande is on me sene.[160]

These things are beyond Joseph's understanding; but an angel reveals to him in a dream that the child is of God. Filled with remorse and with greater love for Mary, he hastens home to beg her pardon but he is afraid to speak to her. Mary, realizing his distress, says,

> Forgiffnesse sir! late be! for shame,
> Slike wordis suld all gud women lakke.[161]

The depth of characterization in the play may well compare with some of the best work of Elizabethan dramatists. Gayley rightly says that without this virgin ideal

[159] C. M. Gayley, *Plays of our Forefathers* (New York, 1907), p. 195.
[160] *Joseph's trouble about Mary*, York Plays, ed. L. Toulmin Smith (OCP, 1885), pp. 108-9, ll. 208-17.
[161] *Ibid.*, p. 111, ll. 297-9.

comedy would have remained farcical, fleshly, or heartless. It is largely by virtue of this ideal that the romantic comedy of Greene and Shakespeare runs with a ruddier blood and beats with a quicker pulse and healthier actuality and nobler spirit than the satire of Aristophanes or the smut of Wyckerley. Comedy is not of the head alone nor of the belly. She is no Phoenician Ashtoreth, nor Aphrodite Pandemos, nor French Lubricity; nor is she any pallid Artemis, or lightning-born Athene, purposive, unfeeling, and serene. *Thalia Urania* is wit and winsomeness; sanity, romance, and tenderness, – in one: the light and love of a life found 'more amusing than we thought.'[162]

Portia and the Virgin

On the subject of the Virgin and the Devil, secularized drama reached its climax and perfection in *The Merchant of Venice* where Portia answers the Virgin ideal expressed in *Annunciacio*, in Mary's reply to Gabriel.

> I lofe my lord all weldand,
> I am his madyn at his hand,
>   And in his wold;
> I trow bodword that thou me bryng,
> Be done to me in all thyng,
>   As thou has told.[163]

Portia, with the same willingness, puts herself at the disposal of her lord.

> You see my Lord Bassiano where I stand,
> Such as I am; ...
> . . . . . .
> Happiest of all, is that her gentle spirit
> Commits it selfe to yours to be directed,
> As from her Lord, her Gouernour, her King.[164]

This attitude of loving submission was by no means merely passive. It had crushed the Devil in *Annunciacio* and it inspired Portia's activity when the need arose. For then we see her carrying on the ancient tradition of the *advocata nostra* pleading for mercy against Shylock's unreasonable demand for justice with the same motives as his prototype Masscheroen and with the same persistency, for as Salerio remarks:

> neuer did I know
> A creature that did beare the shape of man
> So keene and greedy to confound a man.

[162] C. M. Gayley, *Plays of our Forefathers*, p. 197.
Cf. C. S. Lewis, *The Allegory of Love* (Oxford, 1936), p. 42. 'When *Frauendienst* succeeds in fusing with religion, as in Dante, unity is restored to the mind, and love can be treated with a solemnity that is whole-hearted.'
[163] *Annunciacio, The Townely Plays*; ed. A. W. Pollard, EETS, e.s., LXXI (1897), p. 90, ll. 143-8.
[164] *The Merchant of Venice*, III, ii, 156-72; (149-66).

He plyes the Duke at morning and at night,
And doth impeach the freedome of the state
If they deny him iustice. Twenty Merchants,
The Duke himselfe, and the Magnificoes
Of greatest port, haue all perswaded with him,
But none can driue him from the enuious plea
Of forfeiture, of iustice, and his bond.[165]

In the play *Mariken van Nieumeghen* God proclaims that it is only those refusing to repent who will be punished, at which Masscheroen replies:

U gherechticheyt faelt in veel dinghen.
Al heetmen u rechtveerdich God in allen siden.[166]

In the *Processus Sathane*, Satan cries out: 'Ubi est iusticia'[167] Shylock follows the tradition. Seeing that the Duke is unwilling to grant his plea, he brings forward his challenge:

If you deny me; fie vpon your Law,
There is no force in the decrees of Venice;
I stand for iudgment, answer, Shall I haue it?[168]

The trial scene in *The Merchant of Venice* no longer takes place in heaven (the higher part of a two-story pageant) before the judgement seat of Almighty God, but at Venice, in the Court of Justice accessible to anyone who wishes to attend. This brings the scene down to human level in more than one respect. Moreover, whereas the play of Masscheroen with its plea for mercy deals, as it were, with one aspect of the Lord's Prayer 'forgive us our trespasses', the trial scene at Venice is a continuation of it, a further development in which man's own responsibility begins to play an active part. 'As we forgive them that trespass against us' is here laid down as a condition, for as the Duke remarks: 'How shalt thou hope for mercie, rendring none?' It is this which forms the main theme in the play. Mercy is the quality which makes man resemble his Creator, 'It is an attribute to God himself', but it is also a test of true humanity by which man will be judged.

Therefore Iew,
Though Iustice be thy plea, consider this,
That in the course of Iustice, none of vs
Should see saluation: we do pray for mercie,
And that same prayer, doth teach vs all to render
The deeds of mercie.[169]

---

[165] *Ibid.*, III, ii, 291-300; (276-285).
[166] *Mariken van Nieumeghen*, D. v. 'Thy justice fails in many things despite the fact that thou bearest the name of a just God.'
[167] Saxoferrato, *Tractatus Iudiciorum* (Tolosae [1485?]). C. ii.
[168] *The Merchant of Venice*, IV, i, 106-8; (101-4).
[169] *The Merchant of Venice*, IV, i, 207-212; (192-97).

Shylock's answer is what we expect from him.

> I craue the Law,
> The penaltie and forfeite of my bond.[170]

As the duke informs us, he is indeed

> A stonie aduersary, an inhumane wretch,
> Vncapable of pitty, voyd, and empty
> From any dram of mercie.[171]

In Jacob van Maerlant's *Merlijn* The Devil is called 'dat quade dier'.[172] Just so Gratiano, after being assured that no prayers can pierce the Jewish heart of Shylock, regards him as a damned 'inexecrable dogge'.[173] Both Masscheroen and Shylock are pleading for revenge, not justice. 'I will haue the heart of him',[174] no more, no less, and for no further reason than 'a lodg'd hate ... ';[175] if it will feede nothing else, it will feede my reuenge';[176] These are sentiments that confirm Shylock's pedigree and show him in league with Masscheroen. Moreover Shylock wants Antonio's flesh 'to baite fish withall'[177] and the Devil fishing for souls was not an unusual theme in sixteenth-century pictorial art. There is no human sense of value in Shylock. Money to him is worth more than his daughter; 'Would she were hearst at my foote, and the duckets in her coffin:'[178] Such was Portia's adversary.[179]

As in the play of Masscheroen, there is a striking antithesis between the two opponents which is emphasized by the rhythm of their speech and use of vocabulary. Heine has best described it, contrasting Shylock with Portia.

Wie trübe, kneifend, und hässlich sind dagegen die Gedanken und Reden des Shylock, . . . Sein Witz ist krampfhaft und ätzend, seine Metaphern sucht er

---

[170] *Ibid.*, IV, i, 216-217; (201-2).

[171] *Ibid.*, IV, i, 6-8; (4-6).

[172] Jacob van Maerlant, *Merlijn*; ed. J. van Vloten (Leiden, 1880), l. 2306.

[173] *The Merchant of Venice*, IV, i, 136; (128).

[174] *Ibid.*, III, i, 120; (111).

[175] *Ibid.*, IV, i, 64; (59).

[176] *Ibid.*, III, i, 48-9; (45-6).

[177] *Ibid.*, III, i, 48; (45).

[178] *Ibid.*, III, i, 84-5.

[179] An occasional melodramatic outburst has justified Shylock in the eyes of some modern critics, but, as John D. Rea points out in 'Shylock and the Processus Belial', *P.Q.* viii (Iowa, 1929), p. 313: 'It is clear that this substitution of Shylock for the devil, or perhaps one should say his identification with the devil, makes still more evident how far the modern sentimentalized Shylock is from the thought of Shakespeare in creating the character.'

Cf. 'Selestinus A Wyse Emperoure' in *Gesta Romanorum*, ed. Sir F. Madden (1838), p. 137, where in the 'moralitee' at the end of the story, the 'marchaunt' demanding the knight's flesh, is the Devil.

Cf. also E. E. Stoll, *Shakespeare Studies* (New York, 1927), p. 275; and Sidney Lee, 'The Original of Shylock', *Gentleman's Magazine*, n.s. CCXLVI (1880), pp. 185 *et seq.*

unter den widerwärtigsten Gegenständen, und sogar seine Worte sind zusammengequetschte Misslaute, schrill, zischend, und quirrend.[180]

They move in different worlds, the one being confined to the narrow cage of revenge, the other enjoying freedom under the spacious dome of mercy. We are dealing with great-hearted generosity against the mean exacting of a bond. John D. Rea draws attention to the fact that although the plot for the *Merchant of Venice* has been taken from the Italian story of Giovanni Fiorentino,

many features of the great trial scene in which Portia pleads the cause of mercy against strict justice are not to be found in the Italian, but are merely a re-dramatizing of the mediaeval Processus Belial, with Shylock substituted for the devil, Portia for the Virgin Mary, and the passive Antonio playing the rôle of Mankind.[181]

The background against which the trial scene takes place is unmistakably derived from Fiorentino's *Il Pecorone* where we find the expression of two gospel parables on God's mercy: the Prodigal Son and the Lost Sheep, combined in the noble and generous Anseldo who is dejected by the absence of his adopted son.

Disse M. Anseldo, Io ho si grande la paura, che questo mio figliuolo non sia morto, ò che'l mare nō gli faccia male, ch'io non trouo luogo, & non ho bene; tanto è l'amore ch'io gli porto.[182]

Anseldo readily forgives the prodigal on his return; he accepts the damages done to himself, the loss of his ship, providing his son is alive. On hearing that Gionetto is in the city,

... subito M. Anseldo si mosse, & uolle andare à uederlo; & com'egli lo uide subito corse ad abbracciarlo, & disse, Figliuol mio, non ti bisogna uergognar di me, ch'egli è usanza che delle naui rompano in mare: & però figliuol mio non ti sgomentare; poi che non t'hai fatto male, io son contento: & menosselo à casa, sempre confortandolo.[183]

---

[180] Heinrich Heine, Shakspeare's Mädchen und Frauen' (1838) in *Sämtliche Werke*, Bibliothek Ausgabe (Hamburg, 1885) Bd. iv, p. 208: 'On the contrary, how depressing, hurtful and ugly are Shylock's thoughts and words. His wit is strained and biting, he looks for his metaphors amongst the most repulsive objects and his very words are shrill, hissing and dissonant.'

[181] J. D. Rea, *op. cit.*, p. 311.

[182] Giovanni Fiorentino, *Il Pecorone* (In Milano, 1558). Giornata Quarta, Novella prima, f. 34ᵛ. ' "I fear so much", says Anseldo, "that my son is either dead, or that the sea disagrees with him, that I have no rest day or night; so great is the affection I bear him".'

[183] *Ibid.*, f. 34ᵛ-35. 'Anseldo instantly gets up, and runs to find him, and when he sees him, "My dear son", says he, "you need not fear my displeasure for what has happened; it is a common accident; trouble yourself no farther; as you have received no hurt, all is well." He takes him home, all the way telling him to be cheerful and not to worry.'

Bassanio commits the same error as Fiorentino's Gionetto. Once his friend has enabled him to purchase his heart's desire, he is so engrossed in the love for his fair lady that he forgets the donor, until he is suddenly awakened to the fact that his friend is in imminent danger on his account. Bassanio, in a fit of remorse, accuses himself to Portia confessing that he is worse than nothing;

> for indeede
> I haue ingag'd my selfe to a deere friend,
> Ingag'd my friend to his meere enemie,
> To feede my meanes.[184]

Portia, seeing him in this distress, assures him that there is no need to worry for she will provide him with the necessities.

> Pay him sixe thousand, and deface the bond:
> Double sixe thousand, and then treble that,[185]

Indeed she will stop at nothing for 'Since you are deere bought, I will loue you deere'.[186] Antonio's letter informs her that he loves her husband so much that his only desire for recompense is to see him present at his death. Even if Shakespeare was not concerned with allegory and only wished to construct a plot, the implications of the gospel parables and of the medieval play of Masscheroen cannot entirely escape us. Antonio is more than 'passive' mankind, two characters seem to be interwoven here, he is at once father and son. Portia tells Lorenzo what a pleasure it is to her to be of some assistance, for, she says, this Antonio

> Being the bosome louer of my Lord,
> Must needs be like my Lord. If it be so,
> How little is the cost I have bestowed
> In purchasing the semblance of my soule;
> From out the state of hellish cruelty,[187]

Surely such were the motives of the Virgin Mary when she stepped between Mankind and the Devil. Portia forbids Shylock to shed one drop of the blood which cannot be separated from the flesh without causing Antonio's death. According to *Processus Sathane*, in response to the Devil's demand for his share in Mankind, the Virgin equally intimates that it is impossible to damn a part of it without imperilling the entire race.

fili iniquitatis si enim fuit damnatus vnus chorus angelorum cum essent decem nō adhuc remanserunt nouem chori illius. secus vero est in homine quia si genus

---

[184] *The Merchant of Venice*, III, ii, 276-9; (263-5).
[185] *Ibid.*, III, ii, 317-18; (102-3).
[186] *Ibid.*, III, ii, 331; (314).
[187] *Ibid.*, III, iv, 19-23.

humanu*m* in totum deleatur ergo in vanum constitutus fuit home nō in sapientia.[188]

Both Shylock and Satan are forced to an ignominious retreat. Their own excessive cruelty has defeated them, and they have been fooled by a woman. Portia deceives in a masterly fashion. The Virgin Mary, as we have seen from the example quoted and from many other legends, made it her sport to get the better of the Devil. The very name 'Masscheroen' suggests a fool, a clownish fellow. The Eastern 'Maschara' was a court-fool.[189] Shylock, like the Devil, is feared by the Christians, but once his power has been put out of action, he becomes the object of derision. The twittering fun at the court of Venice, no less than the singing and dancing of the angels in heaven, is rude nature expressed in all its spontaneity.

> Gra[tiano].   O learned Iudge, mark Iew, a learned Iudge.
> . . . . . .
>
> A second *Daniel*, a *Daniel* Iew,[190]

In *Processus Sathane* we read, 'Tunc angeli inceperunt cantare. Salve regina misericordie ... Eya ergo advocata nostra ...'[191] It is the quality of loving mercy which got the better of the Devil. The weapon is completely alien to him who acts upon compulsion.

> Iew.   On what compulsion must I? tell me that.
> Portia.   The quality of mercy is not strain'd.[192]

Portia's eulogy remains a timeless monument erected by man in honour of woman in whom he had found all necessary requirements and who, by her feminine qualities, drove the Devil from the court.

---

[188] Saxoferrato, *Tractatus Iudiciorum*, [last leaf] [the passage does not occur in the 1588 edn. of the *Omnia Opera extanta*] 'Son of iniquity, if one choir of angels out of ten was condemned, there would surely be still nine left. The case is different with man for if the human race were totally destroyed, man would have been created in vain, not in wisdom.'

[189] *Ibno 'l-Achîr's Chronicle*, i, 127, in *Nederlandsche Gedichten, van Jan Boendale* etc. ed. F. A. Snellaert (Brussel, 1869), p. lxxvii, records that for two years Moses and Aaron daily knocked at Pharaoh's gate but no one had the courage to announce their arrival until the news was taken to Pharaoh by the Maschara whose task it was to make him laugh.

[190] *The Merchant of Venice*, IV, i, 333-49; (312-28).

[191] Saxoferrato, *Tractatus Iudiciorum*, [last leaf].

[192] *The Merchant of Venice*, IV, i, 193-4; (177-9).

3

The Wanton

8 *He played with the wanton*

3 The Wanton

Womanhood, wanton, ye want;[1]

THE DEVIL TURNS UPON THE WANTON IN AN ORGANIZED INVASION

Just as a coward, defeated by one stronger than himself, takes his revenge upon a weaker enemy; so the Devil, his power broken, spiritually, physically and mentally, when he has been expelled from the court and society by the feminine qualities of a strong woman, now turns upon the weaker among that sex in order to regain something of the lost ground and faded reputation.

Lucifer organizes his legions[2] for the attack and sixteenth-century England is soon infested with devils.[3] The Fiend's strategy is the ancient one, using woman to ensnare man.

Euer since *Euah* was tempted, and the Serpent preuailed with her, weomen haue tooke vpon them both the person of the tempted and the tempter. They tempt to be tempted, and not one of them, except she be tempted, but thinkes herselfe contemptible. Vnto the greatnesse of theyr great Grand-mother *Euah*, they seeke to aspire, in being tempted and tempting.[4]

The daughter of Eve becomes the wanton, the woman who glories in being tempted and in playing the temptress. So successful is the satanic strategy, that Pierce Pennilesse begs Lucifer to remove from the City of London the young damsels that are infected by the Devil's doing:

Lais, Cleopatra, Helen, if our Clyme hath any such, noble Lord warden of the witches and iuglers, I commend them with the rest of our vncleane sisters in

[1] John Skelton, *Womanhod, wanton, ye want*; in *The Poetical Works*, ed. A. Dyce (1843), i, 20.

[2] T. Lodge, *Wits miserie and the worlds madnesse*, (1596); *Works*, ed. Sir. E. Gosse, (1883), iv, 8. 'LEUIATHAN . . . that tempteth with Pride; MAMMON . . . that attempteth by Auarice; ASMODEUS . . . that seduceth by Lecherie; BEELZEBUB . . . that inciteth to Enuie; BAALBERITH . . . that prouoketh to Ire; BEELPHOGOR . . . that mooueth Gluttony; ASTAROTH . . . that induceth Sloth and Idlenesse.'

P. Viret, *op. cit.*, C. i. '*Theo[phrast]*. I am afraied least that Deuill, that is spoken of in the *Apocalips*, whiche was bound for a thousand yeres, be let loose.'

[3] M. Rudwin, *op. cit.* p. 25. 'Johannes Wierus, a pupil of the famous Cornelius Agrippa and author of the learned treatise, *De praestigiis daemonum* (1563), went to the considerable trouble of counting the devils and found that their number was seven and odd millions. According to this German demonologist, the hierarch of hell commands an army of 1,111 legions each composed of 6,666 devils, which brings the total of evil spirits to 7,405,926, "without any possibility of error in calculation".' [Rudwin's source of information was the 1st edn., which I had no opportunity to consult. The editions of Wier vary considerably].

[4] T. Nashe, *Christs Teares ouer Ierusalem*, (1593); *Works* ed. R. B. McKerrow (1904), ii, 136, ll. 30-35.

Shorditch, the *Spittle, Southwarke, Westminster* & *Turnbull streete,* to the protection of your Portership: hoping you will speedily carrie them to hell, there
to keepe open house for all young Deuils that come, and not let our ayre bee
contaminated with theyr six-pennie damnation any longer.[5]

But Lucifer considered them a sound investment, invaluable as an auxiliary
force, and was far more anxious to increase their number. In fact, he was
so emphatic in the statement of his wishes that his answer sent to Pierce
ended with his last will and testament that the fair wench should be made
the target of the day.

Let no yong rigle-eyde Damosell (if her years haue strucke twelue once) be
left vnassaulted, but it must be thy Office to lay hard seige to her honestie:
and to try if the walles of her Mayden-head may be scaled with a ladder of
Angells: for one Acre of such Wenches will bring in more at yeares ende, then
an hundred Acres of the best harrowed Land betwéene Detford and Douer:[6]

The result of it was that in the meantime English literature had begun to
swarm not only with devils but also with maidens who were enticed by
their offer of pleasures and luxuries. There arose a large number of Helenas
who 'wanted no allurements to bewitch the eie; no oratory, to seduce the
eare; no subtilty, to affect the senses'[7] and who tempted a good man to
any of the seven deadly sins, whilst the Devil provided all necessary weapons.

MAN'S DISTRUST AND CONSEQUENT ALARM

It was a frightening situation and man was continuously on the look-out
for any approaching danger. His reverent attitude began to waver when he
detected how woman's 'leadership of love' had been changed into a tyr-
annical domination, the enslaver of his passions, from which it was not easy
to escape.

> Womanhod, wanton, ye want;
> Youre medelyng, mastres, is manerles;
> Plente of yll, of goodnes skant,
>
> ......
>
> Why so koy and full of skorne?
>
> ......

---

[5] T. Nashe, *Pierce Penilesse,* (1592); *Works* ed. McKerrow (1904), i, 217. ll, 3-10.
[6] T. Middleton, *The blacke booke,* (1604), E 2ᵛ-3.
Moreover, from a dialogue in *Iudicium; The Towneley Plays,* ed. A. W. Pollard,
EETS, e.s. LXXI (1897), p. 372, ll. 161-2, we know that hell was already well stocked
with the female sex.

> *primus demon.* has thou oght Writen there/
> of the femynyn gendere?
> *secundus demon.* yei, mo then I may bere/
> of rolles forto render;

[7] T. Lodge, *Wits Miserie; Works,* ed. Gosse, iv, 8.

> Youre key is mete for euery lok,
> > Youre key is commen and hangyth owte;
> Youre key is redy, we nede not knok,
> > Nor stand long wrestyng there aboute;
> > Of youre doregate ye haue no doute:
> But one thyng is, that ye be lewde:[8]

Woman was leading him astray. He feared, seeing that, instead of mediating between him and God, she was siding with Masscheroen and had become the Devil's advocate and supporter. In self-defence, prose-writers, dramatists, ballad-mongers, poets and preachers undertook the task of setting up a bulwark against Woman and the Devil.

A godly Ballad was composed proving by scriptural examples consequent disasters of whoredom. The writer warns men to subdue their 'lusts inordinate' for

> The Fish is by a plesant bait
> Constrained to the deadly bit.[9]

Historical examples were held before man's eyes: Bethsaba bewitching King David's brain; Sampson's lust for Dalila:

> Lo, him that none coulde foil in fight,
> > Whose puissant arme the lion slew,
> Whose strength put thousands vnto flight,
> > By lust one woman ouerthrew.[10]

Lust had impaired the good name of Salomon; Herod by his passion had been misled into beheading the Baptist. Once caught, it was hard to escape. The good Aeneas may temporarily have saved himself, but in the end Dido's ghost caused 'a multitude of vgly fiendes' to drag him off to hell.[11] And in England itself how many poets and gallants claimed to have been slain by false love. Even the dying Falstaff, who, God knows, was not averse to women, 'cryed out of Sack' that 'they were Deules incarnate', and 'A said once the Deule would haue him about Women'.[12]

---

[8] J. Skelton, *Womanhod, wanton, ye want*; in *Poetical Works*, i, pp. 20-21, ll. 1-3, 8, 23-27.

Cf. I. Rolland, *The seuin Seages, translatit out of prois in Scottis meter* (1578); ed. G. F. Black, iii STS, 3rd series (1932), p. 115, ll. 3548-50, who expressed himself more bluntly.

> Thow art a Tratour wylie Tod
> That stinkis in the neis of God,
> Thow art the Deuillis dam.

[9] A. I., *A godly ballad*, (1566); in J. Lilly, *Black-Letter Ballads and Broadsides* (1867), p. 101.

[10] *Ibid.*, p. 103.

[11] *The wandring Prince of Troye*; in *The Shirburn Ballads*, ed. A. Clark, (OUP, 1907), p. 281, verse 23.

[12] *Henry V*, 1st Folio, Histories, p. 75; (II, iii, 30-35).

That women were 'devils who catch men' was no longer spoken of joco-
sely as it had been in one of the stories in the Decameron.[13] It had become
an earnest belief.

> The Net is stronge, the fole caught can nat starte
> The darte is sharpe, who euer is in the chayne
> Can nat his sorowe in vysage hyde nor fayne.[14]

Even Thomas Nashe who almost feared to express his opinion on the situation writes:

For my part I meane to suspende my sentence, and to let an Author of late
memorie be my speaker, who affyrmyth that they [the women] carrie Angels in
their faces to entangle men and deuils in their deuices.[15]

Meeting a fashionable Courtezan, *Dromio Siracusia* asks his master:

> Master, is this Mistress *Sathan*?

ANTIPHOLUS.　It is the diuell.

DROMIO.　Nay, she is worse, she is the diuils dam:
And here she comes in the habit of a light wench,
and thereof comes, that the wenches say God dam me,
That's as much to say, God make me a light wench :
It is written they appeare to men like
angels of light, light is an effect of
fire, and fire will burne : *ergo,* light
wenches will burne, come not neere her.[16]

Spenser's Bower of Bliss, with its 'faire witch' Acrasia, provides ample
warning against the dangerous enticements of woman. As in the case of
Doctor Faustus' Helena, she serves as a narcotic. Cymochles has fallen prey
to her enticements.

> He, like an Adder, lurking in the weeds,
> His wandring thought in deepe desire does steepe,
> And his fraile eye with spoyle of beautie feedes;
> . . .
> Made drunke with drugs of deare voluptuous receipt.[17]

Atin rescues him 'pricking him with his sharpe-pointed dart', but shortly
after Cymochles again succumbs to lascivious woman, this time Phaedria
who is taking him across the Idle Lake.

---

[13] Th. Warton, *op. cit.,* i, 272-3. 'This fable occurs in an old collection of Apologues. . . .
MSS Harl. 463, fol. 2, a. [Wright's *Latin Stories,* p. 7: *De filio regis qui nunquam
viderat mulieres.*]'
[14] S. Brant, *op. cit.,* i, 81, verse 4.
[15] T. Nashe, *The Anatomie of Absurditie,* (1589); *Works,* ed. McKerrow, i, 13, ll. 32-5.
[16] *The Comedie of Errors,* 1st Folio, Comedies, p. 94; (IV, iii, 48-57).
[17] *The Faerie Queene,* II, vi, 17.

Her light behauiour, and loose dalliaunce
    Gaue wondrous great contentment to the knight,
    That of his way he had no souenaunce,
    Nor care of vow'd reuenge, and cruell fight,
    But to weake wench did yeeld his martiall might.
    So easie was to quench his flamed mind
    With one sweet drop of sensuall delight,
    So easie is, t'appease the stormie wind
Of malice in the calme of pleasant womankind.[18]

Lulling him to sleep, she sings:

Why then dost thou, O man, that of them all
    Art Lord, and eke of nature Soueraine,
    Wilfully make thy selfe a wretched thrall,[19]

How true her words were if applied to dalliance with women. Neither Phaedria nor Cymochles realized how they might serve as a warning. But others did and began to rebel.

The Elizabethan outbreak of lovers' revolts in poetry coincided with a great moral reaction against love – brought on by the licentiousness of the courtly lovers, both in literature and actual practice. The purity of their sentiments had been open to serious doubt while they still professed ideal devotion, and in the afternoon of their popularity they became more and more unrestrained in their expression.[20]

There were not many Guyons who attributed this licentiousness to 'the mind of beastly man,/That hath so soone forgot the excellence/Of his creation'.[21] Generally, as in the case of Adam and Eve, woman was blamed.

O dilicat dame/ with Eiris bent
That harknit to that fals serpent[22]
    Thy banis we May sair ban
Without excuse thow art to blame
Thow Iustly hes obtenit that name
    The verry wo of man[23]

---

[18] *Ibid.*, II, vi, 8.
[19] *Ibid.*, II, vi, 17.
[20] L. B. *Salomon, The Devil take her* (Univ. of Pennsylvania, 1931) p. 21.
[21] *The Faerie Queene*, II, xii, 87.
[22] That woman proved a credulous listener is humorously portrayed in the *York Plays* by 'The Tapiteres and Couchers'. The Devil, fearing that with the condemnation of Christ his power will end, has recourse to Pilate's wife, Percula.

I will on stiffely in þis stounde,
Vnto Sir Pilate wiffe, pertely, and putte me
in prese.

The dame responds at once and takes action. (p. 277, ll. 166-67).
[23] *Ane Ballat of the creatioun of the warld*; in *The Bannatyne MS* (1568), ed. W. T. Ritchie, ii, STS, n.s., 22 (1928), p. 31, ll. 155-60. [hereafter referred to as *Bannatyne MS*]

A very proper dittie was issued: *Leaue lightie loue Ladies* in which the powerlessness of man was pathetically transparent.

> If ARGVS were lyuying, whose eyes were in nomber
>   The Peacockes plume painted, as writers replie,
> Yet women by wiles full sore would him cumber,
>   For all his quicke eyes, their driftes to espie;
>   . . . . . .
>
> Suche wiles and suche guiles by women are wrought,
>   That halfe their mischefes men cannot preuent;[24]

Such outbursts were often vituperative or lachrymose, seldom ranking as good literature.

> Throughe frendship is spoyled the seely poore fish
>   That hoouer and shouer vpon your false hookes;[25]

They expressed man's feelings, however, and his bitter disappointment that he could no longer rely on woman, for

> It seemes, by your doynges, that Cressed doth scoole ye, –
>   Penelopeys vertues are cleane out of thought:
> Mee thinkes, by your constantnesse, Heleyne doth rule ye,
>   Whiche both Greece and Troy to ruyne hath brought.[26]

Robert Greene, supplementing, as it were, the faulty and often coarse rhetoric of less gifted contemporaries, justifies their outbursts.

> What meant the Poets in inuectiue verse,
> To sing Medeas shame, and Scillas pride,
> Calypsoes charmes, by which so many dide?
> Onely for this, their vices they rehearse,
> That curious wits which in this world conuerse
> May shun the dangers and entising shoes
> Of such false Syrens, those home breeding foes
> That from their eyes their venim do disperse.
> So soone kils not the Basiliske with sight,
> The Vipers tooth is not so venomous,
> The Adders toung not halfe so daungerous,
> As they that beare the shadow of delight,
> Who chain blind youths in tramels of their hayre,
> Till wast bring woe, and sorrow hasts despayre.[27]

[24] L. Gybson, *Lightie Loue*; in J. Lilly, *op. cit.*, pp. 115-6.
[25] *Ibid.*, p. 114.
[26] *Ibid.*, p. 115.
[27] R. Greene, 'Against enticing curtizans'; in *The Plays and Poems of Robert Greene*, ed. J. Churton Collins (Oxford 1905), ii, 315.

A moralist was expected to call a whore a whore. It was the 'vayne' and wanton poet who called her *Amaryllis*, and surrounded her with goddesses. Urged by necessity, abusive language became permissible.

> Good men of skill doe know it well,
> that these our dayes require such speech;[28]

Vives, quoting St. Jerome, shows the misery which the pursuer of love finds. He refers to the perjury, murder, slaughter, and destruction, love has caused; calling to witness all that happened on account of Helen of Troy, and ends with the grave warning:

O thou vngracious woman/ seest thou nat/ howe thou bryngest hym [the lover] into the possessiō of the deuyll with thy crafte/ whither thy selfe shall go also/ there to receyue thy mede/ wher ye shall both burne/ he for beynge ouer come of the deuyll/ and thou for ouercommynge hym for the deuyll/[29]

Thomas Nashe sees the harm done to husbands and threatens women that, unless they stop tempting, their pains in hell will be doubled,

for millions haue you tempted, millions of men (both in soule & substaunce) haue you deuoured. To you, halfe your husbands damnation (as to *Euah*) will be imputed.[30]

THE DEVIL IS BLAMED FOR WOMAN'S ACTIONS

The Importance of Her State of Mind as Opening the Way to Him

It was a legacy bestowed by the Middle Ages to give all praise to God when things went right.[31] But if anything went wrong, the Devil was blamed.[32] Consequently, if woman fell short of man's high expectations, the

---

[28] Stephen Gosson, *Pleasant Quippes* (1596), in *Remains of the Early Popular Poetry of England*, ed. W. C. Hazlitt; vol. iv, p. 262, ll. 283-4.

[29] J. L. Vives, *the Instruction of a Christen Woman*, tr. R. Hyrde, (1529?), Bk. I, Rii^v; edn. Foster Watson, *Vives and the Renascence Education of Women*, (1912), p. 107.

The editor remarks (p. 23), 'On what we may call the negative side of his teaching – *i.e.*, his protest against women's love of apparel and personal decoration, of banqueting, of frequenting public places, of dancing, of dicing, Vives summarizes the best social and religious outlook, not only of his contemporaries, but even of his successors, for the whole of the Tudor period.'

[30] Th. Nashe, *Christs Teares*; *Works*, ed. McKerrow, ii 140, ll. 33-6.

[31] *Henry V*, 1st. Folio, Histories, p. 89; (IV, vii, 84). Henry after the victory at Agincourt calls out: 'Praised be God, and not our strength for it :'

[32] Many examples of the Devil being blamed for woman's wickedness can be found in medieval romances. In *Morte Darthur*, tr. Malory (edn. 1529), Bk. IV, cap. 13, F. iiij, for example, Morgan le fay discovered by her son Ewayne when at the point of slaying Arthur in his sleep, excuses herself: 'I was tēpted with a deuyll/ wherfore I crye the mercy/ . . .'

In the *Historie of Palmerin D'Oliua*, tr. by A. M[unday]. (1597), Pt. II, C.viii., Palmerin thinks it impossible 'that a maiden, by nature modest and bashfull', would behave in such an audacious fashion unless she was possessed by the Devil.

Devil must be with her. Yet woman must first have given her consent since Mephostophilis, whom we may regard as one of the most truthful devils, assured us,

> Nor will we come, vnlesse he vse such meanes,
> Whereby he is in danger to be damnd:[33]

It was the woman's state of mind, therefore, that mattered and that might, or might not, give access to the Fiend. Once he entered into relationship with her, it generally proved fatal not only to herself, but to her husband, lover, and those around her. That it could effect even her unborn child was clearly portrayed in the 'lyfe of the moost ferefullest/ and vnmercyfullest/ and myscheuous' *Robert the deuyll*. The Duchess of Normandy being discontented with God for not giving her a child, and in an angry state of mind, spoke the following:

In yᵉ deuyles name be it in so moche as god hath not yᵉ power yᵗ I cōceyue/ and yf I be cōceyued with chylde in this houre I gyue it to yᵉ deuyll body and soule and this same houre yᵗ this duke and duches were thus moued the sayd lady was conceyued with a man chylde whiche in his lyf wrought moche myschefe.[34]

In a similar manner Merlin was begotten by the Devil on a woman who went to bed one night in a bad temper and unforgiving mood and forgot to bless the house.[35] Agatha Shipton also was accosted by the Fiend when 'sit-

---

[33] *Dr Faustus*, p. 178, ll. 295-6.

[34] *Robert the deuyll*, [1502?], A.iiiᵛ – A.iiij. See also *Early English Prose Romances*, ed. W. J. Thoms (revised edn., 1858), i, 7. For the historical background of the story see Thoms, i, xxii *et seq*.

There is a fragment in the Bodleian (Douce Fragments 24) in the type of W. de Worde, or Pynson, of rather doggerel verse.

The story is mentioned in *The Complaynt of Scotlande* (1549), ed. J. A. H. Murray (1872), p. 63, ll. 10-11, among the stories of 'A monologue recreative'. For the editor's notes, see pp. lxxiii-iv.

Th. Warton, *op. cit.*, ii, 176. It is a translation of the French prose romance of *Robert le Diable* printed in 1496, and extant in the collection *Bibliothèque Bleue*.

Despite his evil deeds which superseded all humanity and made people strongly suspect that he was indeed a fiend, we still feel sorry for the poor 'devil' who himself could not understand the reason of his wickedness. Finally when everyone flees from him, including his own mother, he decides to ask her the reason for his cursed disposition: 'dere lady moder I praye and requyre you tell me how and by what maner or wherby cometh it that I am soo vycyous and curste for I knowe wel I haue it other by you or of my fader' (*Robert the deuyll*, Biiᵛ; edn. Thoms, i, 181). She confesses her guilt, after which Robert is converted.

[35] *Merline*, in *Bishop Percy Folio MS.*, ed. J. W. Hales and F. J. Furnivall, (1867), i, 447.

The editor draws a comparison between the romantic legend of *Sir Gowther* which is only a different version of *Robert the Deuyll*, and *Merline*.

See *Syr Gowghter*; in *Select Pieces of Early Popular Poetry*, ed. E. V. Utterson (1817), i, 165, ll. 97-100.

> The childe with yn hire was non other
> But Marlyngs half brother,
> On fende gat hem bothe;

ting Melancholy under a Tree by a River Side', and the miserable result was the birth of a child known as 'Mother Shipton' whose entry into the world filled every one with terror and dismay.[36] An even worse tragedy befell Artimaga, who entered English Literature through the Spanish romances. It was said of this lady that

She gaue hir selfe so much vnto all the euils and vices of this world, that for hir abhominable sinnes and wickednesse, God did permit that when this Artimaga came vnto the age of fiftéene yéeres, she was deceiued with the diuell, ...[37]

The fruit of their relationship was 'the diuellish and infernall Fauno, the diuells sonne' who was slain by the Knight of the Sun.

Taking into consideration woman's great responsibility as virgin, wife, or mother, her relationship with the Devil was all the more to be feared. It is not strange that Vives should draw attention to the fact that

it lyeth more in the mother/ thā men wene/ to make the conditions of the children. For she maye make them whether she wyll/ very good/ or very badde.[38]

There was good cause for man's warnings, threats and tears; whilst the Devil had his own reasons for bringing such a powerful instrument into his service. The weapons and artifices invented by the Fiend were particularly designed for womankind, and ingeniously contrived to please her.

THE DEVIL'S WEAPONS DESIGNED FOR WOMANKIND

(a) *Fashions in Clothing, Cosmetics and Male Attire*

It was soon detected that fashions, and particularly woman's fashions, proved one of the Devil's most popular instruments, for here the material of worldly wealth, leisure, and woman's vanity lay at his disposal. Foreigners visiting London expressed the opinion that

Die Weibsbilder haben vil mehr Freyheit/ als ettwan an andern Orten/ wissen sich auch dessen wol zugebrauchen/ dann sie in Kleidern vberauß prächtig/ vil auff Kreser vnnd anders legen/ dergestalt/ das/ wie ich bericht/ wol eine

---

Utterson's edition was reviewed by E. B., 'Notices of reprints of curious old books' in *Blackwood's Edinburgh Magazine*, II (1818), pp. 370 et seq.

[36] R. H[ead]., *The Life and Death of Mother Shipton* (1684) The physiognomy of the infant, p. 9, shows the ingenuity of human imagination.

[37] D. Ortuñez de Calahorra, *op. cit.* f. 59ᵛ.

[38] J. L. Vives, *Instruction of a Christen Woman*, Bk. II L.iiiᵛ; edn. Watson, p. 124.

Cf. Agrippa von Nettesheim, *op. cit.*, tr. Clapam, C. i. 'For as the lawe sayth, the greattest & chiefest offyce and duetye of woman, is to conceyue, and to saue that is conceyued. For which cōsideration we se very many to be lyke theyr mothers, by reson they be begotten of their bloudde : and this lykenes is very oft well perceyued in the proportion and makyng of their bodies, but it is alwayes in their maners. For if the mothers be foolyshe, the chyldren proue foolysshe also. If the mothers be wyse, the chyldren shall haue a sent thereof.'

auff der Gassen/ Sammet/ der ben ihnen gemein/ tragen darff/ die daheimbt im Hauß/ ettwan das trucken Brot/ nicht gehaben mag.[39]

The opinion was confirmed by Thomas Lodge who clearly discerned the workings of the Devil behind it all.

Kind heart *shall not show you so many teeth tipt with siluer in his Sunday hat, as I Deuils incarnate in clokes of the new fashion, . . . some sit on your pillows when you sleepe, . . . dresse ladies heads when they attire them, perfume courteours when they trim them, and become Panders if you hire them: and if you know them not rightly they may hap to leaue their horns behind them among some of you.*[40]

In vain did the valiant puritan Philip Stubbes fight against the 'great ruffes, & neckerchers . . . smeared and starched in the deuils liquore,'[41] In vain did he draw attention to those 'cartwheeles of the diuels charet of pride, leading the direct way to the dungeon of hell'.[42] Ladies of distinction learnt to cover their faces in order to safeguard their complexion when riding abroad with 'inuisories, or visors made of veluet . . . So that if a man, that knew not their guise before, should chaunce to meet one of them, hee would think hee met a Monster or a deuil;'[43]

Proteus, that Monster, could neuer chaunge him self into so many fourmes & shapes as these women doo: belike they haue made an obligation with hel, and are at agreement with the deuil, els they would neuer outrage thus, without either feare of God or respect to their weak Bretheren, whom heerin they offend.[44]

The 'french hood, hat, cappe, kercher, and suche like; . . . some of this fashion, some of that, . . . according to the variable fantasies of their serpentine minds'[45] were an eye-sore to the Puritan, as also were the 'Petticots . . . of scarlet, grograine, taffatie, silk, and suche like, . . .' and the 'kyrtles . . . bordered with gards, lace, fringe . . .'.[46] All were bought at the Devil's shop.

---

[39] [J. Rathgeb], *Beschreibung der Badenfahrt: Welche Herr Friderich/Hertzog zu Württemberg in 1592* verrichtet hat (Tübingen, 1602), f. 13. 'The women have much more liberty than perhaps in any other place; they also know well how to make use of it, for they go dressed out in exceedingly fine clothes, and give all their attention to their ruffs and stuffs, to such a degree indeed, that, as I am informed, many a one does not hesitate to wear velvet in the streets, which is common with them, whilst at home perhaps they have not a piece of dry bread.' [transl. W. B. Rye, *op. cit*, pp. 7-8.]
The rather unusual title given to the description of this journey owes its origin to the rough crossing at which they were washed over by the waves. 'dermassen daß wir zum Dritten mal im wasser biß an die Gürtel sassen' (f. 38).
[40] T. Lodge, *Wits Miserie; Works,* ed Gosse, iv, 5-6.
[41] P. Stubbes, *The Anatomie of Abuses,* Pt. i, 70.
[42] *Ibid.,* Pt. ii, 35.
[43] *Ibid.,* Pt. i, 80.
[44] *Ibid.,* Pt. i, 73.
[45] *Ibid.,* Pt. i, 69.
[46] *Ibid.,* Pt. i, 74-5.

Thus were women 'plumed and decked in the Feathers of deceiptfull vanity'. Then there was the footwear: 'pinsnets, pantoffles, and slippers . . . imbrodered with Gold and siluer all ouer the foote, with other gewgawes innumerable . . . the deuill brocheth soe many new fashions euery day'.[47] The dramatist burlesques the Puritan view in the figure of a young Puritan wife who is tormented in conscience at her new clothes:

What haue I done? Put on too many clothes, the day is hote, and I am hoter clad then might suffice health, my conscience telles me that I haue offended, and Ile put them off, that will aske time that might be better spent, one sin will draw another quickly so, see how the diuell tempts:[48]

But the crowning glory of fashion were the Looking Glasses that the ladies carried about in their gloves:

& to such abhomination is it grown, as they must haue their looking glasses caryed with them whersoeuer they go. And good reason, for els how cold they see the deuil in them? for no doubt they are the deuils spectacles to allure vs to pride, & consequently to distruction for euer.[49]

This threat was actually realised in the Proud woman of Antwerp.[50] This lady, a rich merchant's daughter was invited to a wedding. She made great preparations wishing her apparel to correspond with her reputation as the town's beauty.

For the accomplishment whereof, she curled her haire, she died her lockes, and laied them out after the best maner, she coloured her face with waters and Ointmentes: But in no case could she gette any (so curious and daintie she was) that could starche, and sette her Ruffes, and Neckerchers to her mynde: wherefore she sent for a couple of Laundresses, who did the best thei could to please her humors, but in anywise thei could not. Then fell she to sweare and teare, to cursse and banne, castyng the Ruffes vnder feete, and wishyng that the Deuill might take her, when she weare any of those Neckerchers againe.[51]

A devil, named Rush, seizing this opportunity, transformed himself into the form of a young gallant and under the pretence of wooing, demanded the cause of her displeasure. She told him how she was abused in the setting of her ruff, and immediately he promised to take this task in hand, which he accomplished to her great satisfaction. He then asked her to view herself in the looking glass whereupon she fell in love both with her own appearance and the Devil. The latter, whilst kissing her, wrings her neck. After death

[47] *Ibid.*, Pt. i, 76-77.
[48] G. C[hapman], *An Humerous dayes Myrth* (1599), A. 4ᵛ.
[49] P. Stubbes, *op. cit.*, i, p. 79.
[50] See *Henslowe's Diary*; ed. W. W. Greg (2 parts, 1904-8), Pt. ii, item 223. [91-95, 104. 'frier Rushe & the prowd womon'. . . . Paid on behalf of the Admiral's men, to Day and Haughton, 4 July to 29 Nov. 1601, in full, £5. Paid to Chettle. 21 Jan. 1601/2, 'for mending', 10 s.]
[51] P. Stubbes, *op. cit.*, i, p. 71-72.

the woman was metamorphosed into a black and blue monster. Her coffin was so heavy that four men were unable to remove it. On investigation they found that the body had disappeared

and a blacke Catte verie leane and deformed sittyng in the Coffin, setting of greate Ruffes, and frizlyng of haire, to the greate feare, and wonder of all the beholders.[52]

Thus it came true what the prophet Isaiah foretold

insteade of their Pomaunders, musks, ciuets, balmes, sweet odours and perfumes, they shall haue stench and horrour in the nethermost hel.[53]

Not only in Flanders but in England also the ruffs, those 'cartwheeles of the deuils charet of pride' were turning women's heads and many a one could be found that

had rather view her face a whole morning in a looking Glasse then worke by the howre Glasse, ...[54]

The arrangement of the ruff could hardly be called a harmless pastime. It not only surrounded woman's head but seemed to take possession of it, making such a powerful impact upon her mind that on one or two occasions its imprint was found upon her offspring. Thus we find a ballad entitled

The true Discripcion of a Childe with Ruffes, borne in the parish of Micheham, in the countie of Surrey.[55]

The broadsheet bears the illustration of a dimply baby with an enormous ruff. Needless to say the child is of the 'femynyne gendere'.

This present yeere of our Lord MDLXVJ. the vij. day of June, one Helene Jermin, the wife of John Jermin, husbandman, dwelling in the parishe of Micheham, was deliuered of a woman-childe, named Christian, ...[56]

The description that follows serves as a warning to women to leave their vanities.

> But poets tales may passe and go
> as trifels and vntrueth,
> When ruffes of flessche, as I doo trowe,
> shall moue vs vnto ruthe.[57]

[52] *Ibid.*, i, p. 72.
Cf. U. Fulwel, *Like will to Like*, (1587); ed. J. S. Farmer, The Tudor Facs. Texts (1909), A. ij^v. Nichol Newfangle, the Vice, had been in hell as a prentice to Lucifer and learnt to make 'ruffs like Calues chitterlings'.
[53] P. Stubbes, *op. cit.*, i, p. 77.
[54] T. Nashe, *The Anatomie, Works*, ed. McKerrow, i, 18, ll. 25-26.
[55] H. B., *The true Discripcion of a Childe with Ruffes, borne* in the parish of Micheham, A. D. MDLXVI; in J. Lilly, *op. cit.*, p. 243.
[56] *Ibid.*
[57] *Ibid.*, p. 246.

Several ballads were registered on the birth of divers monsters and deformed, misshapen children, horrible to look at, and all on account of women's vanities.[58]

> These flaming heads with staring haire,
>> These wyers turnde like hornes of ram:
> These painted faces which they weare,
>> Can any tell from whence they cam?
>>> Don Sathan, Lord of fayned lyes,
>>> All these new fangeles did devise.
>
> . . . . . .
>
> These buttons, pinches, fringes, jagges,
>> With them he weaveth wofull harmes.
> He fisher is, they are his baytes,
>> Wherewith to hell he draweth huge heaps.[59]

Much of the cruder sort of literature on our subject owes its existence to a tradition ingrafted by centuries of relentless preaching on the view and treatment of the weaker sex. The Franciscan Friar Waldeby, John Bromyard a Dominican Father and other famous medieval preachers spared neither Woman nor the Devil.[60] Many stories that illustrated their sermons can be found in the *Gesta Romanorum* and in Caesarius von Heisterbach's *Illustrium Miraculorum, et Historiarum Memorabilium.* The following example had furnished popular imagination for many years and its repercussion was still felt in the sixteenth century.

Die quadam dominica, cùm sacerdos in ecclesia, cuius erat plebanus, circuiret, & aqua benedicta populum aspergeret, ad ostium ecum ecclesiæ veniens, matronam quandam pompaticè venientem, & ad similitudinem pauonis varijs ornamentis pictam obuiam habuit, in cuius cauda vestimentorum, quam habebat post se longissimam, multitudinem daemonum residere conspexit. Erant enim parui vt glires, nigri vt aethiopes, ore cachinnantes, manibus plaudentes, & sicut pisces intra sagenam conclusi saltantes. Reuera ornatus muliebris, sagena diaboli est.[61]

---

[58] The *Henry Huth collection* [Brit. Mus. Huth 50] contains several of these ballads; mostly reprinted in J. Lilly, *op. cit.*

[59] Stephen Gosson, *Pleasant Quippes* (1596), ed. W. C. Hazlitt, iv, p. 252, ll. 61-66; p. 254, ll. 86-90.
It is plain that the Royal Proclamations against Women's excess of apparel did not always have the desired effect. Vid. *Tudor Royal Proclamations*, vol. ii (1553-1587) ed. P. L. Hughes and J. F. Larkin (1969), p. 385.
N.B. The ruff was diametrically opposed to the veil. Instead of covering the head, it accentuated it.

[60] See G. R. Owst, *Literature and Pulpit in Medieval England* (CUP., 1933), pp. 392-3.

[61] Caesarius von Heisterbach, *Illustrium Miraculorum, et Historiarum Memorabilium* (Coloniae, 1591), Lib. V, Cap. vii, pp. 364-5. 'One Sunday when a priest was going round in the church blessing the people with holy water, coming to the door, behold, he met there striding haughtily in, a matron dressed out with all kinds of adornments, as gay as a peocock; and on her skirts which she was dragging far behind her, he saw a number

With this medieval background behind them writers grew eloquent when proclaiming the horrors of hell which awaited a wanton woman.

> For thy rich borders, shalt thou haue a number of discoloured Scorpions rould vp together, and Cockatrices, that kill with their verie sight, shall continually stand spirting fiery poyson in thine eyes. In the hollowe Caue of thy mouth, Basiliskes shall keepe house, & supply thy talke with hyssing when thou striuest to speake. At thy breasts (as at *Cleopatras*), Aspisses shall be put out to nurse. For thy Carcanets of pearle, shalt thou haue Carcanets of Spyders, or the greene venemous flies Cantharides. Hels torments were no torments, if inuention might conceite thē.[62]

The prophet Hosea in *A Looking Glasse for London and England* is following the tradition of the English pulpit when he cries out:

> Woe to the traines of womens foolish lust,
> In wedlocke rights that yeeld but litle trust,
> That vow to one, yet common be to all.
> Take warning, wantons; pride will haue a fall.[63]

In Shakespeare, no less than in other poets and dramatists, we can trace the sermonising influence of the Middle Ages. Petruchio surely knocked the devilish spirit out of his shrew by depriving her of the choice of clothes;

> Well, come my *Kate*, we will vnto your fathers,
> Euen in these honest meane habiliments:
> Our purses shall be proud, our garments poore:
> For 'tis the minde that makes the bodie rich.[64]

Antonio in *Twelfe Night*, with Shakespearean conciseness, sums up all that had been said and done by earlier writers and preachers on the subject.

> Vertue is beauty, but the beauteous euill
> Are empty trunkes, ore-flourish'd by the deuill.[65]

For this reason Goneril was called a 'gilded serpent'[66] by her husband. It was all a matter of values. The *Gesta Romanorum* explained that in the story of the Three Caskets, but Shakespeare brought it to life.

---

of demons. They were as small as dormice, and as black as Ethiopians, grinning and clapping their hands and leaping hither and thither like fish enclosed in a net; for in truth feminine extravagance is a net of the devil.'

[62] T. Nashe, *Christs Teares*; *Works*, ed. McKerrow, ii, 140, ll. 16-25.

[63] T. Lodge, *Gent.*, and Robert Greene, *A Looking Glasse for London and England* (1594); in *The Plays and Poems of Robert Greene*, ed. J. Collins, vol. i, IV, iv, 1573-6.

[64] *The Taming of the Shrew*, 1st. Folio, *Comedies*, p. 224; (IV, iv, 165-68).

[65] *Twelfe Night*, III, iv, 370-1; (353-4).

[66] *King Lear*, V, iii, 85; (84).

Looke on beautie,
And you shall see 'tis purchast by the weight,
Which therein workes a miracle in nature,
Making them lightest that weare most of it:[67]

Apart from the moral and religious reasons that gave fashions and womanly vanity such a prominent place in literature, there was a practical point, for men resented the extravagance. Many could not afford to pay for it, and, under the guise of comedy, they expounded on woman's insatiable demands. Man excused himself that even the Devil had been driven to despair by woman's love for fashions. And it was 'no inferiour Deuill, but a Maister Deuill, a principall officer, and commander in Helle'.[68] Balthasar was his name, 'and well spente in yeres, he beganne to waxe wanton, and to doate in the Loue of Mistres *Mildred*'. So great was his affection for this lady 'that he now confessed the fire of Helle to bee but a trifle, in respecte of the scorchyng flames of Loue':[69] Not having any lands, he took upon him an agreeable shape and proposed to Mistress Mildred who accepted him for her husband. Anxious to make a good impression he promised his wife to give her whatever she most desired, providing that thereafter she would trouble him no further with requests. The young woman requested 'a sute of apparell of a gallaunt fashon, but euen then newlie come vp'.[70] Her wish was granted; but later a new fashion was introduced and

Mistres Mildred, beyng now quite out of conceit, for that she had neuer a goune to putte on her backe but of a stale cutte, and the fashion at the leaste of a monethe olde, who would blame the gentlewoman though she tooke it very grieuously : alas her minde was so far out of quiet, that her meate almoste did her no maner of good.[71]

The Devil again relented and supplied her with the latest in '. . . Gounes, Kirtelles, Peticotes, . . . Dublettes, Bombastyng, and Bolsteryng.'[72] But when she came a third time weeping and complaining that she was kept 'like Ione in the Countrey, in a tyre of the olde fassion, deuised a moneth agoe'[73]

the Deuill her housebande was stroke in suche a dumpe, that not able any longer to indure her talke, he not onely auoided hym self from her presence, but also deuised with speede to flie the Countrey, . . .[74]

[67] *The Merchant of Venice*, III, ii, 94-7; (88-91).
[68] B. Rich, *Riche his Farewell to Militarie profession* (1581), facs. edn. Th. Mabry Cranfill, p. 206, ll. 5-6. The story is based on Straparola's novella in *Piacevoli Notti* which appeared at Venice in 1550. It is the fourth tale of the second night, told by Signor Benedetto of Previso. It is similar to Machiavelli's *Belfagor* except that the stress has been laid entirely on the extravagence of clothes and fineries. *Inf.* p. 142.
[69] *Ibid.*, p. 206, ll. 15-17.
[70] *Ibid.*, p. 207, ll. 21-22.
[71] *Ibid.*, p. 207, ll. 29-34.
[72] *Ibid.*, p. 208, l. 11.
[73] *Ibid.*, p. 209, ll. 12-13.
[74] *Ibid.*, p. 209, ll. 15-18.

The Devil, once having started his evil device was unable to stop it. The moralists, carrying this satire to the extreme point, depict the new fashions as invading Hell itself. In *Greenes newes both from Heauen and Hell* Greene and his companions meet a woman on her way to hell carrying a basket of 'Ruffes of the newe sette, newe Cuttes, newe Stitches, newe gardes, newe imbroyders, newe deuysed French Verdingales, newe French bodyes, newe bumbasting . . .' for sale.[75] Greene remarks that it is only fit that such articles should be returned to hell whence they came and where they were devised.

You are much deceyued sir (sayd she) for I haue fashions heere that neuer a Lady nor Gentlewoman that is in hell, euer sawe the like, nor neuer a Curty-san, or any other strumpet that liued in the world, did euer weare the like, such perewigs, curled and firisled [sic] by art, such roules of hayre perfumed and platted by proportion, such ruffes as will aske one whole day to wash and starch, and an other daies labour but to pinne them in the fashion, that (alas poore women) they are faine to take great paynes to goe to the diuell :[76]

And indeed there were women in hell who once used to shroud their age and ugliness with vanities and, on entering, had given great cause for amusement among the devils. Tutivillus, chief Registrar of entries, who in a single hour had brought thousands to hell among whom many of these women, tauntingly remarks:

> When she is thus paynt,
> She makys it so quaynte,
> She lookys like a saynt,
> And wars then the deyle.[77]

They were the type of Elynour Rummynge, the 'comely dame' who – Skelton informs us – thought a great deal of her outward appearance 'upon the holy daye'

> Whan she doth her aray,
> And gyrdeth in her gytes
> Stytched and pranked with pletes;
> Her kyrtel Brystow red,
> With clothes vpon her hed
> That wey a sowe of led,
> Wrythen in wonder wyse,
> After the Sarasyns gyse,
> With a whym wham,
> Knyt with a trym tram,
> Vpon her brayne pan,[78]

[75] B. R[ich]., *Greenes Newes both from Heauen and Hell* (1593); ed. R. B. McKerrow (1911), p. 43, ll. 19-22.

[76] *Ibid.*, p. 43, l. 32 – p. 44, l. 3.

[77] *Iudicium*, *The Towneley Plays*, ed. Pollard, p. 375, ll. 265-8.

[78] J. Skelton, *The Tunnyng of Elynour Rummynge*, in *Poetical Works*, ed. A. Dyce, i, p. 97, ll. 67-77.

'vgly fayre' Skelton describes her, an apt oxymoron; confiding, as we shall see later in the chapter, that 'The deuyll and she be syb'.[79]

Vives not only insists on simple raiment, but bitterly inveighs against any form of cosmetics as the Fiend's invention for

Whan they fell from the heuenly vertue vnto the erthly cōtagiousnes : thā they taught to peynt the blacke of eies/ and ruddines of chekes/ and alter the naturall colour of the heares and visage.[80]

And, indeed, we know from Jewish mythology that it was Azazal who devised the cosmetics and jewelry with which women attract men.[81] Remilia, mistress of the king of Nineveh, illustrates the pains women took to improve God's handiwork with paints and perfumes.

> I haue trickt my tramels vp with richest balme,
> And made my perfumes of the purest Myrre:
> The pretious drugs that Aegypts wealth affoords,
> The costly paintings fetcht fro curious Tyre,
> Haue mended in my face what nature mist.
> Am I not the earths wonder in my lookes?[82]

Thomas Nashe makes Christ himself the mouthpiece of his indignation.

The print of my finger thou hast defaced, and wyth Arts-vanishing varnishment made thy selfe a changeling from the forme I first cast thee in; Sathan, take her to thee, with blacke boyling Pitch rough cast ouer her counterfeite red and white;[83]

Both Vives and Stubbes condemn as wanton the wearing of male attire by a woman[84] for

It is written in the 22 of *Deuteronomie*, that what man so euer weareth womans apparel is accursed, and what woman weareth mans apparel is accursed also.[85]

And even masculine aspects in woman's fashions were regarded with suspicion. William Harrison, describing contemporary apparel, inveighs at the 'galligascons . . . coloured nether stocks of silke, ierdseie, and such like, . . .'

I haue met with some of these trulles in London so disguised, that it hath passed my skill to discerne whether they were men or women.
Thus it is now come to passe, that women are become men, . . .[86]

[79] *Inf.* p. 90.
[80] Vives, *Instruction*, Bk. 1, I, ii^v; edn. Watson p. 74.
[81] M. Rudwin, *op. cit.*, p. 87, note 5.
[82] Th. Lodge and R. Greene, *A Looking Glasse*, ed. J. C. Collins, vol. i, II, i, 426-31.
[83] Nashe, *Christs Teares*; *Works*, ed. McKerrow, ii, 139, ll. 29-33.
[84] Vives, *Instruction*, Bk. 1, K.iiij; edn. Watson, pp. 71-84.
[85] Stubbes, *op. cit.*, i, p. 73.
[86] W[illiam]. H[arrison]., *Description of England* in R. Holinshed, *The Chronicles* (1587), p. 172, col 2, ll. 10-30.
Although in romantic and chivalric traditions women, at times, when driven by necessity or for some good purpose, had recourse to such attire, yet it was generally frowned

The point was that man considered it likely that, if woman wore a 'swashing and a martial outside' she would be tempted to behave as a man, change obedience to demand, and take certain liberties that were otherwise denied her.

Greene in conceipt, New raised from his graue to write the Tragique historie of faire Valeria of London reveals how this wanton, together with her companions 'that troope of trulles', disguised as men, attended a great 'solemnitie' at the Court.

In the midst of their iolitie, they were by the princes commaundemente all forceably vnmaskt, standing then before hir [Grosart reads: him], as stony Images, not blushing ought at this bewraying of their lewdnes, though enuirond, and like monsters gazd on by many eyes, nor making any shewe of sorrowe, for their soueraigns sharpe rebukes, which conceiuing no hope of their amendment, sent them home with open shame vnto their husbāds.[87]

Giraldo, Valeria's husband, died of grief.

(b) *The Attraction of 'Gadding Abroad' in High Places and Low*

Vives maintains that

it neither becometh a womā ... to liue among men/ or speke a brode & shake of her demurenes & honestie/[88]

'Plutarchus saythe/ that hit is a custome in Egypte/ that women shuld weare no showes/ bicause they shulde abide at home.'[89]

Not all women agreed with Vives' exhortation. Indeed many held 'that a harsh place of *Scripture, That women must be no goers or gadders abroad* ...'.[90] A Dutch eye-witness describes the search for attention, excitement and company among the women of sixteenth-century England.

---

upon in sixteenth-century literature. The women characters themselves felt conscious of the incongruity. Rosalind in the Forest of Arden, on hearing that Orlando is near, exclaims:

> Alas the day, what shall I do with my doublet & hose?
> *As you Like it*, III, ii, 214-5; (204).

and Jessica, in her elopement with Lorenzo,

> I am glad 'tis night, you do not looke on me,
> For I am much asham'd of my exchange:
> *The Merchant of Venice*, II, vi, 41-2; (34-5)

Michael Drayton, on meeting a woman dressed up as a man, immediately examined her feet to see if they were cloven. *The Moone-Calfe*; in *Works*, ed. J. W. Hebel (Oxford 1932), iii, 180, ll. 537-42.

[87] I[ohn]. D[ickenson]., *Greene in conceipt* (Richard Bradocke for William Iones, 1598), F. 4ᵛ; ed. A. B. Grosart (Blackburn, 1878), in *Occasional Issues of Unique or very rare Books*, vi, 140.

[88] J. L. Vives, *Instruction*, Bk. 1, E. ijᵛ; edn. Watson, p. 55.

[89] *Ibid.*, K. iᵛ; edn. Watson, p. 79.

[90] D. Lupton, *London and the Countrey carbonadoed* (1632), p. 14.

Sy sitten verciert voor haer Deuren/ om de voorbygaenders te besien/ ofte van die besien te worden: ende in alle Bancquetten ende Maeltijden hebben sy de meeste eere/ aent hooch eynde sittende/ ende worden eerst ghedient/ ende sy dienen dan de Mannen aent neder eynde vande Tafel: voorts den legen tijt besteden sy in wandelen te gaen oft rijden/ met caerten oft anders te spelen/ haer vrienden te besoecken/ ende met haer Gevaders (diesy Gosseps noemen) ende Gebueren te converseren ende vrolick te zijn inde kinderbaringhen/ doopinghen/ Kerckganghen/ ende begravenisse:[91]

Of course this 'gadding about' brought them into the company of men. Vives warns that the Devil is behind the new custom of prolonged discussions with men:

That custome was confermed/ as I trowe/ by the decree of the deuyll/ that women shulde be preysed for talkyng eloquently and prōtly with men: and that by many houres to gether.[92]

By haunting public places, women gave the Devil new opportunities, for here he rallied his forces. The courts especially were looked upon as 'Seates of Satan'. The idea was not without foundation, for in English literature at least, devils were employed as lackeys.[93] Pierce Penniless deplores the Devil's work at the Court of Westminster in London.

Westminster, Westminster, much maydenhead hast thou to answere for at the day of iudgement; . . .
The Court I dare not touch, but surely there (as in the Heauens) be many falling starres, and but one true *Diana*.[94]

[91] E. van Meteren, *Commentarien ofte Memorien* (Schotland/ buyten Danswijck, 1608), A.D. 1587, f. xvij^v, col. ii, Bk. 13. 'They sit in front of their doors, dressed up in fineries to view the passers-by and to be seen by them; and at all banquets and meals they receive the most attention sitting at the head of the table, and are first served before the men at the lower end of the table; moreover they spend their free time in walking or, often, riding, in playing at cards or other games, in visiting their friends and to converse with their equals (whom they call 'gosseps') and their neighbours; and to make merry at child-births, christenings, churchings and funerals.'
Cf. P. Stubbes, *op. cit.*, i, 87. 'Other some spende the greatest parte of the daie, in sittyng at the doore, to shewe their braueries, to make knowen their beauties, to beholde the passengers by, to viewe the coast, to see fashions, and to acquainte themselves with the brauest fellowes: for if not for these causes, I see no other causes why thei should sit at their doores, from Mornyng till Noone (as many doe) from Noone to Night; thus vainly spendyng their golden daies in filthie idlenesse and sinne.'
[92] Vives, *Instruction*, Bk. 1, O. i^v.; edn. Watson, p. 98.
[93] *Henry IV*, Pt. 1, III, i, 152-5; (155-8).

> Hotspur : I tel you what,
> He [Glendower] held me last night at least
> nine houres
> In reckoning vp the seueral Diuils names
> That were his lackies, . . .

[94] Th. Nashe, *Piers Penilesse*; *Works*, ed. McKerrow, i, 216, ll. 12-23.
Cf. Nashe, *The Terrors of the Night* (1594)), *Works*, ed. McKerrow, i, 349, ll. 28-33. 'If in one man a whole legion of diuells haue bin billetted, how manie hundred thousand legions retaine to a Tearme at *London*? If I said but to a Tauerne, it were an infinite thing. In *Westminster* Hall a man can scarce breath for them; for in euery corner they houer as thick as moates in the sunne.'

The Devil's courtly weapons consisted mainly of secular knowledge and worldly pastimes. The liberal arts, particularly eloquence, were fostered there, together with 'pestiferous dancing'.

And this they call the gentill intertaynement of the court, that is to say, of ẏ scole, where they learne other like artes of their mayster the deuill.[95]

Fully aware of these surrounding dangers, Vives had thought it necessary, in order to protect the Princess Mary, to present her with a strong defence:

Accipies igitur satellites ducentos, nam excurrentem numerum nō imputo, quos sic tibi facies familiares, ut nec noctu, nec interdiu, nec domi, nec in publico sinas à tutela animae ac uitae tuae uel latum unguem abscedere, ne his aut certe similibus destituta praedẹ sis diabolo,[96]

But the Courts were not the Devil's only haunts, he could also be found in the lowliest of places, at the ale-houses and brothels of the poor. At one of these Elynour Rummynge held sway, and she as Skelton tells us, was a relation of the Devil. (*sup* pp. 86–7)

> She dwelt in Sothray,
> In a certayne stede
> Besyde Lederhede.[97]

Hither came the dross of humanity

> Wyth all theyr myght runnynge
> . . . . . .
>
> A sorte of foule drabbes
> All scuruey with scabbes:
> Some be flybytten,
> Some skewed as a kytten;
> Some wyth a sho clout
> Bynde theyr heddes about;
> Some haue no herelace,
> Theyr lockes about theyr face,
> Theyr tresses vntrust,
> All full of vnlust;[98]

The dangerous, cheating 'ale-wife' was a popular subject in literature as well as in pictorial art. Man looked upon her with suspicion; but the Fiend had

---

[95] J. L. Vives, *The office and duetie of an husband*, tr. T. Paynell [1555?], Q. iij.

[96] J. L. Vives, *Satellitium siue Symbola* (Brugis, 1524) F. vi^v. 'You therefore shall accept two hundred guards, which should suffice, whom you will make your companions in such a way that neither by day nor night, in private or public, you shall allow them to go away the width of a finger lest, being deprived of these or their like, you fall victim to the devil.

[97] J.Skelton, *The Tunnyng of Elynour Rummynge*; in *Poetical Works*, ed. A. Dyce, i, p. 98, ll. 96-8.

[98] *Ibid.*, i, pp. 99-100, ll. 128, 139-148.

a peculiar affection for her. She was the only woman who was welcomed in hell with great cordiality. In the Chester Play[99] Sathanas himself calls her 'deare darlinge'; 'Secundus Demon' takes her as his wife;

> welckome, dere ladye, I shall thee wedd!
> for manye a heavye and droncken head,
> cavse of thy ale, were broughte to bed,
> farre worse then anye beaste.[100]

'Tercius Demon' looks upon her as his daughter. She is indeed more than a business relation: she is the Devil's own. After the harrowing of hell, when the souls of men have gone to their bliss, the 'ale-wife' is left behind. And now she regrets the time she came hither.

> woful am I, with thee to dwell,
> sir sathanas, sergante of hell![101]

There is a carving of 'The end of the Ale-wife' in Ludlow Church.[102] Among fiendish grins and bagpipe music she makes her entry into hell. All the fun is obviously on the Devil's side.

The disreputable 'guddame', Kynd Kittok, who in her life-time had been 'lyk a caldrone cruk cleir vnder kell', and who had got into heaven through negligence on the part of St Peter, found herself eventually outside the gates because of visiting an ale-house.[103]

(c) The Fairy uses the Dainty Dish, Luxury and Lechery to Compass the Downfall of the Wanton

Like the good woman, the wanton is the subject of attention from 'that fourth kinde of spirites ... called the *Phairie* ...'.[104] His most familiar form in English literature is the Puck,[105] Robin Goodfellow, Friar Rush[106] var-

---

[99] *Descensu Christi ad Inferos*; in *The Chester Plays*, Part II, ed. Dr Matthews, EETS, e.s., cxv (1916), pp. 318 *et seq.*

[100] *Ibid.*, p. 331, ll. 313-16.

[101] *Ibid.*, ii, p. 329, ll. 265-66.

[102] T. Tindall Wildridge, *The grotesque in Church Art* (1899), pp. 102-3.

[103] [W. Dunbar], *My guddame wes ane gay wyfe*; in *The Bannatyne MS*, iii, STS, n.s. 23 (1928), pp. 10-11.

[104] *Sup.* pp. 50 *et seq.*; *inf.* p. 154.

[105] F. T. Hall, *The Pedigree of the Devil* (1883), p. 236.
Puck – the typical house-spirit, a mischievous spirit, generally described as an uncouth dwarfish figure (Shakespeare).
Pouke – an evil spirit (Spenser).
Pug – a fiend (Ben Jonson).
Puk – a goblin (Friesland).
Puki – an evil spirit (Iceland).
Pixy – a mischievous spirit, misleading fairy (Devonshire).
Pooka – an evil spirit (Irish).
Pwcca – an evil spirit (Welsh).

[106] R. Scot, *op. cit.* 1584, Cap. 21, 'A Discourse vpon diuels', p. 522, classes Rush with

iety. These seem to have been the *confusio feminae*. Puck, for instance, causes much havoc in *A Midsommer Nights Dreame* and is himself highly entertained, for all the excuse he can find is: 'this their iangling I esteeme a sport.'[107] He is identified by a Fairy.

> Are you not hee
> That frights the maidens of the Villagree,
> Skim milke, and sometimes labour in the querne,
> And bootlesse make the breathlesse housewife cherne,
> And sometime make the drinke to beare no barme,
> Misleade night-wanderers, laughing at their harme,
> Those that Hobgoblin call you, and sweet Puck,
> You do their worke, and they shall have good lucke.[108]

Though these spirits are whimsical and sometimes even helpful to humans, fundamentally they are sprigs of Satan concerned to make the woman both tempted and tempting. In *The Historie of Frier Rush*,[109] Rush is 'the spirite of the buttery'[110] who sponsors dainty dishes. He is successful with the rich merchant's wife

that will eat no Cherries, forsooth, but when they are at twenty shillings a pound, . . . What should I tel how squeamish she is in her dyet, . . . Is not this the excesse of pride, signior Sathan? Goe too, you are vnwise, if you make her not a chiefe Saint in your Calender.[111]

As the dainty dish was a weapon well fitted to the hand of the woman, Vives warns her:

Loke well on thy selfe: Thou shalt fynde thy selfe one of Satanas officers/ y^t vsest at home so many chosen meates to the ful/ bulkyng out capōs/ pertriges/

Hudgin and Robin Goodfellow. '*Hudgin* is a verie familiar diuell, which will doo no bodie hurt, except he receiue iniurie. . .' Comparing him with Robin Goodfellow he continues: 'Frier *Rush* was for all the world such another fellow as this *Hudgin*, and brought vp euen in the same schoole; to wit, in a kitchen. . .'

Cf. S. H[arsnet]., *A Declaration of egregious Popish Impostures* (1603), ch, xxi, p. 134. 'And if that the bowle of curds, & creame were not duly set out for *Robin Good-fellow* the Frier, & *Sisse* the dairy-maide, . . . then, either the pottage was burnt to next day in the pot, or the cheese would not curdle, or the butter would not come, . . .'

Rush is not a clear type, however, but a mixture of medieval christian Devil and Fairy. Cf. Mr. S[tevenson, W.], *Gammer gurtons nedle* (1575); ed. J. S. Farmer, Tudor Facs. Texts (1910), C. ii^v. III, ii, l. 23, where he is depicted with 'crooked clouen feete, and many a hooked nayle'.

[107] *A Midsommer Nights Dreame*, III, ii, 374; (353).

[108] *Ibid.*, II, i, 33-40.

[109] *The Historie of Frier Rush* (1620); facs. reprint (1810). See also W. J. Thoms, *op. cit.*, i, pp. 253 *ad. fin.*

Thoms, *op. cit.*, (i, 253) remarks that although the earliest English version at present known, bears date only in 1620, it was probably printed at a much earlier period, and a translation from the German, printed at Strasburgh in 1515.

[110] P. Stubbes, *Anatomie*, i, 107.

[111] T. Nashe, *Pierce Peniless*; *Works*, ed. McKerrow, i, 173, ll. 4-20.

phesantes/ delicate cakes/ potages/ sawses/ and soppes/ & al costly/ amonge so many of thy poure neighbours/ that die for hunger :[112]

Luxury and Lechery were the twin weapons of Devil Rush who made his first entry into the world as cook's assistant. In that capacity he knocked at the gate of a Danish monastery.

> Fur das kloster der abt kam gegangen;
> Rausch ward vonn im gar schon enpfangen.
> . . . . . .
> Rausch sprach; 'herr, ich sag uch recht,
> Ich bin ein armer kuchen knecht.[113]

Rush is one of the few sustained anthropomorphic devils in sixteenth-century literature. He seems to have had more than one arrow to his bow. He could woo and flatter a woman both for himself or as a go-between. It was Rush who assisted the woman at Antwerp with the arrangement of her ruff, and Rush who brought women into the monastery where he worked. His cooking was so excellent that he grew into high favour with the prior who confided to him that there dwelt a fair gentlewoman close by the monastery for whom he had a great affection. Rush promises to be his intermediary and visits her.

Rest you merry faire Mistresse, the most fairest creature in the world. My Maister greeteth you by me, desiring you to come and speake with him.[114]

With the procuring of fine dishes and of gentlewomen, Rush was very successful and popular in the monastery until one day his pedigree was exposed and he was consequently dismissed.[115]

Rush now went into service with a husbandman who had an unfaithful wife who in his absence made good cheer with the parish-priest. Rush discovers this time and again and makes fun of the priest until finally he says:

Thou shalt neuer more escape me, thy life is lost. With that, the Priest held vp his hands and said, heere is a hundred peeces of gold, take them and let me goe. So *Rush* tooke the golde and let the Priest goe. And when his Master

---

[112] J. L. Vives, *Instruction*, I, iij^v; edn. Watson, p. 76.

[113] From the German edn. (Strasburgh, 1515); quoted in W. J. Thoms, *op. cit.*, i, 254. 'Rush said he was a poor assistant pastry-cook, and was given a hearty welcome.'

[114] *The Historie of Frier Rvsh*, facs. reprint (1810), p. 5; edn. Thoms, i, 267.

[115] C. H. Herford, *Studies in the Literary Relations of England and Germany* (CUP., 1886), pp. 294-8, mentions an obscure link with the Cistercian convent of Esrow, 'beside the wood-girt and legend-haunted Esrow lake . . .' 'The dissolution of the convent at the Reformation led to the destruction of most of its antiquities; but in Pontoppidan's day there still remained a hugh gridiron and cauldron, and the tradition of a portrait, with incription, of Rus the friar and cook . . . Pontoppidan says himself (Danske Atlas vi, p. 35): "der skal endnu findes Broder Rusis Jerngryde og Rist" . . . The first Danish allusion to his name, which does not occur before the 17th. century in historical documents, is in Christen Hansen's *Dorothea*, 1531 :'

came home, he gaue him the halfe of his money, and bad him farewell, for he would goe see the world.[116]

Although he had given the unfaithful woman many an anxious moment, he had yet taken good care not to rid her of her vice.

(d) *The Devil's Wooing*

Plagued by these spirits, the wanton, like the good woman, had still to face that 'woorser moitie of diuels, . . . that is, waterie . . .'[117] But where the good women of the Elfin group succeed in resisting the Devil, the wantons succumb to his tempting.

The motif of the Devil's wooing plays a prominent part in the legends and literatures of all European countries. In the ballad of the *Daemon Lover*,[118] the Devil, in the guise of a wealthy sea-captain, persuades the Lady to desert husband and babes, and follow him to the sea-shore where the sight of his ship, richly fitted out entices her aboard.

> She set her foot upon the ship,
> No mariners could she behold;
> But the sails were o the taffetie,
> And the masts o the beaten gold.
> . . . . . .
> They had not saild a league, a league,
> A league but barely three,
> Until she espied his cloven foot,
> And she wept right bitterlie.[119]

But her regrets come too late and the daemon pilots her to hell.

A similar motif is found in the Orkney *Play of the Lathie Odivere*,[120] where the Devil appears as a Knight just returned from the Holy Land to bring news of her husband. He tells her many a tale about the victories of the long absent Sir Odivere whilst

> He minted aye, to he never said,
> An skeeted aye i 'ilka teel,
> Dat Odivere wus a rovin bled,
> An liked de lasses ower weel.[121]

His insinuations prepare her for his wooing and she yields.

[116] *The History of Frier Rvsh*, facs. (1810), pp. 33-4; edn. Thoms, i, 257.
[117] *Sup.* p. 55; *Inf.* p. 154.
[118] Child, iv, 367, No. 243, F.
[119] *Ibid.*, iv, 368, F.
[120] *Scottish Antiquary*, VIII (Edinburgh, 1894), pp. 54 *et seq.*
[121] *Ibid.*, p. 54, Second Fit, verse 13.
W. Montgomerie in *Scots Chronicle* (Glasgow, 1951), p. 53, mentions that Mr. Traill

His Relationship with Womankind

Gradually, the Daemon of the ballad subsided into the background, and with the suppression of legend and Mysteries, people had to give up their 'dear delight'. It was the new playwright's responsibility to provide a worthy substitute. In this he succeeded remarkably well, for there appeared a new species of villain: the Jew, the Turk, the Moor, the man of incredible malice. No longer does the plot turn upon the intervention of supernatural beings, but the complications arise through 'the damned ministers of villainy', men who prove themselves 'the adopted sons of hell'. It was natural to cast the Jews in this role for they were outside the pale of Christendom and throughout medieval literature were presented as collaborators of the Devil. Consequently they underwent the same scornful treatment. Launcelot Gobbo, representing common opinion of his day, does not know whether to choose between the Jew or the Devil, whether to run away or stay with his master

(who God blesse the marke) is a kinde of diuell; and to run away from the *Iew*, I should be ruled by the fiend, who sauing your reuerence is the diuell himselfe: certainely the *Iew* is the verie diuell incarnation,[122]

In the end he decides in favour of the Devil. As for the Moor, it was his hue, not his race,

for it was an old superstition, not then extinct, that the Devil when he appeared took the form of a Moor, while the Jews (ye are of your father, the Devil!) were held to be devils born.[123]

In *Lusts Dominion* when Cole and Crabb first catch sight of the Moor's black skin they draw back in fear.

Eleaz[ar].   . . . . ha? are you afraid.

Cole.   Oh? no Sir, no, but truth to tell;
Seeing your face, we thought of hell.[124]

Dennison spent forty years collecting this version in fragmentary scraps from many old people in different parts of Orkney.

Other versions are in Child, ii, 494. No. 113.

Judging from internal evidence Dr. Montgomerie, *op. cit.*, p. 56, considers the Orkney Play the older version.

[122] *The Merchant of Venice*, II, ii, 21-24; (17-22).

[123] E. E. Stoll, *op. cit.*, p. 345.

[124] C. Marlowe, *Lusts Dominion or the Lascivious Queen* (1657), II, iii.

Henslowe's Diary, ed. W. W. Greg (1904), Pt. i, f. 67ᵛ. ll. 16-20. 'Layd owt for the company the 13 of febrearye 1599 for a boocke called the spaneshe mores tragedie vnto thomas deckers wᵐ harton John daye in pte of payment the some of . . .'

Pt. ii, item 197, Greg remarks: 'Identified by Collier and Fleay with *Lust's Dominion*, printed in 1657 as by Marlowe. This seems not unlikely.'

Cf. also the Preface to this play in *Select Collection of Old English Plays*, ed. C. W. Hazlitt, xiv, pp. 95-6.

The Turks, long feared as formidable enemies of Christendom, also fall easily into the role of villain.

> the Turke
> Pure Divell, and allowes enough to fat
> The sides of villany;[125]

For the most part this 'teeming race of glorious villains'[126] inherit the qualities of their demonic predecessors, and sometimes even surpass them in wickedness. Aaron the Moor in *Titus Andronicus*, when at the point of death, confesses:

> If one good Deed in all my life I did,
> I do repent it from my very Soule.[127]

and Eleazar in *Lusts Dominion*:

Devills com claim your right, and when I am, confin'd within your kingdom then shall I, out-act you all in perfect villany.[128]

Their zeal to capture souls was no less than that of Tituvillus in the Mysteries.

> *Eleaz.* Oh for more work, more souls to post to hell;
> That I might pile up *Charons* boat so full,
> Untill it topple o'er, Oh 'twould be sport
> To see them sprawl through the black slimy lake.[129]

In later sixteenth-century literature many of these villains take on a Machiavellian cast, displaying a calculated wickedness combining the qualities of the lion and the fox. These have 'neither pity, loue, nor fear.' Richard III is described by Queen Margaret

> beware of him,
> Sinne, death, and hell haue set their markes on him,
> And all their Ministers attend on him.[130]

Whatever form or quality they adopt, however, they are fully in agreement with the demonic kind in the importance of using women to compass their designs. Typical in his relationship with the wanton is the Moor. This may be due to certain magical charms to which the wanton was susceptible.[131] Eleazar, the Moor, in *Lusts Dominion* bluntly states his plan:

[125] *Lusts Dominion*, I, iv.
[126] A. P. Rossiter, *English Drama from Early Times to the Elizabethans* (1950), p. 158.
[127] *Titus Andronicus*, 1st. Folio, Tragedies, p. 52; (V, iii, 189-90).
[128] *Lusts Dominion*, V, vi.
[129] *Lusts Dominion*, IV, iii.
[130] *Richard III*, I, iii, 304-6; (292-4).
[131] It was not unusual for the Witch's familiar to take on the shape of a Moor. *Cf. inf.* p. 116, note 65. *Cf.* also the history of a Spanish girl, Magdalena à Cruce in J. Wier, *De Praestigiis Daemonum* (Basileae, 1583). Lib. VI, cap. vi, p. 673 *et seq.*

> Love dance in twenty formes
> Upon my beauty, that this Spanish dame
> May be bewitch'd, and doat, her amorous flames
> Shall blow up the old King, Consume his Sons,
> And make all Spain a bonefire.
> This Tragedie beeing acted hers does begin,
> To shed a harlots blood can be no sin.[132]

Aaron in *Titus Andronicus* boasts of his power over Queen Tamara whom he has long held captive by his charms,

> fettred in amorous chaines,
> And faster bound to *Aarons* charming eyes,
> Then is *Prometheus* ti'de to *Caucasus*.[133]

He intends

> To wanton with this Queene,
> This Goddesse, this *Semirimis*, ...
> This Syren, that will charme Romes *Saturnine*,
> And see his shipwracke, and his Common weales.[134]

Once the woman becomes the toy of the Devil, whether he is of the supernatural or the natural variety, she becomes an agent of destruction like Helena in *Doctor Faustus*. She destroys not only her own womanhood but creates havoc all around her even to the wreck of society.

---

[132] *Lusts Dominion*, I, ii.
[133] *Titus Andronicus*, 1st. Folio, Tragedies. p. 35; (II, i, 15-17).
[134] *Ibid.*, Tragedies, p. 35; (II, i, 21-4).

4

The Witch

9 *He lay with the witch*

4 The Witch

one that woorketh by the Deuill.[1]

Legislation and Causes

The wanton was the subject of thundering denunciations from the sixteenth-century moralists; the shrew was burlesqued in prose, poetry and
plays. Only the witch has been the subject of analysis in serious scientific
treatises. Hence we have a carefully worked out definition of the witch, de-
lineating her major characteristics. In *A Discourse of the Subtill Practises
of Deuilles by Witches and Sorcerers*, Gifford defines her as

one that woorketh by the Deuill, or by some deuilish or curious art, either
hurting or healing, reuealing thinges secrete, or foretelling thinges to come,
which the deuil hath deuised to entangle and snare mens soules withal vnto
damnation. The coniurer, the enchaunter, the sorcerer, the deuiner, and what-
soeuer other sort there is, are in deede compassed within this circle.[2]

To understand the major role played by the witch in scientific literature,
in legislation and in actual trials in court, as well as in popular imagination,
it may be helpful to trace the historical background. The idea of the witch
is an old one going back to Ancient History, to Scripture and to the writ-
ings of the Fathers. During the Middle Ages occasional cases of witchcraft
are reported, but there were no mass trials until the thirteenth century.[3]
The early medieval Church was merciful and often attempted to lessen the
belief in witchcraft.

On many different occasions ecclesiastics who spoke with authority did their
best to disabuse the people of their belief in witchcraft. This for instance is the
general purport of the book, 'Contra insulsam vulgi opinionem de grandine et
tonitruis . . .', written by St Agobard (d.841), Archbishop of Lyons (P.L., CIV,
147).[4]

Abbot Regino, historian and codifier of canon law, who taught at Prüm, a
former Benedictine abbey in Lorraine (AD 893–99), when writing about the
supposed powers of witches stresses

[1] George Gifford, *A Discourse of the Subtill Practises of Deuilles by Witches and Sorcerers* (1587), B. ii.

[2] *Ibid.*

[3] Suspected witches were subjected to the ordeal of cold water, but as the sinking of
the victim was regarded as a proof of innocence, we may reasonably suppose that the
verdicts so arrived at were generally verdicts of acquittal.

[4] H. Thurston, 'Witchcraft', *Cath. Encycl.* (New York, 1912), xv, 675, col. i.

'the duty of priests earnestly to instruct the people that these things are absolutely untrue and that such imaginings are planted in the minds of misbelieving folk, not by a Divine spirit, but by the spirit of evil' (P.L., CXXXII, 352; cf. ibid., 284)[5]

Burchard, Bishop of Worms (c.1020)

altogether rejects the possibility of many of the marvellous powers with which witches were popularly credited. Such, for example, were the nocturnal riding through the air, the changing of a person's disposition from love to hate, the control of thunder, rain, and sunshine, the transformation of a man into an animal, the intercourse of incubi and succubi with human beings. Not only the attempt to practise such things but the very belief in their possibility is treated by him as a sin for which the confessor must require his penitent to do a serious assigned penance.[6]

About 1250 the Inquisition began to take an interest in witchcraft as well as in heresy. As we have seen in Chapter I,[7] it was two Dominican Inquisitors, Jacob Sprenger and Hendrick Kramer who composed *Malleorum Quorundam Malificarum* in 1487 which gave definite form to many of the popular beliefs about witches. Moreover, the papal bull *Summis Desiderantes affectibus*[8] attached to the publication appeared to give the full sanction of the Church to the persecution of the witch. Father Thurston looks upon this publication as probably the most disastrous episode in the history of witchcraft. Certainly in the fifteenth century witchhunts became epidemic on the continent with mass trials figuring prominently in Germany, France and Switzerland. The height of the persecution was reached in the sixteenth century and continued into the seventeenth. The persecutions on the continent were marked with an 'insane ferocity that burnt nine hundred witches in the province of Lorraine alone between 1580 and 1595, according to Remigius, and in 1524 put to death one thousand unfortunate wretches in Como according to de Spina.'[9] In England 'there exist details of over two hundred cases of witchcraft between the years 1563 and 1603.'[10]

[5] *Ibid.*, p. 675, cols. i-ii.
[6] *Ibid.*, p. 675, col. ii.
[7] *Sup.* p. 4.
[8] Innocent VIII, *op. cit.*, sup. p. 3.
[9] George Gifford, *A Dialogue Concerning Witches and Witchcraftes* (1593), ed. B. White (OUP., 1931), p.v.
[10] *Ibid.*
According to C. H. L'Estrange Ewen, who examined the Home Circuit Documents, there were more trials during the reign of Elizabeth than during the entire 17c. See *Witch hunting and Witch Trials* (1929), pp. 72-113.
Jacob Rathgeb, secretary and companion of Duke Frederick on his visit to England in 1592, writing his impressions of the country, notes: 'Vil Hexen werden darinnen gefunden/ vnd beschicht offtermaln durch Hagel vnnd ander Ungewitter/ grosser schaden. (*Kurtze vnd Warhaffte Beschreibung der Badenfahrt* Tübingen, 1602), f. 35ᵛ.'
'There are many witches in that country who by producing hailstorms and other bad weather, often cause great harm.'

Legislation became extremely active in England as well as on the Continent. The first Act in the English 'statutes at large' dealing specifically with witchcraft dates from 1541.[11] Henry VIII who was reputed to lend a credulous ear to foolish prophecies, introduced severe penalties against witchcraft.

In 1541, the thirty-third year of his reign, a bill was issued.

that yf any persone or persones, after the first daye of Maye next comyng, use devise practise or exercise, ... any Invocacons or conjuracons of Spirites wichecraftes enchauntmentes or sorceries, ... to waste consume or destroy any persone in his bodie membres or goodes, or to pvoke and persone to unlawfull love, ... or pull downe any Crosse or Crosses, or by such Invocacons or conjuracons of Sprites ... take upon them to tell or declare where goodes stollen or lost shall become, ... shalbe demyde accepted and adjuged a Felon and Felones; And ... suffre suche paynes of deathe losse and forfaytures of their landes tentes goodes and Catalles as in cases of felonie by the course of the Comon lawes of this Realme, And also shall lose p¹vilege of Clergie and Sayntuarie[12]

The Law against witchcraft became more severe as the century progressed. In the fifth year of Elizabeth's reign, the following clause was added to the 1541 bill:

That yf any pson or psons after the first daye of June nexte coming, use practise or exersise any Invocacons or Conjuracons of evill and wicked Spirites, to or for any Intent or Purpose; ....[13]

As Montague Summers remarks, it was

a wide clause which certainly included and was meant to touch 'wise women' and 'white witches', that is to say, those who evoked and raised infernal, or at least mystic and equivocal, spirits, not for harming and bale, but to cure diseases of men and salve cattle, ...[14]

By this act, witchcraft, hitherto often looked upon as a resource for various ailments, and for getting useful or desired information, now began to take on a different hue, and became feared, reviled, and persecuted. The Queen had her agents in the commissions of her Justices who spared no efforts to produce results. There is no doubt that the Devil bore a grudge against Her Majesty for in the *Calendar of State Papers* for 1584 we read, among other confederates who conspired against her life, the names of

"Ould Birtles the great devel, Darnally the sorcerer, Maude Twogood enchantresse, the oulde witche of Ramsbury, several other 'oulde witches,' Gregson

---

[11] J. Ashton, *The Devil in Britain and America* (1896), p. 191.
    Cf. also R. Scot, *op. cit.*, ed. B. Nicholson (1886), p. xxxi. 'Before the time of the eighth Henry, sorcerers were dealt with by the ecclesiastical law, which punished them as heretics.'
[12] 33° Hen. VIII. c. 8; *The Statutes of the Realm*, A.D. 1541-2 (1817), iii, 837.
[13] 5° Eliz. c. 15; *The Statutes of the Realm*, A.D. 1562-3 (1817), iv, Pt. I, p. 446.
[14] R. Scot, *op. cit.*, ed. Summers (1930), xix.

the north tale teller, who was one of them 3 that stole awaye the Earl of Northumberlandes heade from one of the turrettes in York," &c.[15]

It was therefore not surprising that Elizabeth was not immune to fear of these obscure forces, and re-enforced to a large extent the measures taken by her father to exterminate witchcraft. John Jewel in one of his sermons for the Queen gives a vivid description how 'this kind of people, I meane witches, & sorcerers, w'in these fewe last yeres, are marueilously increased w'in this your Grace's realm' and that he had known many who owing to evil spells, had pined away 'euen vnto the death'.

Wherefore, your poore subiectes most humble petitiō vnto your highnes, is that the lawes touching such malefactours, may be put in due execution. For the schole of them is great, their doings horrible, their malice intollerable, the examples most miserable. And I praye God, they neuer practise further, then vpon y[e] subiect[16]

It was not exactly reassuring; consequently the Act of 1581, 23⁰ Eliz., c.2. runs as follows:

That yf any person ... during the Lief of our sayde Soveraigne Ladye the Queenes Ma[tie] that nowe ys, eyther within her Highenesses Dominions or without, shall by setting or erecting any Figure or Figures, or by casting of Nativities, or by calculaōn, or by any Prophecieng Witchcrafte Conjuraōns or other lyke unlawfull Meanes whatsoeṽ, seeke to knowe, and shall set forth by expresse Wordes, Deedes or Writinges, howe longe her Ma[tie] shall lyve or contynue, or who shall raigne as King or Queene of this Realme of England after her Highenesse Decease, ... That then everye suche Offence shalbe Felonye, and everye Offendour and Offendours therein, and also all his or their Aydours ... shalbe judged as Felons, and shall suffer [suche] paynes of Deathe and [forfaieture] as in Case of Felonye ys used, without any Benefite of Cleargie or Sanctuarye.[17]

In Scotland, legislation of witchcraft began even earlier than in England. In 1510, in the 'Proclamation for regulating the proceedings of the Justice-Aire of Iedburghe',[18] the judges are instructed to ask the question 'gif þair be ony Wichecraift or Sossary wsyt in þe realme?' but it was not until 1563 that the regular persecution of these deluded people began. In that year an Act was passed by the Parliament of Mary, Queen of Scots against

---

[15] *Cal. S. P. Domestic Series, 1581-1590* (1865), p. 220, item 90.

[16] John Jewel, *Certaine Sermons preached before the Queenes Maiestie, and at Paules crosse* (1583), M vi[v].

[17] The Statutes of the Realm, A.D. 1580-1 (1817), iv, Pt. I, pp. 659-660.

[18] R. Pitcairn, *Criminal Trials in Scotland from A.D. 1488-A.D. 1624 compiled from the original records and MSS.* (Edinburgh and London, 1833), i, Pt. 1, 64, 66. The editor remarks 'there seems no doubt that this Proclamation was Circular, and addressed to every district of Scotland'.

the hauy and abominabill superstitioun vsit be diuers of the liegis of this Realme be vsing of Witchcraftis Sorsarie and Necromancie and credence geuin thairto in tymes bygane aganis the Law of God[19]

Not only was this law directed against witches and sorcerers, but it included those who sought their advice.

Nor that na persoun seik ony help response or cōsultatioun at ony sic vsaris or abusaris foirsaidis of Witchcraftis Sorsareis or Necromancie vnder the pane of deid alsweill to be execute aganis the vsar abusar as the seikar of the response or consultatioun.[20]

It was sufficient for James to enforce this, a task which was continuously urged by the clergy whose pulpit denunciations of the accursed folk filled every heart with panic and dismay.

Looking back upon the sixteenth century, later generations have sought for explanations of this peculiar phenomenon. One of the first causes to occur to the modern mind is

the utter ignorance of the medical men of the period of the subject of mental disease. The doctors of the time were mere children in knowledge of the science they professed; and to attribute a disease, the symptoms of which they could not comprehend, to a power outside their control by ordinary methods, was a safe method of screening a reputation which might otherwise have suffered.[21]

The trials appealed to many of the uglier passions of humanity. The common people could satisfy a desire for revenge by bringing a disliked neighbour before the court; those whose affairs were not prospering could find an outlet for their dissatisfaction in using the witch as a scape-goat; the gossips and sensation-mongers could feed their unwholesome curiosity with the latest disclosures. For certain people such as the judges and the accusers, the trials proved financially profitable,[22] and even the pamphleteers and ballad-mongers could turn 'a pretty penny' with their lurid versions of the witches' doings. All these factors together contributed towards a kind of mass hysteria.

John Ashton points to another cause.

It is a curious fact, well worthy the thinking over, that England and Europe had a comparative immunity from the assaults of the Devil, until after the Reformation, when for a time he became rampagious, troubling even the arch-Reformer Luther himself.[23]

[19] 'The Actis of the Parliament haldin at Edinburgh [4 June, 1563]'; in *Acts of the Parliament of Scotland* 1424-1567 (1814), ii, 539, 9 ITEM.
[20] *Ibid.*, p. 539.
[21] T. A. Spalding, *op. cit.*, p. 63.
[22] *Cf.* T. C. v. Stockum, 'Friedrich von Spee en de Heksenprocessen', *Mededelingen der Kon. Ned. Akademie van Wetenschappen*, nieuwe reeks, xii, No. 4 (Amsterdam, 1949), p. 287.
[23] J. Ashton, *op. cit.*, p. 202.

Not only did Luther have a strong belief in the Devil but he and Calvin were staunch supporters of witch-hunting. As A. W. Ward points out,

undoubtedly the influence of the Reformation movement, which had widely sapped the popular belief in the remedy provided in the miracles of the Church against the machinations of the Devil, while it strenuously asserted his personality and identified his operations with those of its adversaries, itself increased the popular belief in these perils.[24]

COUNTER-PERSECUTION

Johannes Wier, Reginald Scot, George Gifford

Not everyone in the sixteenth century agreed to the severe measures taken against these suspected women. Several writers raised their voices on behalf of the accused. Doctor Johannes Wier (or Weyer), a Dutch physician,[25] was the first to rebel against the unjust, deplorable treatment and legislation against those pitiable old women who on slight and unreliable evidence were persecuted, tortured and burnt at the stake. *De Praestigiis Daemonum*[26] was in the first place a scientific work. It contained few examples from actual trials. In the preface Wier explains the tenor of the book:

Argumentum est partim Theologicū, quo diaboli actiones & studia, sacrarū literarū testimonijs produntur: & quo ijs mode tutissimè obuiam iri possit, docetur. partim etiam Philosophicum, dum naturalib. conuincuntur rationibus satanae ludibriorum uanitas, & sagarum corrupta imaginatio: partim item Medicum, ubi secundum naturae legem, morbos, eorum causas & symptomata Lamijs perperàm imputata, oriri demonstratur. Partim id etiam Iurisprudentiae placita spectat, quum de magorū infamium, lamiarum & ueneficorum poenis, pro delicti qualitate et magnitudine, alio quàm hactenus usurpatum est mode, agatur.[27]

---

[24] A. W. Ward, ed., *Marlowe's Doctor Faustus, etc.*, pp. xlviii-xlix.
[25] L. Dooren, *Doctor Johannes Wier*, (Aalten, 1940), p. 27 *et seq.*, gives a short biography.
Wier was born at Grave on the borders of Holland and Germany. He was educated at 's Hertogenbosch and Antwerp (where he met Agrippa von Nettesheim), at Bonn, Paris, and Orleans. From 1545 he practised as a physician at Arnhem, and later attended on Duke William III (1550) to whom he dedicated his work.
[26] J. Wier, *De Praestigiis Daemonum* (First edn., Basileae, 1563); *sup.* p. 71, note 3.
[27] J. Wier, *op. cit.*, (Tertia Editione aucti, Basileae, 1566), pp. 11-12. 'The argument is partly theological, by which the actions and endeavours of the devil are brought to light by the witnesses of the Sacred Books, and by which it is taught how they may be most safely resisted; partly philosophical since the vanities of satan's mockeries as well as the corrupt imagination of witches are proved by natural arguments; partly medical, by which it is demonstrated that diseases, their causes and symptoms – wrongly imputed to sorceresses – arise according to the law of nature; partly it pertains jurisprudence which, in a way other than that hitherto exercised, deals with the punishment of infamous magicians, sorceresses and poisoners according to the quality and magnitude of the crime.'

It was the first attempt to refute, systematically, the extraordinary ideas laid down in the *Malleorum Quorundam Maleficarum*,[28] such as the witches' sexual intercourse with devils, their power to destroy crops, and inflict sterility and disease on man and beast. Wier belonged to the reformed Church, but felt no antagonism against the Church of Rome. It is hard to find any opinions in his work that are biased in either direction, though he does not spare the ignorance of clerics

incomparabilis impudentiae, perditissimaeque impietatis homines (uiris pijs, quos unicè ueneror, nihil detractum hic volo) qui medicinae sacrae, quam ne primis quidem labris eos gustasse constat, cognitionem mentientes, facile cuiuis uulgari (Consulares, uel alicuius doctrinae, iudicij, existimationisúe uiros nominare pudet) de morbo sciscitanti, consiliumque quaerenti, è maleficio uel incantatione esse morbum progenitum, ore mendaci respondere, persuadereque non uerentur. ac Pythij hi uates sepenumero incantatricem uel sagam notoria sua arte per indicia, si dijs placet, indigitare nefariè audent : honestae alicui, inculpatae ac piae matronae hoc cauterium crebrò in urentes, à quo illa nunquam, uel eius soboles, ne in multam quidem posteritatem, sanari poterit[29]

Nor is he blind to the ignorance among his own colleagues, physicians and surgeons, upon whom he pours bitter invectives.

Nec interim aliorum quoque ineptorum hominum, medicinae cognitionem impudenter doloseq iactantium, unicum esse asylum inficias eo, ut quum morbi essentiá, multoq magis eius curationem, ignorét, cogantur que ex imperitia uelut caeci de coloribus iudicare, maleficium mox esse affirment: hoc ue lamine suam tegentes in artis sacrae operibus inscitiam, . . .[30]

He blames the judges for their hard-heartedness and lack of humanity.[31] But although Wier appears as the champion of unfortunate women, he does not consider the sex faultless. He attributes to the lack of self-control, credulity and instability of woman the fact that she suffers more from illu-

[28] *Sup.* p. 4.
[29] J. Wier, *op. cit.*, (edn. 1566), Lib. II, Cap. xiv, pp. 187-8. 'men of incomparable impudence, most abysmal impiety (here I do not wish to disparage pious men for whom I have the deepest respect) who, falsely claiming knowledge of sacred medicine, which it is agreed they have never even tasted with their lips, do not fear to answer deceitfully and persuade any common man (it is embarrassing to name governors or men of any learning, judgement or reputation), who inquires about a disease and seeks advice, that the disease was begotten by a curse or a charm. And frequently these Pythic soothsayers in their wickedness dare to call an enchantress or a sorceress to prove through signs well known to her art, if it is pleasing to the gods; often branding onto some honest, blameless and pious matron a stigma from which neither she nor her descendants will ever be able to be cleansed.'
[30] *Ibid.*, Lib. II, Cap. xv, p. 192. 'Nor, meanwhile should you doubt that there is but one asylum of inapt men, impudent and pathetic boasters of a knowledge of medicine, who, since they are ignorant of the essence, much more the cure, of disease and are forced to judge without the necessary skill, like blind men judging colours, often affirm a disease to be a curse, thus covering up their ignorance of the sacred art.'
[31] *Ibid.*, Lib. V, Cap. xii, pp. 663 *et seq.*

sions than does man.[32] Narrowing down the conception of a witch in order to clarify it, he draws a distinction between the different forms of sorcery. The actual witches he names 'sagae' or 'lamiae', those who practise black magic 'magi infames' and those who were adept in the art of poisoning, the 'venifici'. The so-called sterilization by a witch, Wier ascribes to her art of poisoning rather than to any supernatural power.

porrò feminas ab inito ad ueneficium fuisse procliuiores uiris, grauissimi testantur authores.[33]

The Emperor Ferdinand of the Holy Roman Empire was so far in agreement with him that he presented the doctor with a Royal Privilege in order to protect his work against any ill-meaning publishers or rivals opposing his ideas.

Like Wier, Reginald Scot wrote to end the punishment of innocent women, believing that much of the evidence presented against them was ungrounded. In fact, he based his treatise upon Wier's. In many ways Scot was a man well ahead of his time. He saw that people were often bewitched by their own imaginations rather than by the Devil.

The fables of Witchcraft haue taken so fast hold and déepe root in the heart of man, that fewe or none can (nowadaies) with patience indure the hand and correction of God. For if any aduersitie, gréefe, sicknesse, losse of children, corne, cattell, or libertie happen vnto them; by & by they exclaime vppon witches. As though there were no God in Israel that ordereth all things according to his will; punishing both iust and vnjust with gréefs, plagues, and afflictions in maner and forme as he thinketh good: but that certeine old women héere on earth, called witches, must néeds be the contriuers of all mens calamities, and as though they themselues were innocents, and had deserued no such punishments. Insomuch as they sticke not to ride and go to such, as either are iniuriouslie tearmed witches, or else are willing so to be accounted, séeking at their hands comfort and remedie in time of their tribulation, contrarie to Gods will . . .[34]

---

[32] Ibid., Lib. II, Cap. 23, pp. 225 et seq.

Cf. T. Lodge, The diuel coniured (1596); in The Complete Works, ed. E. Gosse, iii, 33, who alleges similar reasons.

[33] Ibid., Lib. V, Cap. 20, pp. 687.

'Moreover, serious writers testify that from the beginning women were more inclined to use poison than men.'

Cf. R. Scot, op. cit. (1584), Bk. 6, Cap. 3, p. 116. 'As women in all ages haue beene counted most apt to conceiue witchcraft, and the diuels speciall instruments therein, and the onelie or chéefe practisers thereof: so also it appeareth, that they haue béen the first inuenters, and the greatest practisers of poisoning, and more naturallie addicted and giuen therevnto than men: according to the saieng of Quintilian; Latrocinium faciliùs in viro, veneficium in foemina credam. From whom Plinie differeth nothing in opinion, when he saith, scientiam foeminarum in veneficijs praevalere. To be short, Augustine, Liuie, Valerius, Diodorus and manie other agrée, that women were the first inuenters and practisers of the art of poisoning.'

[34] R. Scot, op. cit., (1584), Bk. I, Cap. i, p. 1.

Scot had a sceptical frame of mind and although he was genuinely devoted to the cause of these unfortunate women,

he was also actuated, intermittently, by a quality of mind which, if it had come to dominate him completely, would have lifted him right out of his own century and made him more at home in the period of Sprat and Locke. At times he seems on the verge of rejecting the whole outlook which made witchcraft credible. He thinks that the Devil took Christ into the high mountain only 'in a vision' (V, vii). He doubts, with Calvin, whether the Book of Job is *res gesta* or *exempli gratia*. He takes for granted the cessation of all miracles and all prophecy (VIII, i, ii). Finally, in the 'Discourse upon Devils and Spirits', he reduces all that is said of such beings in scripture to something not much more than metaphor.[35]

In the Netherlands where a sceptical attitude was not uncommon, Scot's material was welcomed. It was also appreciated by the Dutch reformed churchman who saw in the writer a staunch ally against any relics of Romish practices or beliefs. Yet as Professor Baschwitz remarks, Scot was not a deep thinker and his imagination was occasionally tripped by the old superstitions. For instance, he did not reject prescriptions for the expulsion of devils, the construction of charms and the like.[36] The anecdotes and stories, often uncouth and based on inaccurate information had their appeal for a certain class of the population whilst his chapters on 'naturall magike' with its spells and conjuring tricks, allured those who were desirous of acquiring the skill. In effect, Scot's refutation of magic evolved into a Magician's handbook. For instance, speaking of the ointment supposed to enable witches to fly, he writes

It shall not be amisse here in this place to repeate an ointment greatlie to this purpose, . . . The receipt is as followeth. R. The fat of yoong children, and séeth it with water in a brasen vessell, reseruing the thickest of that which remaineth boiled in the bottome, which they laie vp and kéepe, vntill occasion serueth to vse it. They put herevnto *eleoselinum, Aconitum, Frondes populeas,* and Soote.

Another receipt to the same purpose. R. *Sium, acarum vulgare, pentaphyllon,* the bloud of a flitter-mouse, *solanum somniferum, et oleum.* They stampe all these togither, and then they rubbe all parts of their bodies excéedinglie, . . .[37]

George Gifford, minister at Malden, a district famous for its superstitions, wrote the only treatise on witchcraft native to England.[38] Unlike Wier and Scot who draw on a variety of continental experiences, Gifford's

[35] C. S. Lewis, *Eng. Lit. in the 16c.,* pp. 435-6.
[36] K. Baschwitz, *De Strijd met den Duivel* (Amsterdam, 1948), pp. 306-7.
[37] R. Scot, *op. cit.,* (1584), Bk. X, Cap. viii, p. 184.
[38] Cf. H. Holland, *A Treatise against Witchcraft* (Cambridge, 1590), B. 1. 'but few haue written to any purpose any thing, which may giue light in this argument, in the english tongue, master George Gifford onely excepted vnto whom we are much bound in the Lorde.'

only sources are the Bible and the daily occurrences at Malden and surrounding country. Experience and meditation had taught this minister of
Malden something of the wiles and snares of the Devil. It appeared to him
that Satan made use of man's anxiety about witches and their puckrels in
order to distract his attention from his own sinfulness, making him seek the
cause of any disaster in others rather than himself.

What shal wee say vnto these things? Is here no packing? Is not here first of
all a way taken by the wiely and wicked serpent to bring men in beliefe that
hee is not nigh them, nor medleth not vnless his dame send him? Hee goeth
about like a roaring Lyon, seeking whom he may deuour, as Saint Peter sayth.
Shall wee bee so sottish to beleeue that hee lyeth at the witches house? hee is a
mighty tyrant, if God do suffer him, that hee beyng a spirite do take vpon him
the shape of some little vermin, as cat or weasill, it is but to deceiue. ... Had
hee power and lay still while shee sent him, not minding to do any thing, un-
lesse hee were requested? what foole can imagine that?[39]

Whilst admitting that there are, indeed, such creatures, his sympathies are
with the unfortunate suspected woman whose guilt is chiefly based on local
gossip and the ignorance of confused judges whom he considers to be often
more ensnared by the Devil than the convict.

This interesting and influential trio, Gifford, Scot and Wier agreed in the
main. Gifford wrote as a minister anxious for his little flock, and his works
being of a more peaceful tenor and smaller dimensions than those of his
contemporaries, had no violent repercussions. With Scot, backed by Wier, it
was a different matter. Scot's style was provocative and he had gone a step
further than Gifford or Wier by more or less denying any supernatural
occurrences.

JAMES I *Daemonologie*

The first to take official offence was King James whose *Daemonologie* was,
in fact, largely directed

against the damnable opinions of two principally in our age, whereof the one
called SCOT an Englishman, is not ashamed in publike print to deny, that
ther can be such a thing as Witch-craft: and so mainteines the old error of the
Sadducees, in denying of spirits. The other called WIERUS, a German Phisi-
tion, sets out a publick apologie for all these craftes-folkes, whereby, procuring
for their impunitie, he plainely bewrayes himselfe to haue bene one of that
profession.[40]

James's work was to exercise a great influence over later literature. Although Montague Summers holds it as 'a great mistake to suppose that
either in scope, authority or importance the *Daemonologie* is for a moment

---

[39] Gifford, *A Discourse*, G. 3. ʳ⁻ᵛ.
[40] James I, *op. cit.*, ed. G. B. Harrison, pp. xi-xii.

to be compared with the classic volumes of Boguet, Remy or De Lancre',[41] yet as far as sixteenth-century England and Scotland are concerned, James's is one of the principal books reflecting the mind of his age. James expressed the opinions that were accepted freely by the multitudes at home; and if his dialogue is accused of being – in part – 'rank folly', it is no more than an echo of his subjects' mental perturbation. Wier had been instigated to write *De Praestigiis Daemonum* in order to stop the alarming increase of superstition, and in defence of innocent women; Gifford, after attending witch-trials at Malden, perceived the inadequacy of the evidence on which convictions were made and produced *A discourse of the subtill practises of Deuilles* in order to enlighten the judges; the St. Osyth's trials are said to have induced Scot to write the *Discoverie of Witch-craft*; these were critics that looked upon the case objectively, as it were, and their sympathy was with the accused. With James it was a different matter. He had been personally involved with witches, his life and throne had been endangered by them, consequently he looked upon witchcraft from a different angle. The famous trial of the North Berwick witches who had attempted to murder him, and at which he himself had been present, as a young man, was still fresh in his memory when he produced *Daemonologie*. It is to be admired in the author that, notwithstanding this personal experience, he states his facts with moderation and reserve.

EPI[STEMON]. For although all that they confesse is no lie vpon their parte, yet doubtlesly in my opinion, a part of it is not indeede, according as they take it to be: And in this I meane by the actiones of their owne persones. For as I said before, speaking of *Magie* that the Deuill illudes the senses of these schollers of his, in manie thinges, so saye I the like of these Witches.[42]

James has never been known as a champion of the female sex.

PHI[LOMATHES]. ... What can be the cause that there are twentie women giuen to that craft, where ther is one man?

EPI[STEMON]. The reason is easie, for as that sexe is frailer then man is, so is it easier to be intrapped in these grosse snares of the Deuill, as was ouer well proued to be true, by the Serpents deceiuing of *Eua* at the beginning, which makes him the homelier with that sexe sensine.[43]

Daemonologie is an attempt to expose the snares of the Devil. Here it touches common ground with Gifford's work. Epistemon being asked by what means the Devil allures persons, answers:

EPI. Even by these three passiones that are within our selues: Curiositie in great ingines: thrift of revenge, for some tortes deeply apprehended: or greedie appetite of geare, caused through great pouerty.[44]

[41] R. Scot, *op. cit.*; ed. Summers (1930), p. xxii.
[42] James I, *op. cit.*, Bk. II, Ch. iii, p. 35.
[43] *Ibid.*, Bk. II, Ch. v, pp. 43-4.
[44] *Ibid.*, Bk. I, Ch. ii, p. 8.

He further explains that it is Magicians or Necromancers who are attracted by curiosity, whereas the Devil's bait for witches is revenge and greed.

Epi. Surelie, the difference vulgare put betwixt them, is verrie merrie, and in a maner true; for they say, that the Witches ar servantes onelie, and slaues to the Devil; but the Necromanciers are his maisters and commanders.[45]

Magicians seek the satisfaction of their curiosity, honour and esteem, but

Phi. These Witches on the other parte, being intised ether for the desire of reuenge, or of wordly riches, their whole practises are either to hurte men and their gudes, or what they possesse, for satisfying of their cruell mindes in the former, or else by the wracke in quhatsoeuer sorte, of anie whome God will permitte them to haue power off, to satisfie their greedie desire in the last poynt.[46]

The approach of the Devil to these wretched women, James maintains, is due to their ignorance, joined with an evil life, or a carelessness and contempt of God.

Phi. And finding them in an vtter despair, for one of these two former causes that I haue spoken of; he prepares the way by feeding them craftely in their humour, and filling them further and further with despaire, while he finde the time proper to discouer himself vnto them. At which time, either vpon their walking solitarie in the fieldes, or else lying pansing in their bed; but alwaies without the company of any other, he either by a voyce, or in likenesse of a man inquires of them, what troubles them: and promiseth them, a suddaine and certaine waie of remedie, vpon condition on the other parte, that they follow his advise; and do such thinges as he wil require of them: Their mindes being prepared before hand, ... they easelie agreed vnto that demande of his:[47]

In Book III James divides the evil Spirits into four categories: The first, *Lemures* or *Spectra*, spirits haunting houses or solitary places, were fairly common.[48] The *umbrae mortuorum* that appear in likeness of the defunct are also classed in this category. The second class of spirits are those which follow persons and trouble them. These include the *Incubi* and *Succubi*. *Aniles fabulae* James sceptically names them. He also mentions *ab incubando* a natural sickness as having no connection with the incubus.

---

[45] *Ibid.*, Bk. I, Ch. iii, p. 9.
[46] *Ibid.*, Bk. II, Ch. iii, p. 35.
[47] *Ibid.*, Bk. II, Ch. ii, pp. 32-3.
[48] L. Lavater, *Of Ghostes and Spirites*, tr. R[obert]. H[arrison]. (1572); ed. J. Dover Wilson and May Yardley (OUP., 1929), p. 191, also implies their existence. 'Be not dismayde, although thou heare some spirit stir and make a noyse, for in case hee rumble onely to make thee afrayde, care not for him, but lette hym rumble so long as he wyll, for if hee see thee wythout feare, hee wyll soone depart from thee.'

EPI. because it being a thick fleume, falling into our breast vpon the harte, while we are sleeping, intercludes so our vitall spirites, and takes all power from vs, as maks vs think that there were some vnnaturall burden or spirite, lying vpon vs and holding vs downe.[49]

The third kind are the spirits that enter into a person and possess him. Lastly he mentions those we have met before,

PHI. That fourth kinde of spirites, which by the Gentiles was called *Diana*, and her wandring court, and amongst vs was called the *Phairie* ... or our good neighboures, ...[50]

and finally concludes that all four are species of the same genus: the Devil. James was careful to distinguish possession from the other categories in his *Daemonologie*.

POSSESSION

The idea that man could actually be possessed by the Devil was not uncommon in the sixteenth century. In this matter the Devil proved quite impartial. He did not confine his presence to the mean and humble but aspired even to a royal abode. Henry More in *Historia Provinciae Anglicanae Societatis Iesu* records the following incident of William Weston, a Jesuit who made a name for himself by his exorcisms.[51] Father Weston gallantly defended the Queen against the Devil's invasion. On a certain occasion

... quod cùm à quopiam in Anglia malum daemonem insidentem pelleret, rogatus à daemone vt Elizabetham Reginam permitteretur ingredi, renuit *Westonus,* omnia animae & corporis ornamenta illi optans, nefas autem existimans mali quidquam inferre ei quam licet in fide dissidentem Reginam tamen suam & Principem agnoscebat. Tum daemon, visne vt in te ingrediar? Si Deo ita visum fuerit, non recuso, inquit *Westonus.* At cauebo ego mihi, ait daemon; Tantundem enim in Te solatii inuenirem quantum si in Aquae Benedictae vas immergerer.[52]

Philip Caraman informs us that Fr. de Peralta, relating the same story, says that

[49] James, *op. cit.*, Bk. III, Ch. iii, p. 69.
[50] *Ibid.*, Bk. III, Ch. v, pp. 73-4.
[51] William Weston was born at Maidstone and educated abroad. He returned to England in 1584. His missionary activities were frowned upon by the Reformed Church and he was imprisoned two years after his arrival.
[52] Henricus Morus, *Historia Provinciae Anglicanae Societatis Iesu* (Audomari, 1660), Lib. IV, p. 155. '. . . that when he was driving out an evil spirit from someone possessed in England, he was asked by that spirit whether he might be allowed to enter into Queen Elizabeth. Weston refused, wishing her every adornment of soul and body, but considering it wicked to cause any evil to her whom, although differing in religion, he yet recognised as his Queen and sovereign. At which the devil, – "Would you mind if I came into you?" "If it seems right to God, I will not refuse" answered Weston. "I'd rather beware" said the devil; "I probably find in you just as much solice as if I entered a holy water stoup".'

the incident was 'public and widely-known and reached the ears of the Queen's Council', for it was described in full in the records of the exorcism which fell into the Council's hands on the arrest of Anthony Tyrrell. de Peralta adds that 'Many think that this was why the Queen never permitted him (W.W.) to be executed.'[53]

Catholics and Protestants alike were then credulous upon this subject.

So far, however, as we can now discover, the subjects were not suffering from diabolic possession, but only from hysteria (then called 'mother'). Yet there is no reason to doubt the sincerity of the exorcists.[54]

THE ENGLISH WITCH UNIMAGINATIVE AND VENGEFUL

Her Familiars and Her Covens

It now remains to look more closely at the English Witch as she appeared to her sixteenth-century contemporaries both in fact and fiction. Undoubtedly we must agree with Beatrice White that

In contradiction to the scientific demonology of France and Germany, English witchcraft of the sixteenth century was a flat, dull, vulgar, unimaginative affair. . . . In England popular ideas on witchcraft had none of the fine exuberance of the Scottish witch cult or the wild imagination of the cult as it revealed itself on the Continent.[55]

The English witch has no trace of the Sibyl, the Prophetess, the woman learned in divination, the Old Testament Witch who made Saul tremble. There is little romanticism attached to her style of living. As Scot describes her, she is a poor woman

[53] William Weston. *The Autobiography of an Elizabethan*, tr. from the Latin by Philip Caraman (1955), p. 29, note 9.

[54] J. H. Pollen, 'William Weston', *Cath. Encycl.* xv, p. 238. Father Weston's exorcisms were burlesqued by Samuel Harsnet, in *A Declaration of egregious Popish Impostures* (1603) (*sup.* p. 92, note 106), the tenor of which is best seen in the exorcism of Sara Williams, servant to the family of Sir George Peckham of Denham, pp. 48-9.

'The Exorcist askes *Maho, Saras* deuil, what cōpany he had with him, and the deuil makes no bones, but tels him in flat termes, *all the deuils in hell*. Heere was a goodly fat *otium* this meane while in hell : the poore soules there had good leaue to play : such a day was neuer seene since hell was hell : not a doorekeeper left, but all must goe a maying to poore *Saras* house . . . . . .
Frateretto, Fliberdigibbet, Hoberdidance, Tocobatto were foure deuils of the round, or Morrice, whom *Sara* in her fits tuned together, in measure and sweet cadence. And least you should conceiue, that the deuils had no musicke in hell, . . . the Fidler comes in with his Taber, & Pipe, and a whole Morice after him, with motly visards for theyr better grace.'
Father Francis Edwards, SJ, Dpt. of Historiography and Archives, 114 Mount St. London, assures me that, in the one remaining letter written by William Weston addressed to Fr. Persons and signed E[dmund] H[unt] 'Stonyhurst MSS. Anglia', No. 28, of which half a page is devoted to an account of exorcisms, no specific mention is made of any women demoniacs.

[55] G. Gifford, *A Dialogue*, ed. B. White, p.v.

which be commonly old, lame, bleare-eied, pale, fowle, and full of wrinkles; poore, sullen, superstitious, and papists; or such as knowe no religion: in whose drousie minds the diuell hath gotten a fine seat; so as, what mischéefe, mischance, calamitie, or slaughter is brought to passe, they are easilie persuaded the same is doone by themselues; imprinting in their minds an earnest and constant imagination thereof. They are leane and deformed, shewing melancholie in their faces, to the horror of all that sée them.[56]

She is completely centred around her own discontentment with life to which she tries to provide an outlet by taking revenge upon her neighbours. If they refuse to respect her, they shall at least fear her. It is the last trump she is able to play on this earth. Scottish witches were far more colourful: they had their sabbaths, their airy excursions, even voyages to sea in sieves; they lived with the 'good neighbours' and were often taken into the Devil's confidence with regard to future events. Their power was extended to do harm to king and country. Compared to these, English witches were just 'bad-tempered old women with a grudge against individuals or the world at large and the victims of their own spite'.[57] Thus Gifford describes

The poore old witch, pined with hunger, goeth abroad vnto some of her neighbours, and there begge a little milke which is denied. She threatneth that she will be euen with them. Home shee returneth in great fury, cursing, and raging. Forth shee calleth her spirite, and willeth him to plague such a man. Away goeth hee. Within few howres after the man is in such torment, that he can not tell what hee may doe. Hee doth thinke himselfe vnhappy that he was so foolish to displease her.[58]

Vengeance for petty slights often motivated her. Thus Mother Nokes was revenged upon a young 'Seruant to Thomas Spycer of Lamberd Ende in Essex' because he stole her daughter's gloves. He was lamed in the legs.[59] Elizabeth Fraunces, who, by the way, was only twelve years old when she was first taught the art of sorcery, turned to witchcraft when she 'required some olde yest'[60] of a neighbour and was denied. Mother Staunton, of Wimbishe, escaped execution although the evidence brought against her was sufficiently sinister to put fear into the bystanders. The accuser's imagination was perhaps a little too colourful, deviating from the usual witchcraft routine in England, to be taken as the basis for execution.

4 Item, she came on a tyme to the house of one Richard Saunder of Brokewalden, and, beeyng denied Yeest, whiche she required of his wife, she went her waie murmuryng, as offended with her aunswere, and after her departure, the yonge child in the Cradle was taken vehemently sicke, in a merueilous strange

<hr>

[56] R. Scot, op. cit., (1584), Bk. I, Cap. iii, p. 7.
[57] G. Gifford, A Dialogue, ed. B. White, p.v.
[58] G. Gifford, A Discourse, (1587), G. 3.
[59] A Detection of damnable driftes, practized by three Witches arraigned at Chelmisforde in Essex [1579], B. iᵛ -ij.
[60] Ibid., A. iiij. Cf. inf. p. 117.

maner, wherevppon the mother of the childe tooke it vp in her armes to com-
forte it, whiche beyng doen, the Cradle rocked of it self, sixe or seuen tymes, in
presence of one of the Earle of Surreis gentilmen, who seyng it stabbed his
dagger three of fower tymes into the Cradle ere it staied : Merily iestyng and
saiyng, that he would kill the Deuill, if he would bee rocked there.[61]

This kind of vengeance seems trivial and indeed the unimaginative English
witch seldom went beyond the ordinary round of domestic catastrophes.
But in the eyes of the villagers

shee is the very pestilence of the earth, all calamity is brought vpon men by
her. Shee killeth men and beastes. Shee tormenteth men, & she destroyeth
mens goods. No man can be in safety so long as shee liueth. Woe bee vnto him
whiche doth diplease her, thrice happy are they which do not meddle with
her.[62]

George Gifford on asking his parishioners how it is possible that a poor old
woman should cause such havoc among her neighbours, receives the
answer:

O syr, they do it not by themselues. They haue their spirites which they keepe
at home in a corner, some of them twoo, some three, some fiue: these they
send when they be displeased, and wil them for to plague a man in his body,
or in his cattle.[63]

And indeed, we find in 'The Euidence giuen against Elleine Smithe of Mal-
don' that

the sonne of this Mother Smith, confessed that his mother did keepe three
Spirites, whereof the one called by her greate Dicke, was enclosed in a wicker
Bottle: The seconde named Little Dicke, was putte into a Leather Bottle: And
the third termed Willet, she kepte in a Wolle Packe. And thereuppon the
house was commaunded to bee searched. The Bottles and packe were found,
but the Spirites were vanished awaie.[64]

These creatures were known as familiars.[65] The witch was supposed to feed
them, and at regular intervals they sucked her blood, which left the Devil's
mark upon her body.[66] It was usual at the trials to look for such a mark.

[61] *A Detection of damnable driftes,* A. vii[v].
[62] G. Gifford, *A Discourse,* G 2[v] – 3.
[63] *Ibid.,* G. 3.
[64] *A Detection of damnable driftes,* A. vi[v].
[65] T. Heywood, *The Hierarchie of the Blessed Angels* (1635), p. 475. 'Grillandus is of
opinion, That euerie Magition and Witch, after they haue done their homage to the
Diuell, haue a familiar Spirit giuen to attend them, whom they call *Magistellus, Magister
Martinettus*; or *Martinellus*; and these are somtimes visible vnto them in the shape of a
Dog, a Rat, an Aethiope, &c. So it is reported of one *Magdalena Crucia,* that she had
one of those *Paredrij* to attend her, like a *Blacke-More* . . .' (Heywood further mentions
how these '*Paredrij*' are kept in rings, boxes, etc., of their own free will and voluntary
motion).
[66] *Cf.* M. Summers, *The History of Witchcraft,* pp. 70 *et seq.* The Devil's Mark was
the sign and seal of Satan upon the actual flesh of his servant. This mark was said to be
insensible to pain and, when pricked, did not bleed. It varied in shape and colour.

116

Thus instead of having a written contract with the Devil, the witch was believed to have this blood-pact. Gifford's *Dialogue* mentions the state of an old woman who made the following confession :

that she had thrée spirits : one like a cat, which she called *Lightfoot*, another like a Toad, which she called *Lunch*, the third like a Weasill, which she called *Makeshift*. This *Lightfoot*, she said, one mother *Barlie of W.* solde her aboue sixteene yeares agoe, for an ouen cake and told her the Cat would doe her good service, if she woulde, she might send her of her errand: this Cat was with her but a while, but the Weasill and the Toad came and offered their seruice : The Cat would kill kine, the Weasil would kill horses, the Toade would plague men in their bodies. She sent them all thrée (as she confessed) against this man:[67]

Fear of these creatures was exceedingly great. Samuell, in Gifford's *Dialologue*, seems to be completely obsessed by it:

I may tell it to you as to my friend, when I goe but into my closes, I am afraide, for I see nowe and then a Hare; which my conscience giueth me is a witch, or some witches spirite, Shée stareth so vppon me. And sometime I sée an vgly weasell runne through my yard, and there is a foule great catte sometimes in my Barne, which I haue no like vnto.[68]

Sometimes witchcraft ran in families. A grandmother or mother, familiar with the art, would teach the daughters. From the examination of certain witches, for example, we know that Elizabeth Fraunces of Chelmsford, who was tried in 1566,

learned this arte of witchcraft at the age of xii yeres of hyr grandmother whose nam mother Eue of Hatfyelde Peuerell, disseased[69]

There was the famous case of the Warboys, father, mother and daughter so skilled in bewitching that 'the like hath not been heard of in this age'.

The most strange and admirable discouerie of the three Witches of Warboys, arraigned, conuicted, and executed at the last Assises at Huntington, for the bewitching of the fiue daughters of Robert Throckmorton Esquire, and diuers other persons, with sundrie Diuellish and grieuous torments:[70]

gives details of the very long and quite incredible process which began in 1589. In it all the unoriginality of English witchcraft is displayed, including

[67] G. Gifford, *A Dialogue*, ed. B. White, C. 1.
[68] *Ibid.*, A 4ᵛ.
[69] *The Examination and Confession of Certain Witches, Anno 1556*, ed. H. Beigel, Philobiblon Society, VIII (1863-4), p. 24.
    Cf. sup. p. 115.
[70] (1593). They were John Samuel, the father; Alice Samuel, the mother; and Agnes Samuel, their daughter.
    In H. E. Rollins, 'An Analytical Index to the Ballad-Entries in the Registers of The Company of Stationers of London', *S.P*, XXI (Chapel Hill, 1924), Item 1419, we find : 'lamentable songe of Three Wytches. of Warbos and executed at Huntingdon, a (Dec. 4, 1593, II, 641, Jno Danter)'.

the feeding of the spirits in the form of small pet animals of which Pluck, in this case, was the guilty one. The entire account smacks of advertisement, and serves as a sample of the kind of pamphlet literature so highly popular amongst the superstitious subjects of Elizabeth I, and which poisoned the minds of the ignorant.

Witches also worked in organized groups known as covens, although these were rare in England. The notorious trial at St. Osyth[71] was the first to discover the witch as member of a coven. The trial began with Grace Thurlowe, 'a poore and needie woman' laying information before the magistrate concerning Ursley Kempe *alias* Grey.

When the accused was committed on ample evidence to the assizes she appeared before Justice Brian Darcy, a man of sound common sense and vigour, who, having straitly examined her, soon perceived that he had to deal with no ordinary malice and malignancy. He probed the black business to the very heart. Eventually he caught in his kiddle some sixteen persons all found to be deeply involved, of whom thirteen, as it was proved beyond all question, were held to be guilty of murder owing to their sorceries.[72]

This was the trial in which Reginald Scot had taken a special interest and which had inspired him to write his *Discoverie of Witchcraft*.

The above examples show us the range of witchcraft in England, and there is little evidence that the full cult, as it was known on the Continent, was practised at all widely.[73]

THE SCOTTISH WITCH

In Scotland witchcraft was a different matter. Here, in Pierce Pennilesse's phrase, the 'noble Lord Warden of the witches and jugglers' took charge both in person and by proxy. Imagination was here coloured by the depth and darkness of the mountain ranges, by the mysterious haunts and the desolation of the countryside. From the evidence given by *Agnes Tompson* we get a lurid picture of a Scottish coven celebrating All-Hallow's Eve. She confessed that

[71] W. W., *A true and iust Recorde, of the Information, Examination and Confession of all the Witches, taken at S. Oses in the countie of Essex*: (Thomas Dawson 1582), A 1-2.

[72] R. Scot, *op. cit.*, ed. Summers, (1930), pp. xxvii-xxviii.

The Trial of the Lancaster Witches (1612); ed., G. B. Harrison (1929) p. ix, mentions other, 'similar organisations, such as the beggars' fraternities'. It is not impossible, he suggests, that these beggars had some connection with the witch-cult. 'The "upright-man" enjoyed the same privileges over the "doxies" and other female wanderers as the master devil in a coven or witch fraternity'. Mother Samuel, the Warboys Witch, for instance, confessed that she received her 'spirit' from an upright-man.

[73] G. B. Harrison, *op. cit.*, p. viii. 'Apart from the Lancaster case [1612] there is no known account of a witches' sabbat before 1620;'

Ibid., p. xli, the writer points out that the causes of Witchcraft in Lancashire go back to the end of the 16th century, when the country was upset by changes brought about by the Reformation. The new ministers had no hold over the people, and the Law was

118

with a great many other witches, to the number of two hundreth: ... all they
together went by Sea each one in a Riddle or Ciue, and went in the same very
substantially with Flaggons of wine making merrie and drinking by the waye
in the same Riddles or Ciues, to the Kerke of North Barrick in Lowthian, and
that after they had landed, tooke handes on the land and daunced this reill or
short daunce, singing all with one voice,

> Commer go ye before, commer goe ye,
> Gif ye will not goe before, commer let me.

At which time she confessed, that this *Geilles Duncane* did goe before them
playing this reill or daunce, vpon a small Trump, called a Iewes Trump, vntill
they entred into the Kerk of north Barrick.[74]

Here they performed their rites with the Devil, who appeared to them in
the form of 'ane mekle blak man' and gave them a sermon from the pulpit.
Afterwards he opened the graves for them so that they could prepare the
necessary powders and ointments. The actual purport of this meeting was
to consult with their Master 'the deuell' 'how they might most efficaciously
kill King James'.

The contriver of this far-reaching conspiracy was indeed none other than Francis Stewart, Earl of Bothwell, ... It was he, no doubt, who figured as 'the
Devil' at the meeting in the deserted and ill-omened kirkyard.[75]

At which time the Witches demaunded of the Diuell why he did beare such
hatred to the King, who answered, by reason the King is the greatest enemy
he hath in the worlde:[76]

Dr Fian, alias John Cuningham, master of the school at Saltpans in Loth-
ian, was the only man present at this meeting. He confessed

he was their Regester, and that there was not one man suffered to come to the
Diuels readinges but onlye he:[77]

Taking into consideration that the witches' sieve was well furnished with
flagons of wine, that the time was midnight and the setting of the rendez-
vous a haunted old church, the description of the Devil given by Anny
Sampson, the oldest witch at the trial, becomes quite explicable. She said
that

---

defied by Catholic priests celebrating the sacraments in secret. Under these conditions
of pressure and uncertainty secret societies began to flourish. The actual trial was recorded
by Thomas Potts in *The Wonderfull Discoverie of Witches in the Covntie of Lancaster*
published in 1613, and has been reproduced by Harrison from a copy of the original.

[74] *Newes from Scotland* (for William Wright, 1591); ed. G. B. Harrison, IX (Bodley
Head Quartos, 1924), pp. 13-14.

[75] J. Sprenger and H. Kramer, *op. cit.*, tr. M. Summers (1928), p. xxii, col. i. [This
edition is named *Malleus Maleficarum.*]

[76] *Newes from Scotland*, p. 15.

[77] *Ibid.*, p. 18.

the deuell [was] cled in a blak gown with a blak hat vpon his head ... his faice was terrible, his noise lyk the bek of ane egle, gret bournyng eyn; his handis and legis were herry, with clawes vpon his handis and feit lyk the griffon, ...[78]

THE WITCH'S RELATIONSHIP WITH THE FAIRY

And with the Pseudo-Devil

How the idea of 'the Phairie' was intrinsically interwoven with those of Devils and Familiars is clearly manifested in the confessions of Elizabeth Dunlop, of Lyne, in the Barony of Dalry, Ayrshire. She was tried for sorcery on 9 November 1576. In (5.) Item, we are told that a certain Thom Reid, her familiar, showed her a fairy-like apparition,

twelf persounes, aucht wemene and four men: The men wer cled in gentil-mennis clething, and the wemene had all plaiddis round about thame, and wer verrie semelie lyke to se; and Thome was with thame:[79]

They invited her to go with them but she refused. Thom told her that 'thai war the gude wychtis that wynnit in the Court of Elfame;'[80]

Just as in the previous chapter we have seen the wanton's relationship with human villains who pride themselves in wearing the Devil's crest, so among the witches we frequently meet with satanical rogues who shamelessly usurped the title of 'great Devil'.

Thus, among a list of suspected persons in the reign of Elizabeth we have 'Ould Birtles, the great devil,[81] ... The evil William, Lord Soulis, of Hermitage Castle, often known as 'Red Cap', was 'The Devil' of a coven of sorcerers.[82]

Thom Reid is another case in point. He seems to have played his part with forethought since he warned Elizabeth Dunlop not to speak to him when she saw him at work in the city.

Doubtless these so-called witches were often the victims of unscrupulous and designing knaves who impersonated Satan for their own purposes. They took advantage of the unsettled conditions and of the ignorance and superstition of the simple people; they played upon their terrors and reduced many to an abject slavery.

THE WITCH IN LITERATURE

On the whole the witch in literature is a great deal more interesting than the Malden witch described by Gifford. In order to produce 'a tale which

[78] Sir James Melville, *Memorialis* 1549-93, ed. G. Scott, Bannatyne Club (Edinburgh, 1827), pp. 395-6.
[79] R. Pitcairn, *op. cit.*, i, Pt. 2, pp. 52-3.
[80] *Ibid. Cf. sup.* p. 52, note 119.
[81] *Cf. sup.* p. 103.
[82] M. Summers, *The History of Witchcraft* (1926), p. 7.

holdeth children from play, and old men from the chimney corner',[84] it is necessary to turn the brazen world into a golden one. Being thus transformed, the witch became

a Magicien, whiche hath power to rule the Heauens, to bringe downe the skie, to beare vp the earth, to turne the waters into hilles, and the hilles into runninge waters, to lift vp the terrestiall spirites into the ayre, & to pull the Goddes out of the heauens, to extinguishe the Planetes, and to lighten the déepe darkenes of hell.[85]

Calib who did great harm to Christendom by confining the seven Champions to a cave, had all spirits at her disposal. When the time of her death was approaching, she commanded in a loud voice,

Come when I call, venite, festinate, inquam. At which wordes the earth began to quake, and the very elements to tremble: for all the spirits both of aire of earth, of water, and of fire, were obedient to her charmes, and by multitudes came flocking at her call:[86]

In literature, the witch was granted in full measure the success to which she had aspired in real life and for which she had bartered her soul to the Devil. Among other gifts, she was able to prophesy. This was not considered strange in one so closely allied to the supernatural world. Thus in *The Ballad History of the later Tudors*, we come upon *Ane Exclamation maid in England upone the delyverance of the Earle of Northumberland*, in which Mary Douglas is endowed with supernatural gifts.

> My mother she was a witch woman,
> And part of itt shee learned mee;
> Shee wold let mee see out of Lough Leven
> What they dyd in London cytye.[87]

She is in love with Northumberland and warns him of the plot laid by her brother, false William, against him. However, Northumberland refuses to heed her warning and goes to his doom.

But the Devil, master of lies, also teaches the witch to equivocate. Often she used obscure and ambiguous forecasts of the future to bring about the ruin of some unhappy man, as in the case of the Earl of Flanders

quha maid mortal veyr contrar the kyng of France. he, his mother and his vyfe, past til ane augure in holland, til inquyre of the fyne of the veyris betuix hym and the kyng of France. the augure ansuert, quod he, thou sal entir in Paris, quhair that gryte tryumphe and ioye sal be maid at thy entres. ferrand

[84] P. Sidney, *An Apologie for Poetrie*, ed. J. C. Collins (OCP, 1907), p. 25, ll. 22-24.
[85] Lucius Apuleius, *The xi bookes of the golden asse*, tr. W. Adlington (1566), Bk. I, cap. 3, f. 4.
[86] R. Johnson, *op. cit.*, p. 10.
[87] C. H. Firth, *The Ballad History of the Reigns of the Later Tudors*, reprint from *The Transactions of the Royal Hist. Soc.*, iii, (1909), p. 87.

beand rycht glaid of the ansuere of his augure, he enterit in France vitht ane gryt armye; bot or he cam to Paris, he and his armye var venqueist, and he vas tane presoner and led to paris. than al the parisiens maid gryt triumphe and ioye for blythtnes be cause that ferrand there mortel enemye vas disconfeist. Of this sort, ferrand exponit the ansuere of his augure til ane vrang sens.[88]

It appears that the Earl's mother was a witch and co-responsible for the augurer's communication. She is mentioned in *the Bruce*:

> The erll ferrandis moder was
> Ane nygramansour, and sathanas
> Scho rasit, and him askit syne,
> Quhat suld worth of the fichtyne
> Betuix the franch kyng and hir sone.[89]

In a similar way confusion is caused by the weird sisters in the story of Macbeth recorded in Holinshed, from which Shakespeare borrowed almost verbatim. Macbeth is warned to 'beware Macduff', and promises are made to him by

a certeine witch, whome hee had in great trust, had told that he should neuer be slaine with man borne of anie woman, nor vanquished till the wood of Bernane came to the castell of Dunsinane.[90]

In consequence he cast off all fear and committed many crimes with impunity.

The English witch as we know her from Gifford moved in a humble village circle; but the literary witch casts her spells upon Kings and Queens. Thus in *Richard III* Queen Elizabeth and Mistress Shore are held responsible for the Lord Protector's withered arm.

> Looke how I am bewitch'd: behold, mine Arme
> Is like a blasted Sapling, wither'd vp:
> And this is *Edwards* Wife, that monstrous Witch,
> Consorted with that Harlot, Strumpet *Shore*,
> That by their Witchcraft thus haue marked me.[91]

In *Henry VI* Margery Jourdain, the cunning witch, and Eleanor Cobham, Duchess of Gloucester, consort together

> Raysing vp wicked Spirits from vnder ground,
> Demanding of King *Henries* Life and Death,[92]

---

[88] *The Complaynt of Scotlande*, ed. Murray, p. 84.
[89] *Ibid.*, p. lxxiv.
[90] R. Holinshed, *The Historie of Scotland* (1587), p. 174, col. ii, ll. 14-18.
[91] *Richard III*, III, iv, 77-81; (69-74).
[92] *Henry VI*, Pt. 2, 1st Folio, *Histories*, p. 127; (II, i, 169-70). *Cf.* Sir Richard Baker, *a Chronicle* (1730), AD 1440, p. 187.

The witch could enchant the mind of a Prince as well as of a commoner. The Duchess of York, mother of Edward IV, fearing her son to be under a spell when he chooses Elizabeth for his wife, cries out:

> O *Edward, Edward,* flie and leaue this place,
> Wherein poore sillie King thou art inchanted,
> This is her dam of Bedfords worke her mother,
> That hath be witcht thée *Edward* my poore childe,[93]

In literature, as in life, the label 'Witch' was sometimes attached to one's enemy. Hence Joan of Arc appears in *Henry VI* as a 'Foule Fiend of France, and Hag of all despight'.[94] Any formidable enemy was looked upon with suspicion, but for a woman clad in armour, harassing the English troops, only one name was applicable.

> Deuill, or Deuills Dam, Ile coniure thee:
> Blood will I draw on thee, thou art a Witch,
> And straightway giue thy Soule to him thou seru'st.[95]

Seeing no reason why God should be on the side of their enemy, and unwilling to admit that the English forces could be overthrown by mere natural power, Joan la Pucelle, whom most of the world regard as a saint, is depicted throughout the play as one who enticed, a sorceress, an 'accursed minister of hell!' Like any other witch Joan has her

> . . . Familiar Spirits that are cull'd
> Out of the powerfull Regions vnder earth,[96]

whom she feeds with her blood. At length she is forsaken by them and, burning at the stake, she dies cursing her enemies.[97]

Most spectacular was the witch's power of transforming humans into beasts. Many playwrights and poets waved their wands in order to produce this magic effect. George Peele in *The Old Wiues Tale* introduces Sacrapant, son of the witch Meroe who was famous and much feared in ancient literature.

> In *Thessalie* was I borne and brought vp,
> My mother *Meroe* hight a famous Witch,
> And by hir cunning I of hir did learne,
> To change and alter shapes of mortall men.

---

[93] Th. Heywood, *King Edward IV* (1600), A 3ᵛ.
[94] *Henry VI, Pt. 1,* 1st. Folio, *Histories,* p. 107; (III, ii, 52).
[95] *Ibid.,* p. 100; (I, v, 5-7).
[96] *Ibid.,* p. 115; (V, iii, 10-11).
[97] Montague Summers in *The History of Witchcraft and Demonology* (1926), p. 288, takes the matter rather seriously and criticizes these passages as 'the most foul and abominable irreverence that shames English literature. It is too loathsome for words, and I would only point out the enumeration in one scene where various familiars are introduced of the most revolting details of contemporary witch-trials, . . .'

There did I turne my selfe into a Dragon,
And stole away the Daughter to the King;
Faire *Delya*, the Mistres of my heart:[98]

Meroe had method in her magic.

Semblably she chaunged one of her neighbours, being an olde man and one that solde wine, into a frogge, in that he was one of her occupation, and therefore she bare him grudge, and now the poore miser swimminge in one of his pipes of wine, and welny drowned in the dregges, doth crie and call with a hoarse voice, for his olde gestes and acquaintance that passe by.[99]

An advocate, because he pleaded against her, was turned into a Ram, and a certain man, because he loved another woman beside her, was changed into a Beaver.[100]

In the same manner the witch was able to transform herself. Spenser's Duessa, by her art, took on many forms but was finally exposed as 'A loathly, wrinckled hag, ill fauoured, old,' who made the Muse blush for shame to describe her. She emerges complete with 'foxes taile',

And eke her feete most monstrous were in sight;
For one of them was like an Eagles claw,
With griping talaunts arm'd to greedy fight,
The other like a Beares vneuen paw:
More vgly shape yet neuer liuing creature saw.[101]

Doblessa, in *A Fig for Fortune*, copied the device and

... gan with Magick-spels and sorcerie
Faire Virgin-like to falsifie her figure,[102]

The incident in *A Midsommer Nights Dreame*, of Bottom's 'translation' is interesting as it recalls the story of the witch at Salamin in Scot's *Discoverie of Witchcraft*, who transformed an English sailor into an ass.[103] This must have amused even the King of Scots who, however credulous he may have been in certain respects, 'could not swallow lycanthropy'.[104] Dromio of Syracuse, in *The Comedie of Errors*, thinks he is transformed, at which Luciana aptly remarks 'If thou art chang'd to ought, 'tis to an Asse.'[105] His master, Antipholus Erotes is no better at ease, for here at Ephesus there are 'Soule-killing Witches, that deforme the bodie'.[106] In fact the city seems

---

[98] G. P[eele]., *The Old Wiues Tale* (1595); ed. W. W. Greg, The Malone Society Reprints (1908), C 2 ʳ⁻ᵛ.
[99] L. Apuleius, *op. cit.*, Bk. I, Cap 4. f. 4ᵛ.
[100] *Ibid.*
[101] *The Faerie Queene*, I, viii, 48.
[102] A. Copley, *op. cit.*, p. 77, verse 3.
[103] R. Scot, *op. cit.*, (1584), Bk. V, Cap. 3, pp. 94 *et seq.*
[104] J. Ashton, *op. cit.*, p. 179.
[105] *The Comedie of Errors*, 1st Folio, *Comedies*, p. 89;; (II, ii, 198).
[106] *Ibid.*, p. 87; (I, ii, 100).
Keith Thomas in *Religion and the Decline of Magic* (1971) p. 607, draws attention to

pervaded by the supernatural. Dromio, being particularly sensitive to the atmosphere, crosses himself for a sinner for

> This is the Fairie land, oh spight of spights,
> We talke with Goblins, Owles and Sprights;
> If we obay them not, this will insue:
> They'll sucke our breath, or pinch vs blacke and blew.[107]

Here is Scot's *Discoverie* brought on to the stage, in spirit as well as in substance. All things, however improbable, become acceptable as 'here we wander in illusions.'[108]

Magic and witchcraft became intrinsically interwoven. The witches of Robert Greene appear in the nature of enchantresses, good fairies who come to man's aid. Melissa in *Orlando Furioso* resembles a 'sacred Goddes' who makes the Satyrs play their music in order to restore Orlando to his right senses.

> *O vos Siluani, Satyri, Faunique, Deaeque,*
> *Nymphae Hamadriades, Driades, Parcaeque potentes*
> *O vos qui colitis lacusque locosque profundos,*
> *Infernasque domus et nigra palatia Ditis!*[109]

Here is the 'golden Witch'. Melissa's very name suggests her nature. She is a good fairy 'I am she that cured thy disease'.[110]

In *Alphonsus, King of Aragon* we meet with Medea, likewise a mighty witch who comes to the assistance of Fausta, the Empresse, and Iphigina, her daughter, by calling up Calchas to foretell the future for them.

> Thou wich wert wont in *Agamemnons* dayes
> To vtter forth *Apolloes* Oracles
> At sacred *Delphos*, ...
>
> . . . . . .
>
> I coniure thee by *Plutoes* loathsome lake,
> By all the hags which harbour in the same,
> By stinking *Stix*, and filthie *Flegeton*,
> To come with speed, and truly to fulfill
> That which *Medea* to thee streight shall will.[111]

---

the fact that 'The Anglo-Saxons had described persons smitten with a supernatural malady as 'elf-shot', and the term was applied to sick animals in Celtic areas until modern times.'

[107] *The Comedie of Errors*, p. 89; (II, ii, 187).

[108] *Ibid.*, p. 94, (IV, iii, 38).

[109] R. Greene, *Orlando Furioso*; in *The Plays and Poems* ed. J. C. Collins (OCP., 1905), vol. i, IV, ii, 1160-4.

> O you creatures of the woodlands, satires and fauns, nymphs,
> hamadryads, dryads, and lords of the grasslands;
> O you who inhabit the lakes and the places of the deep,
> the infernal regions and dark palaces of Pluto !

[110] *Ibid.*, IV, ii, l. 1214.

[111] R. Greene, *Alphonsus King of Aragon*; in *The Plays and Poems*; ed. J. C. Collins (OCP., 1905), vol. i, III, ii, 860-4.

It is the voice of authority. There is no less majesty in Medea than there is in Hecate, or in Calib. Later in the play Medea turns match-maker bringing about the marriage between Alphonsus and Iphigina. There is indeed a vast difference between enchantresses like these and the witches Meroe and Calib who confined the seven Champions to a cave. Whereas the fairy-witch is often good-natured, using her art to help mankind, the wicked kind displays all aspects of revenge, evil and hatred of society. But whether their art is of the black or white variety, the Stygian fumes never fail to rise to the surface. Thus the definition of a witch given by Gifford at the beginning of this chapter holds good, even in literature. She is 'one that woorketh by the Deuill . . .'.

5

The Shrew

10 *He humoured the shrew*

5 The Shrew

I fynd thair haill affectioun
so contrair thair cōplexioun.[1]

In the newly revised version of *The Norwich Play, The Story of þe Crea-cion of Eve* (1565), Adam speaks:

> O my Lord God, Incomprehensyble, withowt mysse,
> Ys thy hyghe excellent magnyficens.
> Thys creature to me ys *nunc ex ossibus meis*,
> And *virago* I call hyr in thy presens,
> Lyke on to me in natural preemynens.[2]

It was the picture before the fall. No sooner had Eve abused her power than God spoke:

> Thou, woman, ...
> ... be subiect to thy husbonde, & thy lust shall pertayne
> To hym: I hav determynyd this ever to remayne.[3]

Ever since strife came into the world by sin, the question of equality of the sexes has been a serious problem. For woman, who had disobeyed God himself, surrender to her husband became at times most difficult. A world literature sprang up in which her 'wayward shrew-shaken' disposition was emphasized. Rabbinical, cabbalistic, heathen and christian legends vied in the portrayal of this quality. M. D. Conway mentions an ancient Persian legend of the first man and woman, Meschia and Meschiane, and how they lived happily together for a long time. They hunted together and disco-vered fire, and made an axe, and with it built themselves a hut. But no sooner had they set up house-keeping than they began to fight terribly, and after wounding each other, they parted.[4] Ancient literature was often unfa-vourably disposed towards woman. Pagan philosophers, Rabbis, and Fathers of the Church here found common ground for their inspiration. Thomas Nashe mentions that

Aristotle doth counsell vs, rather to gette a little wife then a great, because alwaies a little euill is better then a great, ... *Pythagoras* ... affirmeth it to be the only means to escape all euills, is to eschew womens counsaile and not to

---

[1] A. Scott, *Of Wemenkynd*; in *The Poems*, ed. J. Cranstoun, STS, No. 36 (1896), p. 68.
[2] O. Waterhouse, *The non-Cycle Mystery Plays*, EETS, e.s. civ (1909), p. 8, ll. 17-21.
[3] *Ibid.*, p. 16, ll. 87-9.
[4] M. D. Conway, *Demonology and Devil-lore* (1879), ii, 100.

129

square our actions by their direction. The olde Sages did admonish young men, if euer they matcht wyth any wife, not to take a rich Wife, because if she be rich, shee wyll not be content to be a wife, but will be a Maister or Mistresse, in commaunding, chiding, correcting & controlling. ... *Socrates* deemed it the desperatest enterprise that one can take in hand, to gouerne a womans will.[5] ... *Demosthenes* saide, that it was the greatest torment, that a man could inuent to his enemies vexation, to giue him his daughter in marriage, as a domesticall Furie to disquiet him night and day. ... Another hath these words: ... *A woman loues that she may entrappe, she deceiues that she may spoyle, she loues that thou hast, not that thou art.*[6]

In *Malleus Maleficarum*, in the midst of its treatise on witches, we find:

But as to domination by women, hear what Cicero says in the *Paradoxes*. Can he be called a free man whose wife governs him, imposes laws on him, orders him, and forbids him to do what he wishes, so that he cannot and dare not deny her anything that she asks?[7]

If we add to this the many 'edifying' remarks uttered by the Fathers of the Church with regard to woman,[8] we have most of the underlying thought governing shrew literature.

In her relationship with the Devil, the shrew differs from the wanton and the witch. Whereas it might be said that the witch had a master, – the Devil; in this Chapter we shall witness how the Devil had a mistress, – the shrew:

As sharp as a thystyll/ as rugh as a brere;
She is browyd lyke a brystyll/ with a sowre loten chere;[9]

From time immemorial, according to ancient legends and sagas, the shrew has been related to Lilith who in rabbinical myth was the first wife of Adam.[10] John B. Noss in *Man's Religions* points to the fact that the first Hebrews

believed in spirits having a human shape, though possessed of an inhuman character, like the Jinn of later Arabia, and they let their imaginations play

---

[5] He spoke from experience.
Cf. The Taming of a Shrew, 1st Folio, *Comedies*, p. 213; (I, ii, 68-9).

... as curst and shrow'd
As *Socrates Zentippe*, ...

[6] T. Nashe, *The Anatomie of Absurditie; Works*, ed. McKerrow, i, p. 12, ll. 14-37; p. 13, ll. 4-8; p. 14, ll. 31-3.
[7] J. Sprenger and H. Kramer, *op.cit.*, tr. M. Summers (1928), pp. 45-46.
[8] Nashe, *The Anatomie; Works*, ed. McKerrow, i, 14, ll. 14-19. quotes the ancient fathers: '*Quid aliud est mulier nisi amicitiae inimica, &c. What is a woman but an enemie to friendshippe, an vneuitable paine, a necessary euil, a naturall temptation, a desired calamitie, a domesticall danger, a delectable detriment, the nature of the which is euill shadowed with the coloures of goodnes.*'
[9] *Pagina Seconda Pastorum, The Towneley Plays*, ed. Pollard, p. 119, ll. 101-2.
[10] G. G. Scholem, *Major Trends in Jewish Mysticism* (Schocken Books, 1946), p. 175.
The only place where the name of Lilith occurs in the Bible is Isaiah xxxiv, 14, variantly translated as Lamia, Kobold, shrichowle (auth. version, 1611).

130

with the thought of seductive female night-demons like glamorous Lilith in the Hebrew tradition, who led Adam astray.[11]

According to the legend it was this shrill-voiced and ill-tempered wife who, because of her wicked jealousy and possessiveness, was the cause of Eve's fall and subsequent misery. Cast off, she took upon her the form of a serpent and became the first temptress.[12] By the same cabbalistic legends Lilith

11 *A fine serpen made with a virgyn face*

was made the mother of the jinns or demons, including Asmodeus, the Persian demon of lust, and Leviathan, the demon of pride, who in course of time succeeded to the highest rank in the demonic hierarchy, as can be seen

[11] John B. Noss, *Man's Religions* (1969), p. 364.
[12] M. Rudwin, *op. cit.* pp. 43-4. 'The idea of the Devil, in the representation of the temptation of Eve, as a serpent with the head of a woman is not earlier than the Middle Ages. According to the Venerable Bede, Lucifer chose to tempt Eve through a serpent which had a female head because "like is attracted to like". Vincent of Beauvais accepts Bede's view on the female head of the serpent in the Garden of Eden. Pierre Comester, in his *Historia scholastica* (c. 1176), concludes from this fact that, while the serpent was yet erect, it had a virgin's head.'
   Cf. *De Creatione Mundi, The Chester Plays*, Part I, ed. H. Deimling, EETS, e.s. LXII (1892), p. 28, ll. 193-6.

> A manner of an Adder is in this place,
> that wynges like a byrd she hase,
> feete as an Adder, a maydens face;
> her kinde I will take.

Cf. also O. Waterhouse, *op. cit.*, p. xxxiv.

> Lucifer incarnates as 'a fyne serpen made
> with a virgyn face & yolowe heare vpon her
> head'. [f. 66, *Grocer's Book*, Norwich].

The description of a fiend in *The Faerie Queene* (V, xi, 20) reads: 'For of a mayd she had the outward face'. The idea, therefore, was fairly common.

in Chapter III where we meet them among the potentates of hell.[13] This is the reason why the shrew, in truth, may be titled 'the deuils damme'[14] in her own right. That she indeed asserted her ancient privilege is known from the *Bihar Proverbs* 'a Shrew strikes terror into a demon even'.[15] The Reverend John Christian relates a story of Jagdipa, a termagant who by her constant brawling caused, by and by, the entire evacuation of her village. Having no one left on whom to wreak her anger, she began to attack dumb nature part of which was inhabited by demons.

Every morning, armed with her broom, she would attack the tree and vociferate. A demon, who dwelt in this tree, unable any longer to stand this daily invasion, also left his abode and sought refuge elsewhere.[16]

That indispensable article, the broomstick, was here put to harder usage than it ever was by the witch, as is fully implied by the Dutch term for shrew, the 'helleveeg' (hell-sweep).

The influence of these eastern stories is, as we shall see, clearly felt in sixteenth-century literature. The earliest shrew in Christendom, however, who was to make her début in English drama, was the virago, the scold depicted in the sermons, the disobedient, bad-tempered woman who upset the happiness and peace of the family. A universal prayer was sent up to heaven:

> O god aboue: a kynge moste glorious
> Of heuen and erth the whiche has rauysschyd hell
> Delyuer vs from the tungys venemous
> Of frowarde wymen, cursyd and cruell[17]

THE FIRST SHREW IN CHRISTENDOM : NOAH'S WIFE

This frowardness in women was personified as Noah's wife in the Mystery Plays. When Noah and his sons are grateful to God for saving them from the oncoming flood, his dame thinks otherwise:

> Trowes þou þat I wol leue þe harde lande,
> And tourne vp here on toure deraye?[18]

Preachers had warned against this unnatural condition of contrariety or wilfulness which the intending husband must be prepared to face;[19]

---

[13] *Sup.* p. 71 note 2.

Cf. M. D. Conway, *op. cit.* ii, p. 100: ' "Samaël is the fiery serpent, Lilith the crooked serpent," and from their union came Leviathan, Asmodeus, and indeed most of the famous devils.'

[14] *The Taming of the Shrew*, 1st Folio, *Comedies*, p. 220; (III, ii, 152). 'TRANIO. Why, she's a deuill, a deuill, the deuils damme.'

[15] Proverb 392, quoted in W. E. A. Axon, *The Story of Belfagor in Literature and Folk-lore* (1902), p. 20.

[16] in *Bihar Proverbs*, p. 182; quoted in Axon, *op. cit.*, p. 20.

[17] S. Brant, *op. cit.*, ii, 4.

[18] *Noah and his wife, York Plays*, ed. L. Toulmin Smith, p. 47, ll. 77-8.

[19] In the *Faust-Book*, p. 10, even Mephostophilis, disguised as a Friar, warned his

Father Bromyard, a medieval Dominican monk, spent many of his sermons on woman's disobedience to the wishes of her rightful lord.[20] Noah's wife gives a practical display of it. She tells her husband that she is annoyed at not having been taken into his confidence when he was building the ship, and Noah explains that it was God's will that it should be kept a secret.

> Vxor.   What? wenys þou so for to go qwitte?
>   Nay, be my trouthe, þou getis a clowte.
>
> Noe.   I pray þe, dame, be stille.
>   Thus god wolde haue it wrought.
>
> Vxor.   Thow shulde haue witte my wille,[21]

Already in Chaucer's days the theme was popular.

> 'Hastow nat herd', quod Nicholas, 'also
> The sorwe of Noë with his felawshipe
> Er that he mighte gete his wyf to shipe?'[22]

M. Carey draws attention to the transitional speech after God has departed. It reveals Noah's domestic situation. His dignity and patriarchal prestige which made him able to talk with God on almost equal footing, are gone. 'The very thought of Uxor arouses misgivings in his breast. He is the craven husband pure and simple, terrified of his formidable wife.'[23]

> My [wife] will I frast/ what she will say,
> And I am agast/ that we get som fray
>   Betwixt vs both;
> ffor she is full tethee,
> ffor litill oft angre,
> If any thyng wrang be,
>   Soyne is she wroth.[24]

Of all the Uxors, M. Carey remarks, Gille in *the Towneley Plays* is the most stubborn. From the beginning unto the end she exhibits her shrewish disposition. Ever active and wanting to take the lead, she is a three-dimensional character throughout the play, more personal than others also on account of her proper name.[25] The reason for the wickedness of Noah's

---

protégé. 'Therefore sweet Faustus, thinke with what vnquiet life, anger, strife & debate thou shalt liue in when thou takest a wife: ...'
[20] G. R. Owst, *op. cit.*, pp. 389 *et seq.* Cf. *sup.* p. 83.
[21]*Noah and his wife, York Plays*, ed. L. T. Smith, p. 49, ll. 119-23.
[22] G. Chaucer, 'The Milleres Tale', *The Canterbury Tales*; in *The Complete Works*, ed. W. W. Skeat (OCP., 1924), p. 102, ll. 352-4.
[23] M. Carey, *The Wakefield Group in the Towneley Cycle*, (Baltimore 1930), p. 96.
[24] *Processus Noe, Towneley Plays*, ed. Pollard, p. 28, ll. 183-89.
[25] F. L. Utley, 'The One Hundred and Three Names of Noah's Wife', *Speculum*, XVI

wife is given by the Shipwrights' Gild of Newcastle-upon-Tyne which introduced the Devil into their play. With his entry, peace and Noah's plans are upset, the Devil making use of the dame's inclinations. After the news has reached him that Noah and his family, and through them the human race, will be saved, he laments and then resolves:

> To Noah's wife will I wynd,
> Gare her believe in me;
> In faith she is my friend:
>
> She is both whunt and slee.
> Rest well, rest well, my own dere dame!

Uxor Noah dicat.   Welcome, bewschere; what is thy name?
> Tyte that thou tell me![26]

The Devil, knowing that his name will not daunt her, confides in her and swears by his crooked snout that Noah's actions bode no good and that she must try and prevent them. Thereupon he mixes a drink which the dame is to offer her husband when he comes home and which will cause him to confess all. Taking his departure, he assures her,

> Believe, believe, my own dame dere,
> I may no longer bide;
> To ship when thow shall fayre,
> I shall be by thy side.[27]

Noah, overcome by the Devil's broth, tells his wife what is about to happen and she says:

> Who, devil, made thee a wright –
> God give him evil to fayre – [28]

Despite all obstacles put in the way by his wife and the Devil, Noah completes his craft with the help of an angel.

G. R. Owst's suggestion that 'the age-long tradition of sacred oratory itself tends to support belief that it was the preacher who taught the dramatist, rather than *vice versa*',[29] can certainly be applied to the story of Noah; in popular sermons the Devil came into the story and even entered the ark.

(Cambridge, Massachusetts, 1941), p. 430, No. 32, mentions 'Gill (fifteenth century English mystery play),' and considers that possibly it is the short for 'Gillian' or 'Jellot'.

Pollard in *The Towneley Plays*, p. 29, l. 219, does not capitalize the name. 'haue at the, gill!' and p. 33, l. 336: 'Sir, for Iak nor for gill/ will I turne my face'

In *The Towneley Mysteries*, ed. Surtees Society, III (1836), however, the name is capitalized.

[26] *The Newcastle Play Noah's Ark*; O. Waterhouse, *op. cit.*, pp. 22-23, ll. 111-17.

[27] *Ibid.*, p. 23, ll. 138-41.

[28] *Ibid.*, p. 24, ll. 172-3.

[29] G. R. Owst, *op. cit.*, p. 473.

Miss Anna Jean Mill[30] draws attention to the editor's comment in Jansen Enikel's *Weltchronik*:[31] how Wolfgang Bütner (Epitome Historiarum 1579, bl. 54) remembered a sermon at Erfurt, in which the preacher spoke about the tricks of the Devil, how he stole into the Ark by the help of Noah's wife in order to drown the human race. The preacher may well have found his material in the ancient chronicles where the story occurs at considerable length and great detail. Noah, in various ways having persuaded his wife to enter the Ark loses his patience and calls out:

> 'ginc, tiufel, drât dar in!
> dû hâst nindert rehten sin.'
> dô er daz wort volgesprach,
> der tiufel wider sich selber jach:
> 'wol mich! mir hât erloubt Noê,
> daz ich in die arc gê,
> die er gesegent hêt sô sêr,
> daz dhein tiufel was sô hêr,
> der in die arc moht komen.
> nû hân ich williclîch vernomen,
> daz er mich hiez dar în gên.'[32]

Once the Devil has worked his way in, mischief begins, and acting as go-between among the sons and daughters of Noah, he causes much havoc. Abstinence which was commanded them by Noah is no longer observed until one day the Devil is discovered and cursed by Noah. Unable to bear a Patriarch's curse he gnaws a hole in the ark and disappears, a toad filling up the hole.

Miss Mill, in her article, points to two lines in the Newcastle Play which, at first sight, seem insignificant.[33]

> To ship when thow shall fayre,
> I shall be by thy side.[34]

It seems that the snouted demon did work his way into the English *Mysteries* but that the theme remained undeveloped or that part of the original text has gone astray. 'The Noah Legend in the early fourteenth century *Queen Mary's Psalter*,' Miss Mill suggests, 'may well be an iconographical

---

[30] A. J. Mill, 'Noah's Wife again', *PMLA*, LVI (New York, 1941), p. 619.

[31] Jansen Enikel, *Die Weltchronik*; hg. von P. Strauch in *Monumenta Germaniae Historica. Deutsche Chroniken und andere Geschichtsbücher des Mittelalters*, iii (Hannover und Leipzig, 1900), p. 36, note 2.

[32] Jansen Enikel, *op. cit.*, p. 36, ll. 1805-15. 'Get in! thou Devil, thou art always contrary. No sooner had Noah uttered these words than the Devil laughed up his sleeve. Good for me! Noah hath permitted me to enter the ark which he blessed so carefully to keep me out. Now I hear with pleasure that he orders me to enter in.'

[33] A. J. Mill, *op. cit.*, p. 625.

[34] O. Waterhouse, *op. cit.*, p. 23, ll. 140-1.

reflection of earlier dramatic texts or performances'. Yet to look for a strict chronological approach is here impossible. The illustration 'may reflect or initiate literary motives'. There is no text or performance of the Newcastle Play before early 15c. The earliest record of a Corpus Christi Play in Newcastle is 1426.[35]

That the theme was widespread appears also from various paintings. In an early sixteenth-century Russian picture, 'Satan and Noraita', the Devil offers Noraita a bunch of Khmel (hops) with which to brew *kvas* and make Noah drunk;[36] Miss Mill mentions a scene painted in the vaulting of Risinge church (Ostergotland) of the embarkation with Uxor and the Devil.[37]

Conway draws attention to an old version given by Buslaef 'after apocryphal tradition used by heretics' in which Satan addresses Noah's wife as 'Eve'.[38] The importance of the lady is emphasized by the many names attributed to her. F. L. Utley discovered no less than one hundred and three, among which are Eve, Delilah, Naamah, Wahila (Lot's wife), Pandora and Semiramis.[39] Gille looks innocent compared to these. It is the Biblical overtone, however, which is lacking in other shrews, that adds to her glory.[40]

OTHER SHREWS IN LITERATURE

Man Cannot Cope with the Shrew; He Warns Her but Cannot Tame

Shrews figure in merry jests and tales; in numerous ballads in the *Percy*, *Child*, and *Huth* collections as well as in the *Bannatyne* and *Maitland MSS*. They fill several items in *Henslowe's Diary*.[41] Medievalist and humanist

[35] A. J. Mill, *op. cit.*, p. 626; *Queen Mary's Psalter.* fols. 6-8.
[36] M. D. Conway, *op. cit.*, ii, 412.
[37] A. J. Mill, *op. cit.*, p. 623.
See A. Lindblom, 'Den Apokryfa Noahsagan i medeltidens konst och litteratur'; in *Nordisk Tidskrift för vetenskap konst & industri*, Femte Häftet (Stockholm, 1917), pp. 358-68.
Cf. also *De Deluvio Noe; The Chester Plays*, Pt. I, ed. H. Deimling, p. 56, ll. 219-20, where Noah, in the midst of the rising flood, shouts:

> Come in, wife, in 20 devills waye,
> or els stand there without.

[38] M. D. Conway, *op. cit.*, ii, p. 412.
[39] F. L. Utley, 'The One Hundred and Three Names of Noah's Wife'; *Speculum*, xvi (1941), p. 450.
In the apocryphal account of Eve, whose apple-eating was not the only sin she learned from Satan, it is said that she was seduced by the Devil.
Naamah, according to rabbinical commentators, was involved in a romance with the fallen angel, Azazal, of which the demon Asmodeus and others were the offspring.
Semiramis, a semitic type of woman's wickedness, wife of the King of Niniveh, seized her husband and threw him into a dungeon.
[40] Actually, in the Bible no mention is made of her wickedness.
[41] The *Bishop Percy Folio MS*, ed. J. W. Hales and F. J. Furnivall; F. J. Child, *op. cit*; The *Henry Huth Collection* (Brit. Mus. Huth 50) mostly reprinted in J. Lilly, *op. cit*; *The Bannatyne MS.*, ed. W. T. Ritchie; *The Maidland Folio MS.*, ed. W. A. Craigie; *Henslowe's Diary*, ed. W. W. Greg.

here found common interest; More and Erasmus vied with the ballad-mongers in jests and anecdotes on the subject. Often it was treated in an uncouth manner; at times man obtained the mastery by brute force as in *The Wife wrapt in wether's skin*.[42] Shakespeare immortalized the topic in *The Taming of the Shrew*; Spenser expressed his warnings in tactful terms:

> Ye gentle Ladies, in whose soueraine powre
> Loue hath the glory of his kingdome left,
> And th'hearts of men, as your eternall dowre,
> In yron chaines, of liberty bereft,
> Deliuered hath into your hands by gift;
> Be well aware, how ye the same doe vse,
> That pride doe not to tyranny you lift;
> Least if men you of cruelty accuse,
> He from you take that chiefdome, which ye doe abuse.[43]

For this is what had happened to Radigund, the Amazonian fury (Bk. V). Spenser agreed, in principle, with Knox that a regiment of women was monstrous and *contra naturam*. So did Shakespeare's Petruchio. The peace and calm of a woman's surrender to the will of her lawful lord was considered her grace and charm; by it her quality was determined.

... and she that is shamfaste/ sobre and reasonable of mynde/ shall neither be ragious angre/ nor falle to raylynge/ crueltie/ or bestlynes. For whan hit is naturall for women to be kynde and gentyl/ bicause they be feble/ and neden the ayde of other/ who can be cōtent with out-ragious ire and cruelte in a woman:[44]

The advice based on Radigund's and disdainful Mirabella's misfortunes (Bk. VI) applied to all women.

> And as ye soft and tender are by kynde,
> Adornd with goodly gifts of beauties grace,
> So be ye soft and tender eeke in mynde;[45]

Katharina's eyes had been opened by bitter experience.

[42] Child, V, 104, No. 277.
Cf. *The Wife lapped in Morels skin* in Select Pieces, ed. E. V. Utterson (2 vols. 1817) ii, p. 169; reviewed by E. B. in *Blackwood's Edinburgh Magazine*, ii (1818)), p. 376, col. ii. The Ballad, E. B. remarks, is an imitation of one of the early French fabliaux, 'which is full of spirit and vivacity; and having been printed by Hugh Jackson, who, according to Herbert, printed no book with a date later than 1590, preceded the Play of 'The Taming of the Shrew', the earliest edition of which is that of 1607, and was therefore not improbably familiar to Shakspeare.'
[43] *The Faerie Queene*, VI, viii, 1.
[44] Vives, *Instruction*, M. iᵛ; edn. Watson, p. 91.
[45] *The Faerie Queene*, VI, viii, 2.

Fie, fie, vnknit that thretaning vnkinde brow
And dart not scorneful glances from those eies,
To wound thy Lord, thy King, thy Governour.
It blots thy beautie, as frosts doe bite the Meads,
Confounds thy fame, as whirlewinds shake faire budds,
And in no sense is meete or amiable.
A woman mou'd, is like a fountaine troubled,
Muddie, ill seeming, thicke, bereft of beautie,
And while it is so, none so dry or thirstie
Will daigne to sip, or touch one drop of it.[46]

Generally speaking, man agreed with these last lines of Katharina. The Petruchios were few and their taming had little effect upon future literature. Man felt that there was indeed no remedy, and that, if he wished to preserve peace, there was only one thing left for him to do.

If the goodwife speake aloft,
See that you then speake soft;
Whether it be good or ill,
Let her doo what she will;[47]

Under the guise of jocular treatment, this grave and irremediable evil was exposed, and it was made clear that man resented the situation as an insult to his masculine dignity. To be ruled by a woman showed up his own weakness, it meant loss of freedom, and this may well have been the reason why a shrew, considered the most unnatural of her kind, was depicted as a devilish creature, the worst evil on earth. For,

Such is the crueltie of womenkynd,
When they haue shaken off the shamefast band,
With which wise Nature did them strongly bynd,
T'obay the heasts of mans well ruling hand,
That then all rule and reason they withstand,[48]

As the century progressed, the incongruity of such a situation became more and more apparent and the shrew grew to be a stock figure for laughter and amusement,

Ane evill wyfe is the werst aucht,
That ony man can haif;
For he may nevir sit in saucht,
Onless he be hir sklaif:
Bot of that sort I knaw nane uder,
But owthir a kukald, or his bruder;[49]

[46] *The Taming of the Shrew*, 1st Folio, *Comedies*, p. 229; (V, ii, 136-145).
[47] R. T[arlton], *A prettie newe Ballad, intytuled, The Crowe sits vpon the wall*; in J. Lilly, *op. cit.*, p. 256.
[48] *The Faerie Queene*, V, v, 25.
[49] Flemyng, *Ane Ballat of evill Wyffis*; in *Ancient Scottish Poems* published from the MS. of George Bannatyne (1568), for John Balfour (Edinburgh, 1770), p. 179, verse VI.

Man realized that it was foolish to try to appease a shrew. She was a creature fit for the Devil to deal with, and where he failed it was useless for man to try.

THE DEVIL CANNOT COPE WITH HER

There is no lack of evidence that the Devil himself had difficulty in coping with the situation. In *The Farmer's Curst Wife* a minor devil confesses his inadequacy:

> A wee reekit deil lookit owre the wa:
> 'O tak her away, or she'll ruin us a'.
>
> 'O what to do wi her I canna weel tell;
> She's no fit for heaven, and she'll no bide in hell.[50]

But even Satan could not control her and carried her back to her husband.

> Againe she kickt and prickt,
>   and sate so stiffe and well,
> The Devill was not [half] so plagu'd
>   a hundred yeares in hell.
>
> . . . . . .
>
> 'Here, take her!' quoth the Devill,
>   'to keep her here be bold;
> For hell will not be troubled
>   with such an earthly scold.'[51]

As will be seen by the following examples, most of the Devils related to shrew literature were of a congenial type, less malignant than their brethren in charge of the witches and wantons. Some were even endowed with conjugal affections and it must be said that whereas woman's reputation had descended the scale, seen side by side with the shrew, the Devil appeared in a more favourable light than he had ever done before. Man was convinced that

> The diuill Is not to daly stryf
> Comparesone to a wicket wyfe
> A womanis malice Is so fell
> Exceiddis all the devillis in hell[52]

In *The two angrie women of Abington*, Philip says of his own sister Mall that she 'will floute the diuel and make blush, the boldest face of man'.[53]

---

[50] *The Farmer's Curst Wife*, Child, V, 108, No. 278 B.

[51] *The Devil and the Scold*; in *The Roxburghe Ballads*, ii, ed. W. Chappell (1874), Pt. 2, p. 370, ll. 105-8; p. 371, ll. 129-32.

[52] *The diuill is not to daly stryf*; in *The Bannatyne MS*, iv, STS, n.s. No. 26 (1930), 23-4.

[53] H. P[orter]., *The Pleasant History of the two angrie women of Abington* (1599), ed. W. W. Greg, The Malone Society Reprints (1912), E 3ᵛ, l. 1081.

And Agrippa's enthusiastic treatise on the excellence of womankind was to be spoiled completely by a remark of the Dutch translator who took a very practical view of the matter.

> Wel Vrouw; uw' Naam is Engeltje; maar
> in de gantsche Hel,
> En is geen Duiveltje, soo Trots, soo Boos,
> soo Fier, soo Vinnig, nog soo Fel.[54]

We have the Devil's own words for it in *Der Teüffel mit dem alten Weyb*, one of Hans Sachs's Fastnachtspiele where 'das alt Weyb' proves too much for him.

> Ich förcht dein betrüg vnd arglist,
> Weyl du tausendt mal ärger bist,
> Dann ich, der Teüffel auß der Hell.[55]

The old scold had done the Devil a good turn by causing strife among her neighbours, a married couple. For thirty years the Devil has tried in vain to achieve this; the old woman succeeds in a day.[56] When the Devil is enjoying himself watching the fray, she calls him to his account and demands her fee, a pair of new shoes. He is terrified and hands her the shoes at the end of a long stick. When the scold asks him why he behaves in such fashion, he says:

> Ja, ich förcht mich so hart vor dir.
> Ich bin ein ainiger Sathan,
> Du hast ein gantze Legion
> Teüffel, . . .[57]

COMPLETE LOSS OF FAITH IN WOMAN AND IN THE DEVIL

At times the Devil was compared so favourably with this specimen of womankind and was depicted as so good-natured, that it seemed as if man had lost his faith in him as well as in woman. The best literary repre-

---

[54] Agrippa von Nettesheim, *Vermaakelyk Tractaat* (Amsterdam, 1733), *Voor-reeden* [f. 1ᵛ.] [This is a translation by J. d. V. of *De Foeminei sexus praecellentia* which has been placed in a humorous light by the translator.] 'Woman, thy name is Angel; but there is no Devil in the whole of hell who is as proud, as wicked, or as shrewd as thou art.'

[55] Hans Sachs, *Sämmtliche Fastnachtspiele*, ed. E. Goetze (Halle a/S, (1880-87), Bändchen ii, p. 67, ll. 250-2. 'I fear thy deceipt and tricks since thou art a thousand times worse than I, the Devil from Hell.'

[56] *Cf. Arthur of Little Britaine*, tr. Iohn Bourghcher [1582], f. 158. 'for if a woman be minded to cast forth her hookes & lines to take any man, therewith, it is verie hard to scape out of their daunger for in such a case a woman is more subtil then the diuell, for he causeth a woman of such disposition to doe that thing that he cannot do himselfe, . . .'

[57] Hans Sachs, *Sämmtliche Fastnachtspiele*, Bändchen ii, p. 68, ll. 273-6. 'Yay, thou holdest me in great fear. I am only one Satan but thou hast a legion of devils.'

sentation of the subject in English Literature is *The playe called the foure PP*, by John Heywood. The characterizations of both Shrew and Devil are superb, and a neat epitome of current views is shown in the definite and unanimous opinion reached by four men, each representing a different class of society: a Palmer, a Pothecary, a Pardoner and a Pedlar. The Four have a dispute about the merit of their respective callings which is to be determined by the quality of a lie each in turn has to tell. The Pardoner gives an account of his search for the soul of Margery Corson with whom he had failed to keep an appointment at the hour of death. After knocking at the gate of Purgatory, he is informed that there is no one there of that name.

> Then ferd I muche it was nat well
> Alas thought I she is in hell
> For with her lyfe I was so acqueynted
> That sure I thought she was nat sainted[58]

That same evening he repairs to hell and bargains with Lucifer that one of the devils may come to earth and choose any soul he likes, in exchange for the one he wishes released.

> Nowe quoth the deuyll we are well pleased
> What is hys name thou woldest haue eased
> Nay quoth I be it good or euyll
> My comynge is for a she deuyll
> What calste her quoth he thou whoryson
> Forsoth quoth I Margery coorson.
> Now by our honour sayd Lucyfer
> No deuyll in hell shall withholde her
> And yf thou woldest haue twenty mo
> Were nat for iustyce they shulde goo
> For all we deuyls within thys den
> Haue more to do with two women
> Than with all the charge we haue besyde[59]

Taking his leave of Lucifer, the Pardoner is now led into the kitchen where Margery Corson is turning the spit in such a furious fashion that the spit was burnt before the meat was half roasted. He describes the joy and roaring of the devils at her delivery;

> And how the cheynes in hell dyd rynge
> And how all the soules therin dyd synge[60]

But the Palmer whose turn has now come, dryly remarks that he cannot understand how women in hell can be such shrews when on earth they are

---

[58] J. Heywood, *The playe called the foure PP*. [1545?]; ed. J. S. Farmer, The Tudor facs. Texts (1908), D. ii.
[59] *Ibid.* D.iii[v], – iiij.
[60] *Ibid.* D.iiij[v].

so gentle. He has travelled many miles but admits that in all the places visited, he never saw, nor knew, in his conscience, 'any woman out of patience'.

> POTYCARY.   By the masse there is a great lye
> PARDONER.   I neuer harde a greater by our lady
> PEDLER.   A greater nay knowe ye any so great.[61]

The Pedlar acting as judge, decides that whereas he cannot check up on the lies told by the others, the Pardoner's can be tried anywhere, here in the very borders. For whether a woman be 'of the yongest' or 'of the oldest', 'of the hotest' or 'the coldest', of 'the fayrest' or 'of the maddest', of whatever degree she might be, at least two in every three you will find are shrews.[62] Never did men agree so unanimously.

In *A C Mery Talys* one could find 'the thre pointes belonging to a shrewd wyfe,' so that it was not difficult to recognize her.

The *i point is* that if a woman have a shril voyce, it is a gret token that she is a shrew.

The ii point is that, if a woman have a sharp nose, then most commenly she is a shrew.

The iii point that neuer doth mis that if she were [a] kerchefer, ye may be sure she is a shrew.[63]

This ought to have given sufficient warning to man, but as so often is the case, love in its blindness denied all reason and evidence. Machiavelli's *novella piacevolissima, Belfagor*[64] reveals the lamentable results of such folly. It is recorded in the old histories of Florence, that a certain devout person saw in a vision vast numbers of souls descending into hell,

... tutte, ò la maggior parte si doleuano non per altro che per hauer tolta moglie essersi à tanta infelicità condotte.[65]

Lucifer anxious to investigate further into this matter, calls a council at which it is determined that one of the devils shall go to earth and marry a woman. The choice falls on Belfagor, a senior devil of gentle disposition. The conditions are that in all things he has to adapt himself to the life of a human. He is forthwith furnished with a sum of money, and establishes

---

[61] *Ibid.* E. i.
[62] *Ibid.* E. ii.
Cf. Henry IV, Pt. 2, V, iii, 33.
      For women are Shrewes, both short, and tall:
[63] *A C Mery Talys*; (1526) in *Shakespeare Jest Books*, ed. W. C. Hazlitt, (3 vols, 1864), i, 123.
[64] N. Machiavelli, *Belfagor*; in *Tvtte le Opere* (Geneva, 1550), Quinta Parte, p. 71 *et seq.*
[65] *Ibid.*, p. 71. 'The greater part of which complained that it was their wives who sent them thither.'

himself in Florence as Roderigo di Castiglia. Soon he marries the beautiful Honesta, who proves the proudest shrew alive, and possessed

tanta superbia, che non n'hebbe mai tanta Lucifero, & Roderigo che haueua prouata l'vna & l'altra, giudicaua quella della moglie superiore.[66]

As soon as she discovers that Roderigo is enamoured of her, she never ceases to make unreasonable requests and to revile him with the most opprobrious and provocative names. She is unable to keep servants for longer than two or three days, and even the devil-servants who form part of Roderigo's retinue, desert him, preferring to live in hell than to be ordered about by such a vixen. Finally, driven to despair, Roderigo takes to flight. His life is saved by a farmer, Giovanni Matteo, with whom he enters into partnership. After many games of possession he enters into the daughter of the King of France and this time refuses to let his confederate Matteo drive him out. However, Matteo outwits the Devil by creating an impression that Honesta is coming, at which news Roderigo makes off immediately.

B. M. Ranking comments that the *Marriage of Belphegor* expresses the downfall of belief: 'neither manhood is worthy nor womanhood to be worshipped, nor the faith venerable.'[67] As in Heywood's *the foure PP*, man, woman and the devil are burlesqued.

The earliest imitation of Machiavelli's *Belfagor* is perhaps Hans Sachs's *Der dewffel nam ain alt weib*, one of the *Fastnachtspiele* dated July 13, 1557. Here the Devil is in his dotage and wants to marry an old woman.

> Ain jůnge die wer mir zw gail;
> Ich pin auch alt aůf meinem dail;
> Ein jůnge thet mir leicht kain gůet.[68]

He meets a woman in the forest who is looking for berries, and immediately proposes. He promises to gratify all her demands at which the marriage is concluded. It is not long before the Devil discovers that he has found his match. The old woman, taking advantage of his willingness, demands sacks full of money and orders him about.

> Das, das wirt mir ain rechtes spil!
> Der deuffel thůet als, was ich wil,
> Und gieb im doch kain gůetes wort.
> Ich wil in entlich an dem ort
> Gar zv aim wintelwascher machen;
> Můs mir meinr schalkheit selber lachen,

---

[66] *Ibid.* pp. 73-4. 'such a pride that Roderigo, who was well acquainted with both parties, thought she excelled Lucifer in that quality.'

[67] B. M. Ranking, *Streams from Hidden Sources*, (1872), p. xii.

[68] H. Sachs, *Sämmtliche Fastnachtspiele*, Bändchen vii, p. 21, ll. 30-33. 'A young damsel is too sweet to my liking. I am old myself and a young partner won't do me any good.'

Das er so gar ainfeltig ist
On all petrüeg vnd hinterlist.[69]

She makes him so miserable that finally he runs away and, meeting with a travelling physician, he enters into partnership with him. The rest of the play is similar to that of Machiavelli's story.[70] The first mention that I have been able to discover in English literature is in *Riche his Farewell to Militarie profession* in 1581, already discussed in a previous chapter.[71] In *Grim the Collier of Croyden* the entry of Belfagor (here known as Belphegor) upon English soil is officially announced by St. Dunstan in his opening speech:

> Women beware, and make your bargains well,
> The Devil, to choose a Wife, is come from hell.[72]

Here, as in Machiavelli's novella, the action originates in the infernal regions. The first stage direction indicates a 'place for the devils' consistory'. Disguised as a Spaniard and introducing himself as Castiliano, Belfagor comes to London, determined to marry Honorea, the Earl of London's dumb daughter. He is accompanied by Robin Goodfellow (Acercock). In order to win the lady, the infernal wooer frees her tongue.

> Now lovely *Honorea* thou art free,
> Let thy Celestial voyce make choyce of me.[73]

But Honorea's reply is different from what he expects:

> Go, get thee gone, the shame of my esteem,
> And seek some drudge that may be like thy self.[74]

---

[69] *Ibid.*, Bändchen vii, p. 21, ll. 138-45. 'It is going to be good fun! The Devil does exactly what I want him to; and I don't give him a kind word either. I'll make him a slave. I am amused at my own knavery. How simple he is and unaware of all deceipt and trickery.'

[70] W. E. A. Axon, *op. cit.*, p. 11, refers to 'a French adaptation in Gabrielle Chaphuys's *Facétieuses Journées* in 1584'.

[71] *Sup.* p. 85 *et seq.*

[72] I. T[atham]., *Grim the Collier*; in *Gratiae Theatrales* (1662). I, i, p. 8.

See W. C. Hazlitt, *A Manual for the Collector and Amateur of Old English Plays* (1892), p. 99. *Grim the Collier of Croydon; or, The Devil and his Dame*: . . . 'This is probably a modernized text of a drama, which may be rightly identified with one mentioned by Henslowe under date of March 6, 1600-1, when he pays William Haughton "in respect of a book which he would call *The Devil and his Dame*".'

Cf. Henslowe's Diary, ed. W. W. Greg (1904), Pt. II, item 204, where Greg considers it clear from internal evidence that it is a 16 c. play. 'Grim is mentioned in Edwards' *Damon and Pythias* (entered S. R. 1567-8, and printed 1571), and is a character, together with the devil, in Fulwel's *Like will to like* . . . (entered S. R. 1568-9, and printed the former year), which may have been the same as the "historie of the Collyer" performed, according to the Revels' Accounts, by Leicester's men at Hampton Court, 30 Dec. 1576.'

[73] I. T[atham]., *op. cit.*, I, iv, p. 16.

[74] *Ibid.*, p. 17.

Even Lacey, her proposed fiancé, exclaims: 'I would to God her tongue were tied again'. At which Castiliano,

> I marry Sir, but that's another thing,
> The Devil cannot tye a woman's tongue,
> I would the Fryer could do that with his Beads.[75]

Very soon Honorea and her friend Marian prove too much for the devils. Robin Goodfellow makes his appearance in the third act *'with his head broken'*[76] and decides to run away from the bastinadoes. 'Zounds, I had rather be in hell than here;'

> But I'le no longer serve so curs'd a Dame,
> I'le run as far first as my leggs will bear me:
> What shall I do? to Hell I dare not go!
> Untill my Master's Twelve months be expired.
> And here to stay with Mistress *Marian*,
> Better to be so long in purgatory.
> Now farewell Master, but shrewd Dame, fare il
> I'le leave you, though the Devil is with you still.[77]

Castiliano himself, at the end of his probation, is able to escape into hell just in time to release himself from an intricate maze of troubles.

THE SHREWISH TONGUE IS OF THE DEVIL'S MAKING

Although the tongue of a scold so discomforted the Devil that he cried out:

> Mir stehn gen Berg all meine Haar
> Vor diem gifftigen, bösen maul.[78]

it was yet an instrument of his own making. He foments a quarrel between the shrewish old women in *Gammer Gurtons Nedle*:

> Sticke to her gammer, take her by the
>   head, chil warrant you thys feast.
> Smyte I saye gammer,/ Byte I say gammer,
>   I trow ye wyll bekeene:
> Where be your nayls? claw her by the iawes,
>   pull me out bothe her eyen,
>   . . . . . .
> Hoyse her, souse her, bounce her, trounce her,
>   pull out her throte boule.[79]

---

[75] *Ibid.*, p. 17.
[76] *Ibid.*, stage directions, Act III, p. 37.
[77] *Ibid.*, III, i, pp. 37-38.
[78] Hans Sachs, *Der Teüffel mit dem alten Weyb*; in *Sämmtliche fastnachtspiele*, Bändchen ii, p. 68, ll. 281-2. 'Your poisonous, evil tongue makes my hair stand on end.'
[79] [W]. S[tevenson]., *Gammer Gurtons Nedle* (1575), C. iiiᵛ.

The names they call each other come straight from the Devil's vocabulary: 'doting drab, olde witche, thou old gyb, yᵉ rampe, thou ryg, Hogge, thou arrant witche, thou bawdie bitche, thou slut, yᵉ kut, yᵉ rakes, yᵉ iakes, thou skald, thou bald, thou rotten, yᵉ glutton, thou drunken beaste, old hore, strong stued hore, thou scalde callet, thou hoddy peke, doll, losell, thou withered witch, yᵘ old tarlether.'[80]

> Theyr furour passyth, in dede and in langage
> All men in erth: none may with them compare
> He is well happy whiche may of them be ware.[81]

As in the case of Honorea in *Grim the Collier*, so with the 'dome wyfe' in *A C Mery Talys*,[82] once the weapon of speech had been fashioned, he was unable to retain the mastery.

... vpon a day as he [the husband] walked alone ryght heuy in harte, thynkynge vpon his wyfe, there came one to him and asked hym, what was the cause of his heuynesse; ...[83]

The Devil suggests that he put an aspen leaf under his wife's tongue when she is asleep. In order to make sure of the remedy, he put three leaves instead of one. The following morning he asks her how she did, whereupon the woman: 'I beshrowe your harte for wakenynge me so erly;'

... her speche so encreased day by day, and she was so curste of condycyon, that euery daye she brauled and chydde with her husbande so moche, that at the laste he was more vexed, and hadde moche more trouble and disease with her shrewde wordes, than he hadde before whan she was dome.[84]

On asking the Devil to give him a medicine to cure the evil, he receives the reply:

All be it yet I haue power to make a woman to speke, but and if a woman begyn ones to speke, I, nor all the deuyls in hell that haue the more power, be nat able to make a woman to be styll, nor to cause hir to leaue her spekynge.[85]

Among John Heywood's *dialogue of prouerbes* we find:

> I would
> *Thy tongue* were cooled to make thy tales more cold;
> *That aspen leaf*, such spiteful clapping have bred,
> That *my cap is better at ease than my head.*[86]

[80] *Ibid.*, C. iii., ll. 10 - C. iiiᵛ. *ad fin.*
[81] S. Brant, *op. cit.*, ii, p. 1.
[82] Erasmus tells the same tale in his *Coniugium*, which shows the popularity of the theme even amongst scholars.
[83] *A C Mery Talys*; in *Shakespeare Jest-Books*, ed. Hazlitt, i, p. 87.
[84] *Ibid.*, i, pp. 87-88.
[85] *Ibid.* p. 88.
[86] J. Heywood, *A dialogue conteinyng all the prouerbes in the englishe tongue* (1562), ed. J. S. Farmer Pt. 2, Ch. vii, p. 85.

In the *Maitland Folio MS.* the husband meets with

> Ane greit grim man be chance
> quhilk fast at him did fraine
> quhy he sa sadlie went
> quhat angwisch greif or paine
> purturbit his intent[87]

After having supplied the remedy of the aspen-leaf, the man warns him

> Scho sall spek out haif thow na dout
> And mair than thow desyreis[88]

Here, too, the 'greit grim man' is unable to assist him any further, for although

> The leist deuill yat is in hell
> Can gif ane wyff hir toung
> The gritest I ʒow tell
> Cannot do mak hir dum[89]

The aspen-leaf theory persisted for a long time though it was refuted by *The Wanton Wife of Bath* who valiantly defended herself and her sex against all the saints in heaven, including St Thomas.

> 'They say', quoth Thomas, women's tongues,
> Of aspen-leaves are made.
> Thou unbelieving wretch, quoth she,
> All is not true that's sayd.[90]

But then it must be admitted that she herself was a potential shrew and only escaped being banished from heaven by begging pardon for her sins.

LIFE IS MADE RESTLESS BY THE SHREW BOTH HERE AND HEREAFTER

She is Kept at Bay by Both Man and the Devil

Clearly, life was made uncomfortably restless by the workings of the shrew, both in this life and the hereafter. In *the hye way to the spyttell hous*, Robert Copland, on being shown through the chambers of the diseased by the porter, enquires,

---

[87] *The Dumb Wife* in *The Maitland Fol. MS*, ed. W. A. Craigie, vol. i, STS, n.s. No. 7 (1919), p. 69, ll. 12-16.
[88] *Ibid.*, i, 70, ll. 43-4.
[89] *Ibid.*, ii, STS n.s. No. 20 (1927), p. 67, ll. 105-8.
[90] T. Percy, *Reliques of Ancient English Poetry* 3 vols., (1876-77), iii, p. 336, ll. 77-80.

Come hyther ony of these wofull creatures
　　That be sore wounded/and moche wo endures
With a shrewd wife/and is neuer quyet
　　Bycause that she wold haue all her dyet
But bralle and chyde/babble/crye and fyght
　　Euer vncontented bothe day and nyght[91]

The porter explains how they have special chambers set aside for these victims, for that otherwise they would have to go to Bedlam, for,

　　By good fayth, the very deuyll of hell
　I trowe to my mynd hath not moche more payne
　　One were in a maner as good be slayne
　For there is no ioye but euer anguysh.[92]

That the 'shrew-shake' had its repercussions even in the underworld, we
know from Dante who, in asking one of the restless whirling creatures who
he is and how he came to be in such a state, receives the reply,

　　Ed io, che posto son con loro in croce,
　　　Jacopo Rusticucci fui; e certo
　　　La fiera moglie più ch'altro mi nuoce.[93]

Even if man was not eligible for hell, he would rather forgo heaven and re-
main a restless spirit than be re-united to a shrew. Such a one was, for instance, the bricklayer in *Greenes Newes both from Heauen and Hell*. St
Peter invites the bricklayer into heaven, but

　　The fellowe hastily replyed, saying: I pray sir let mee first aske you a question, doo vse to let any women come into Heauen amongst you?[94]

St Peter is surprised that the man should doubt such a matter, and the
bricklayer now cautiously enquires whether six weeks ago perhaps a woman
did arrive 'with a bleare eye, a snottie nose, a blabber lippe, a stincking
breath, her voyce was very shrill, and her speech thicke and short', with the
name of Margery Sweete, nicknamed Mannerly Margery.

　　Why she is in heauen (saide S. *Peter*) and if thou hast any thing to say to
her, thou mayst there finde her?
　　Mary God blesse me from thence (saide the other) if shee be there, I know
her fashions too well, to come any more where she is, shee was my wife, and I

　　[91] R. Copland, *The hye way to the Spyttell hous* (1536), D.ii.
　　[92] *Ibid*. D. ii[v].
　　[93] A. Dante, *Divina Commedia*, Heath's Mod. Language Series (1909-13), *Inferno*,
Canto xvi, ll. 43-5. 'As for myself, who partake with them of this torment I was
Rusticucci who no doubt was brought to this evil by the shrewish temper of my wife,
more than by anything else.'
　　[94] B[arnabe]. R[ich]., *Greenes Newes both from Heauen and Hell* (1593); ed. McKerrow
(1911), p. 27, ll. 27-29.

was married to her sixteene or seuenteene yeeres, and I faith all heauen would be too little for her and mee, and if we should once meete againe, but I am now ridde of her, and I hope I will keepe mee so, she shal not cast it in my teeth, that I was so far in loue with her to follow her, as she hath many times doone: telling me, that if I had not beene she might haue had a Minstrell, that would haue got more money in a weeke with his Fiddle, than I could get in a moneth, with laying of Brick.[95]

HER FAILURE AS WOMAN

The shrew was considered far worse than either the witch, or the wanton. The latter, though untrue to her nature, possessed a peculiar charm which enticed men to follow her. The witch, wicked and revengeful, tempted him to persecute her, in which he often succeeded and from which he received a certain satisfaction. Besides, there were occasions when she could be of use. But the shrew, unkinder and more unnatural than any of her sex, held no attraction for mankind. On her account, man sank into a servility and was degraded contrary to his nature.

If a *homo faber* was angry, disagreeable, or uncouth, he was still accepted by society for his labour;[96] but as far as women were concerned, they were expected to 'Conforme to þair cōplexioun'.[97] Man looked in them for the qualities of the 'femynyne gendere'; 'Faire, kinde, and true',[98] both inwardly and outwardly, was his argument, and he was bitterly disappointed to find them otherwise.

[95] *Ibid.*, p. 28, ll. 3-15.
[96] F. J. J. Buytendyk, *op. cit.*, p. 13.
[97] A. Scott, *Of Wemenkynd*; in *The Poems*, ed. J. Cranstoun, STS, No. 36 (1896), p. 70.
[98] Shakespeare, *Sonnets*, 105.

Conclusion

In sixteenth-century literature almost all possible relations between Woman and the Devil are exemplified. It is the Virgin who makes him tremble, the saint who treads him under foot, the good woman who chases him away at the hour of death. It is the fair lady who inspires her knight to conquer him; and even the country lass breaks his spell. Not one phase of her dealings with the Devil has been neglected and the point that this literature makes unceasingly is that while every woman is potentially either a saint or a sinner, the outcome depends entirely on how she deals with the Evil One.

In this book the Devil is depicted on a descending scale. There are great gaps between, for instance, Masscheroen, the Advocate, who has access to the Court of Heaven, and pleads his case with all the power of his angelic intelligence, and the mischievous Fairy who plays tricks upon the dairy-maids. Still lower in the scale is the witch's familiar kept in a wool box, and the dotard or the 'wee reekit deil' under the thumb of the shrew.

In his descent he drags the woman down with him. The wanton, the witch and the shrew, in different ways, diminish or degrade their woman-hood. The Devil achieves his greatest triumphs through the wanton. Being 'Natures fairest ill'[1] she is the most dangerous to man. The witch, for all her grisly intimacy with the Devil, does not seem to succeed in greatly increasing the numbers of the damned. The shrew overcomes the Devil by her own self-will but in doing so she loses everything for even 'hell will not be troubled with such an earthly scold.'[2] Woman's debasement has now run its term and she appears as a travesty with a 'Tygres Heart wrapt in a Womans Hide.'[3]

When this point is reached in literature, we find that we are no longer dealing with a real woman or a real devil as they have been portrayed in the early chapters, for the sixteenth-century writer has lost faith in both.

The essence of womanhood in the tradition of the time is summed up in the free and loving submission to her lord's will, her selfless, courageous co-operation and merciful disposition, and equally in her sense of initiative and unflinching stand in the face of danger. The wanton, the witch and the shrew all contradict these ideas; the wanton by a self-centred love which lacks all nobility; the witch by embodying malice instead of love; while the

---

[1] [R. Greene], *Orlando Furioso*; in *The Plays and Poems*, ed. Collins, vol. i, II, i, 672.
[2] *The Devil and the Scold*; in *The Roxburghe Ballads*, ii, Pt. 2, p. 370, ll. 107-8.
[3] *Henry VI, Pt. 3*, Ist. Folio, *Histories*, p. 151; (I, iv, 137).

shrew personifies self-assertion, thus forming a direct antithesis to the good woman.

Man is invariably involved. The good woman brings out the best in him; the wanton seduces his virtue; the witch makes him a coward; and the shrew saps his very manhood.

Although the wantons, witches and shrews may always outnumber the good women in literature, and, in Nashe's phrase 'there . . . be many falling starres', yet there will always be found a 'true *Diana*'.[4] And when the prose-writer, poet and playwright, with their distrust of the wanton, and their abhorrence of the witch, have finally made their escape from the shrew, they will perforce retrace their steps to the good woman whom they will still find 'Faire, kinde, and true'.[5]

[4] Th. Nashe, *Pierce Pennilesse, Works*, i, p. 216.
[5] Shakespeare, *Sonnets*, 105.

Appendices

POPE JOAN

The story of Pope Joan[1] is unique in sixteenth-century literature. Although she manifests certain characteristics of all three: the wanton, the witch and the shrew, yet she cannot be classed with any one of them. Like the wanton, she puts on the attire and behaviour of a man, but the temptations of the senses do not figure in her story. Like the witch she was popularly credited wih a knowledge of magic. And there is something of the shrew's self-will in her aspiration to power, not just any power, but power in the Church, which she achieves by the help of the Devil.

The most interesting dramatic version of her life, which I came upon, is Theodorich Schernberk's *Ein schön spil van Fraw Jutten*.[2] The play is introduced by Lucifer himself who informs the audience that Joan will henceforth be named 'Johannes aus Engellant'. The Devil promises her

> Ir sullet werden klug und weise.
> Auch sage ich euch mehre,
> Ir sollet komen zu großen ehren.[3]

That was his bait, to hold before her 'die edle kunst grammaticam', further 'das latein', 'die hubsche kunst logica', 'rethorica', and other arts. Clericus, the Devil, accompanies Joan to Paris and is her companion in study. After they have taken their doctorates, they decide to seek further honour in service of the Pope, and soon rise to the rank of Cardinal. Finally, Joan is elected Pope. Now that she has achieved what is known as the highest

---

[1] This mythical female Pope gave material for much controversy. She was supposed to have intervened as John VIII between Leo IV and Benedict III in the ninth century.
The idea was refuted by F. de Raemond, *Erreur populaire de la papesse Jeanne* [no place of publication mentioned, possibly Lyons?] (1588).

[2] in *Fastnachtspiele aus dem fünfzehnten Jahrhundert*, Bibliothek des Litt. Vereins, xxix, Bd. ii (Stuttgart, 1853), pp. 900 *et seq*. The play was first published in 1565. The MS. dates from 1480. It was yearly produced as one of the Fastnachtspiele.
G. B. Harrison, *An Elizabethan Journal* (1928), p. 112 mentions among the plays of the week, 4th March, 1592. 'The plays at the Rose Theatre this past week were *Cloris and Ergasto, Muly Mullocco, Pope Joan, Machiavel, Harry the Sixth* (for the first time), *Bindo and Richardo*.'
In *Henslowes Diary*, ed. Greg, Pt. 2, the following item appears p. 152, item 9. '[7 14. "poope Jone". Performed by Strange's men, as an old play, 1 Mar. 1591/2.]'

[3] T. Schernberk, *op. cit.*, p. 905, ll. 31-2. 'Thou shalt become wise and learned and, moreover, attain to great honour.'

place in Christendom, her womanly nature takes its revenge and she is found with child. A devil, whom she has exorcised, spitefully gives her secret away.

> Der bapst der tregt fürwar ein kind.
> Er ist ein weib und nicht ein man.[4]

Although the verses frequently lapse into doggerel, we may presume, from Schernberk's stage directions, that the pageant must have been highly spectacular. Joan dies after publicly giving birth to a child, and her death is celebrated in a three-storied *finale*, with action taking place on the upper, middle and nether regions simultaneously.

> *Hie gehen die cardinel mit ihrem gesinde*
> *in der procession, mit kerzen und fahnen.*
> *Nu folget, wie Bapst Jutten Seel durch*
> *der jungfrawen marien und S. Nicolai*
> *Fürbitt aus dem Fegfewr erlöset sein sol.*
> *Lucifer rüft sein Hellisch Gesinde zu*
> *haufe:* ...[5]

'DIUELRIE'

Apart from the explanation of Fairy-lore in Chapter II,[1] there was a widespread theory in the sixteenth century reconciling popular belief in greater and lesser devils. This was based on Psellus' *de operatione daemonum* (cap.8) mentioned in Scot's *Discoverie of Witchcraft*:

he saith, that there are six principall kind of diuels, which are not onelie corporall, but temporall and worldlie. The first sort consist of fier, wandering in the region néere to the moone, ... The second sort consisting of aire, haue their habitation more lowe and néere vnto vs : ... The third sort of diuels *Psellus* saith are earthlie; the fourth waterie, or of the sea; the fift vnder the earth; the sixt sort are *Lucifugi*, that is, such as delight in darkenes, & are scant indued with sense, and so dull, as they can scarce be mooued with charmes or conjurations.

The same man saith, that some diuels are woorse than other, but yet that they all hate God, and are enimies to man. But the woorser moitie of diuels are *Aquei, Subterranei*, and *Lucifugi*; that is, waterie, vnder the earth, and shunners of light:[2]

---

[4] *Ibid.*, p. 925, ll. 34-5. 'The Pope is great with child. He is a woman and no man.'

[5] *Ibid.*, p. 944, ll. 4-7. 'Whilst the Cardinals and Clergy process through the streets of Rome with candles and banners; St. Nicholas and the Virgin Mary prostrate themselves before God's judgement-throne to entreat for mercy; and Lucifer calls up all the fiends of hell to come to the defence.'

[1] *Sup.* p. 51 *et seq.*

[2] R. Scot, *A Discourse vpon diuels and spirits*, which was added by the author to *The discoverie of witchcraft* (1584), cap. 3, pp. 493-4.

12 *Deuilrie*

The same theory had also been mentioned by Dirc van Delf in *Tafel van der Kerstenghelove*, a late fifteenth-century treatise on the fall of the angels and their nature. Spirits of woodland, air or water, all were identified by him with devils. He describes how Lucifer with the rebel angels was flung down from heaven, but some never quite reached hell as the depth of their fall was determined by their guilt and wickedness.

een deel int ondersceyt vander lucht, een deel vielen in dat meer, een deel in moerbosken, wildernisse ende braem, na dat haer toekeer quaet ende groet was. Ende hier om ist dat wi in lucht, in water, in velde dicwil aenstorm der quader geesten liden.[3]

[3] Dirc van Delf, *Tafel van der Kerstenghelove*, quoted in C. G. N. de Vooys, *Mid-*

Thomas Heywood mentions a similar division in *The Hierarchie of the Blessed Angels*.[4] It is clear that the lesser spirits were more accessible and consequently appeared more frequently to man. The important devils only interfered when a crisis occurred, as for instance in *Dr Faustus* when Mephostophilis was no longer able to cope with the situation.[5] Despite the lesser guilt and occasional show of humanity of the air and woodland kind, they were nevertheless the emissaries of the greater fiends whose evil designs they carried into action. The majority of the devils mentioned in this book belong to this category, including Mephostophilis, Moenen, Rush, and also the nameless variety. They not infrequently appear in literature as the servants of a greater devil, for instance, in *Grim the Collier* where Akercock, alias Goodfellow, attends on Belphegor.[6]

These spirits were often employed as messengers and they maliciously rejoiced when they could report success.

> a lorges, a lorges, lorddes alle at onys!
> ȝe haue a servant fayer and afyabylle,
> for she is fallyn in ower grogly gromys;
> ȝa, pryde callyd corioste, to hur is ful lavdabyll.[7]

If the news was bad, they were beaten as in the case of Mary Magdalene's conversion.[8]

The names they bore were derived from biblical, pagan and christian sources, or they were based on local superstition. In *the Digby Plays*, for instance, Mercury runs messages for Belial.

In literature there is no strict dividing line between fairies and devils and it is impossible to explain its whole devil-lore by any one theory. We can

---

delnederlandsche Legenden en Exempelen ('s Gravenhage, 1900) p. 161. 'One part remained up in the air, another part fell in the sea, and some landed in forests, on moors and heaths, according to the measure of their punishment. And this is the reason why we are troubled with the attack of evil spirits in the sky, water and on land.'

[4] Th. Heywood, *The Hierarchie*, pp. 503 *et seq.*

[5] They were sometimes used in the attacks on big cities when great leadership was required. In Ben Jonson, *The Divell is an Asse*; the *Works* ed. C. H. Herford Percy and Evelyn Simpson, vol. vi (OCP, 1938), I, i, 29-31, Satan himself said,

> The state of *Hell* must care
> Whom it imployes, in point of reputation,
> Heere about *London*.

It seems that women's fashions were considered sufficiently important for Pluto to be put in charge. J. L. Vives in *Instruction of a Christan woman* (1540?), I, iiiᵛ, accuses the woman that goes about in silks and fine garments: 'Nay nay/ thou art rather yᵉ disciple of riche Pluto'.

[6] I[ohn]. T[atham]. *op. cit.*, I, iii *et seq.*

[7] *Mary Magdalene, The Digby Plays*, ed. F. J. Furnival, EETS, es. lxx (1896), p. 75, ll. 547-50.

[8] *Ibid., sup.* p. 42.

Cf. also *sup.* p. 34, where a little devil has the awkward task of facing the Virgin Mary who demands the pact signed by Theophilus.

only admit that, judging from sixteenth-century evidence there might be some truth in Toby's statement, 'the whole worlde is nothing els but a Diuelrie, altogether diuelished'.[9]

THE *Processus Sathane* OR THE PLAY OF MASSCHEROEN

The earliest sources of this play date back to the end of the twelfth century.[1] Hope Traver in his extensive study of the subject mentions sermons and commentaries by Peter de Blois, Stephen de Tournai,[2] Caesarius von Heisterbach, St. Bernard and Hugo. The idea of the Devil appearing in heaven among the Sons of God, is derived from *the Booke of Iob*.[3] Mariolatry was at its height and since many theologians also studied Canon and Civil Law, a theme developed based on Theology, Mysticism, Mariology and Law.

At first it took the form of a simple debate but gradually refinements of legal chicanery were added. In the 1588 version of Bartolus de Saxoferrato,[4] for instance, full citations from the Canon Law are given to support the statements made by the Virgin or by Satan.[5] The *Processus Sathane* as it is generally named, became a miscellany of much learning then prevalent such as the distinction between the sin of man and of Lucifer from Thomas Aquinas, and the purpose of man's creation from Anselm. Bede had mentioned a book recording good and evil deeds.[6] Further, since Pope Alexander III (1159–1182) a ceremony was instituted preceding the process of Canonisation in which an *Advocatus Diaboli* appointed for the occasion, had the task of putting forward any points against the canonisation.[7] Legendary material was also interwoven to make this law-suit palatable to the imaginative medieval mind.

[9] Viret, *op. cit.*, G. 4ᵛ. (5th Dialogue).
[1] The actual evolution of the *Processus Sathane* was spread over more than a thousand years going back to apocalyptic and gnostic sources. See R. Hope Traver, *The Four Daughters of God, Bryn Mawr College Monographs*, VI (Bryn Mawr, Pennsylvania, 1907).
[2] Stephen de Tournai studied theology at Paris, Canon and Civil Law at Bologna and he wrote a summa on Gratian's *Decretals*, a famous digest of Canonical Law (1140).
[3] *Booke of Iob*, ii, 1.
[4] Tractatis Questionis . . .; in *Opera omnia* (Basileae, 1588-89), vol. v., pp. 349 *et seq.*
[5] Jacopo da Teramo's *Belial* (1381) and the French *Advocacie* by Jean de Justice are of a similar nature.
Saxoferrato was a Professor at the School of Law in Bologna.
[6] Hope Traver, *op. cit.*, pp. 57-8, mentions 'the Legend of *Piers Toller*, which had its origin in the life of the sixth-century John of Alexandria. A paire of scales appear to Piers in a vision. In one scale the fiends heaped up his sins and the angel could find nothing to put in the other side except the little loaf which he had thrown at a beggar.'
[7] R. Stinzing, *Geschichte der populären Literatur des römisch-kanonischen Rechts in Deutschland am Ende des fünfzehnten und im Anfang des sechszehnten Jahrhunderts* (Leipzig, 1867), p. 260. 'Seit Papst Alexander III (1159-1182) gehört bekanntlich zu dem der kanonisation voraufgehenden weitläufigen Verfahren unter Anderem auch ein förmlicher Prozeß, in welchem der Teufel durch einen bestellten Anwalt (Advocatus diaboli) als Partei auftritt.'

The earliest extant version and the one which is most complete is found in Jacob van Maerlant's *Merlijn*[8] (*ca.*1260), a translation of Robert de Boron's *Merlin*. It does not occur in the French text, however, and must have been inserted by van Maerlant.[9] The oldest extant Latin version is in the *Tractatus Questionis* of Bartolus de Saxoferrato who adds the canonical citations lacking in van Maerlant. The 1485 edition (*sup.* pp. 66–7) also contributes its own colouring.

It became a fit subject for drama. F.A.Snellaert thinks it likely that it was produced as a pageant in the fourteenth century.[10]

Taking van Maerlant's version, the contents run as follows: the devils, fearing that all their labours will be in vain now that man can obtain forgiveness of his sins, and that they will be cheated of their rightful prey, decide to send a representative to the Court of Heaven to plead for justice on their behalf. Masscheroen is elected for the task. He appears before God with the request that mankind shall be summoned before the Court and he be allowed to plead against him. God consents and suggests Good Friday as a suitable day. Masscheroen objects since it is a holy day but God says that He will give dispensation.

On that day Masscheroen enters heaven very early and places himself in a corner from where he can choose a vantage point as the accuser, and form his strategy. He is well prepared and has the Bible in his pocket for reference. Keeping his eyes and ears wide open, he waits till noon, but nothing happens. He grows impatient but God tells him that the day is long. When it grows dark, he begins to scream and expostulate:

> 'Al desen dach heb ick gebeit
> In dat rike der Gerechticheyt,
> Ende en vonde gene gerechtichede.'[11]

[8] Hope Traver, *op. cit.*, p. 68. See *sup.* p. 64.

[9] J. van Maerlant was known as Jacob de Koster (sacristan) of Maerlant (c. 1235-1300).

J. P. Wickersham Crawford, in 'the Catalan Mascarón and an Episode in Jacob van Maerlant's *Merlijn*' *PMLA*, XXVI (1911), pp. 47-8, suggests: 'It is likely that the Catalan version was translated into French, and this lost French version was translated into Dutch and Latin. Not only does the primitive character of the Catalan text furnish evidence that it was the earliest, but also the name Mascarón points to Spain. Van Maerlant and the Latin translator added the two new elements, both of which were popular themes in medieval literature.'

Hope Traver *op. cit.*, pp. 49-69, considers it more likely that an older Latin version has influenced both the Dutch and Catalan. The version of Caearius von Heisterbach, though older than the Dutch and Latin, he regards as being too slight and perverted to have served as the original form.

Jan Boendale who was a pupil of van Maerlant based his version on that of his master. (see Snellaert, *Nederlandsche Gedichten*, pp. 493 *et seq.*)

[10] F. A. Snellaert, *Nederlandsche Gedichten*, p. lxxv.

E. K. Chambers, *op. cit.*, p. 64, mentions *ludus de Bellyale* given at Aberdeen in 1471 incorporating the Four daughters (*inf.* p. 160). For further influence on English drama see Hope Traver, *op. cit.*, p. 125.

[11] Van Maerlant, *op. cit.*, ll. 2185-7. 'I have spent all this day in the kingdom of justice, but there is no justice.'

But since the accused has not appeared, God postpones the session till the following day. Meanwhile the Virgin Mary, hearing of the difficulty in which man finds himself, offers to represent him and be his advocate. When Masscheroen appears on the following morning, he is unpleasantly surprised at the entry of Mary accompanied by a host of angels, prophets and patriarchs. She takes her place at the side of the Judge, her Son. Despite many protests from Masscheroen, she is allowed to proceed as man's advocate.[12] Although the Devil knows that everyone is against him, yet he is stubborn in his cause, and pulling the Bible from his pocket, reads how God spoke to Adam and Eve:

> 'dat zult gy weten:
> Van aller vrucht zult gy eten
> Sonder van deser, ende op wat uren
> Gy daervan etet, zuldy dat besuren
> Ende sterven van dode te dode.'[13]

Masscheroen demands that these words shall be executed at all times. But Mary accuses him of falsehood in beguiling Adam and Eve by his promises and blames him for man's fall.[14] The Devil, seeing he is laughed at, quotes from the Law book how a public offence should be punished even if there is no accuser and that, therefore, neither the Virgin nor himself can bear any influence on the case, since man sinned publicly. Mary now grows anxious and, at a loss for argument, she makes a compassionate appeal, tearing her clothes and uncovering her breasts, reminding Christ that she bore and nourished Him and leaving Him the choice between herself and Masscheroen.

> Dus wert die Sone wt den Vader
> Beroert, daer hy sine moeder sach an
> So wijflecke wenen,[15]

and, as a result, Masscheroen was denied his demand. Then said the Devil:

---

[12] At the Tower of London in the Byward Tower a 14c. wall-painting reveals the figure of the Virgin Mary pleading for souls in an imaginary Judgement scene. St. Michael holding the scales, gives it a very human interest. Workmanship and colouring are superb.

[13] van Maerlant, *op. cit.*, ll. 2485-9. 'This thou shalt know: thou mayest eat from all fruits except this one and thou shalt regret the hour thou eatest thereof, for thou shalt die the one after the other.'

[14] *Cf.* Saxoferrato, *Opera omnia*, v, 354, col. ii, ll. 23-4. Mary here maintains that it is the Devil who deserves punishment, and not man. 'Quia qui occasioné dáni dat, damnú dedisse uidetur : . . .'
'because he who gives the occasion for damnation must be responsible for the consequences.'

[15] van Maerlant, *op. cit.*, ll. 2612-14. 'The Father's son was moved at seeing his mother weep in such womanly wise.'

> 'vleesch ende bloet
> Hevet dy geraden, dat gy dit doet
> Ende niet die hemelsche gerechticheit;
> Ick hadde dat wel te voren geseit,'[16]

'It is hard to have the Judge's mother as opponent,' he says. Everyone thinks that here the case will end but Masscheroen now starts afresh. He pleads that a common possession should be divided and that, therefore, he has a right to at least a portion of mankind, and he claims the largest one, for the good people are only a mustard seed; 'therefore,' he says, 'it ought to be carefully weighed out what is mine and thine.' 'This was done long ago', is Our Lady's reply, and, turning to her son, she continues, 'when thou didst hang on the cross, and bought mankind. We shall, therefore, have no further weighing.' The Devil begins to fear, and roars terribly. He demands two advocates, Justice and Truth who are granted him. The angels advise Mary also to choose advocates and she asks for Mercy and Peace.

The debate now continues between the allegorical figures of Justice, Mercy, Peace and Truth.[17] The Devil's advocates, Justice and Truth finally give way to Mercy and Peace, so that all four side with the Virgin, and Masscheroen is forced to make an ignominious retreat.

[16] *Ibid.*, ll. 2617-20. 'Flesh and blood have counselled thee and not the justice of heaven. I knew this would happen.'

Cf. Saxoferrato, *Opera Omnia*, v. 350, col, ii, ll 42-6. 'Respond, daemon: Sancte pater, non moueat te caro & sanguis tuus, nec etiam amor matris tuae: argumen. ext. de praebend cap. graue. ibi, carnalitatis sequentes affectum, &c. sed tota iustitia: quia uos estis iustitia: ut 14. distinct. cap. . . .'

'The devil responded: 'Holy father, let not flesh and blood, nor even love of your mother, move you . . . but total justice because you are justice.'

[17] There is an interesting version of this, though not connected with Masscheroen, in W. Forrest, MS. 'Harley, 1703', f. 82ᵛ et seq. where the debate is conducted in a homely fashion. On f. 83ᵛ, for instance, we read:

> The lady peace: tooke mercyes parte,
> and sayde sisters: do not thus thwarte,
> mercye, shee doth: but pleate her arte:
> yee, of longe time haue borne the bell,
> let mercye now: in youre place dwell.

Cf. sup. p. 8.

The allegory does not occur in Saxoferrato.

Bibliography

All works published in London unless otherwise stated.

Annunciacio in *The Towneley Plays* (*qv*); ed. A. W. Pollard.

Apuleius, Lucius. *The xi Bookes of the Golden Asse* (Henry Wykes, 1566).[This is a translation by William Adlington of *Metamorphoses seu de Asino Aureo*.]

Arthur, King. *Thus endeth thys boke entytled la morte darthur reduced in to Englysshe by syr Thomas Maleore Knygt.* (Wynkyn de Worde, 1529). [The 1st edn. was printed by William Caxton, 1485.]

Arthur of Little Britaine. *The history of the most Noble and valyant Knight, Arthur of little Britaine, translated out of French by Iohn Bourghcher Knight, Lord Barners* (Thomas East [1582]). [1st edn. 1555?]

Ashton, John. *The Devil in Britain and America* (1896).

Assumption and Coronation of the Virgin, The. York Plays (*qv*), ed. L. Toulmin Smith.

Axon, William E. A. *The Story of Belfagor in Literature and Folk-lore* (Reprinted from the Transactions of the Royal Society of Literature, 1902).

B., E. 'Select Pieces of Early Popular Poetry', in *Blackwood's Edinburgh Magazine*, ii (1818). [Notices of reprints of curious old books]

B., H. *The true Discription of a Childe with Ruffes, borne in the parish of Micheham, in the countie of Surrey, in the yeare of our Lord MDLXVI the xx of August* (John Allde and Richarde Johnes, 1566); in the *Henry Huth Collection* Brit. Mus., Huth 50; reprinted in *Black-Letter Ballads and Broadsides* (1867) for J. Lilly (*qv*).

Bacon, Francis. *The Essays or Counsels Ciuill and Morall* (Iohn Haviland for Hanna Barret, 1625), in *A Harmony of the Essays, etc.*; ed. Edward Arber, (*qv*) (1871).

Baker, H. C. 'Classical Material in Broadside Ballads', *PMLA*, liv (1939).

Baker, Sir Richard. *a Chronicle* (1730).

Ballat of the creatioun of the warld, in *The Bannatyne MS.* (*qv*) (1568); ed. W. T. Ritchie, ii STS, n.s. 22 (1928).

Bannatyne MS, The; written in tyme of pest (1568), ed. W. T. Ritchie, STS (4 vols., 1928-34).

Barnouw, A. J. 'Mary of Nimmegen', in *The Germanic Review*, vi (Columbia Univ., 1931).

Baschwitz, K. *De Strijd met den Duivel* (Amsterdam, 1948).

Beatrijs, Facs. uitgave MS '76 E 5' [1237-1374?] (Koninklijke Bibliotheek 's Gravenhage) bewerkt door A. L. Verhofstede (Antwerpen, 1948).

────── Uitgave D. C. Tinbergen (Groningen, 1938).

Bede's Account of the Poet Caedmon; in *Sweet's Anglo-Saxon Reader* (Oxford, 1950).

Bible, The Holy. Conteyning the Old Testament and the New (Robert Barker, Printer to the Kings most Excellent Maiestie, 1611).

Boendale, Jan. *Dit. es van Maskeroen*; in *Nederlandsche Gedichten uit de 14ᵉ eeuw*, bewerkt door F. A. Snellaert (*qv*) (Brussel, 1869).

Brandl, Alois. 'Thomas Elyot's verteidigung guter Frauen' (1545), *Deutsche Shakespeare Gesellschaft Jahrbuch*, 51 (Berlin, 1915).

Brant, Sebastian. *The Shyp of folys of the Worlde* (R. Pynson, 1509); ed. T. H. Jamieson, 2 vols., 1874). [This is a translation by Alexander Barclay of *Das Narren-schiff* first published in the Swabian dialect, 1494].

Butler, E. M. *The Fortunes of Faust* (Cambridge, 1952).
———— *The Myth of the Magus* (Cambridge, 1948).
Buytendyk, F. J. J. *De Vrouw, haar natuur, verschijning en bestaan. Een existentieel – psychologische studie.* (Utrecht – Antwerpen, 4ᵉ oplage, 1951).
Calahorra, Diego Ortuñez de. *The third part of the first booke of the mirrour of princely deedes and knighthood.* (Thomas Este, [1598-99?]) This is a translation by R. P. from the Spanish.
Caraman, Philip. *William Weston. The Autobiography of an Elizabethan.* (1955).
Carey, Millicent. *The Wakefield Group in the Towneley Cycle.* (Baltimore, 1930).
Catholic Encyclopedia, The; ed. C. G. Herbermann, E. A. Pace, C. B. Pallen, T. J. Shahan, J. J. Wynne (New York, 15 vols., 1912), xv.
Chambers, E. K. *English Literature at the Close of the Middle-Ages* (Oxford, 1945).
Chambers, M. C. E. *The Life of Mary Ward.* (2 vols., 1882), i.
C[hapman], G. *A pleasant comedy entituled: An Humerous dayes Myrth* (Valentine Syms, 1599).
Chaucer, Geoffrey. *The Canterbury Tales* in *The Complete Works*; ed. W. W. Skeat (2nd edn. OCP, 1924).
Chelmsford. *A Detection of damnable driftes, practized by three Witches arraigned at Chelmisforde in Essex,* 1579 (for Edward White [1579]).
Chester Plays, The. EETS, e.s. *Part I*, ed. Hermann Deimling, lxii (1892). *Part II*, ed. G. W. Matthews, cxv (1916).
Child, F. J. *The English and Scottish Popular Ballads* (5 vols., 1882-1898). This is the edn. used throughout unless otherwise stated.
———— *English and Scottish Ballads* (Cambridge, 8 vols. in 4 bks. 1860).
Christian Church, Oxford Dictionary of the. ed. S. L. Cross and E. A. Livingstone, 2nd edn. (OUP, 1974).
Coinci, Gautier de. *Les Miracles de Nostre-Dame,* publiés par V. F. Koenig (Genève, Lille, 1955) Tome i; Textes Litteraires Français.
Collins, J. Churton; ed. *The Plays and Poems of Robert Greene.* (OCP, 2 vols., 1905).
Complaynt of Scotlande, The. (1549); ed. J. A. H. Murray, EETS, e.s. xvii (1872).
Concise Cambridge History of English Literature ed. G. Sampson (Cambridge, 1941).
Conway, M. D. *Demonology and Devil-lore* (2 vols., 1879).
Copland, Robert. *The hye way to the spyttell hous* [1536?].
Copley, A. *A Fig for Fortune* (Richard Iohnes for C. A., 1596) printed for the Spenser Society (Manchester, 1883).
Corbet, Dr. Richard. *The Faeryes Farewell*; in *The Poems*, ed. J. A. W. Bennett and H. R. Trevor-Roper (OCP, 1955).
Crawford, J. P. Wickersham. 'the Catalan Mascarón and Episode in Jacob van Maerlant's Merlijn', *PMLA*, xxvi (1911).
Creatione mundi et Adami et Evae, De Pagina Secunda. De eorumque tentatione. The Chester Plays, (qv) Part I; ed. H. Deimling.
Dante, Alighieri. *Divina Commedia*, Heath's Mod. Language Series (3 vols., 1909-13).
Daemon Lover, The; in *The English and Scottish Popular Ballads*, ed. F. J. Child (qv) iv.
Descensu Christi ad Inferos; in *The Chester Plays, (qv) Part II*; ed. G. W. Matthews.
Devil and the Scold, The. (for Henry Gosson); in *The Roxburghe Ballads (qv)*, ii, ed. W. Chappell (1874).
D[ickenson]. I[ohn]. *Greene in Conceipt: new raised from his graue to write the tragique historie of faire Valeria of London.* (Richard Bradocke for William Iones, 1598); in *Occasional Issues of Unique or very rare Books*, ed. A. B. Grosart (Blackburn, 1878).
Dictionary of National Biography, ed. L. Stephen and S. Lee (1908).
Digby Plays, The; ed. F. J. Furnival, EETS, e.s. lxx (1896).

diuill is not to daly stryf, The; in *The Bannatyne MS*, (*qv*), ed. W. T. Ritchie, iv, STS, n.s. 26 (1930).

Dooren, L. *Doctor Johannes Wier* (Aalten, 1940).

Drayton, Michael. *The Moone-Calfe*; in *The Works*; ed. William Hebel, (Oxford, 5 vols. 1931-41), iii.

Dream of Pilate's Wife, The. York Plays (*qv*); ed. L. Toulmin Smith.

Dumb Wife, The; in *The Maitland Folio MS* (*qv*); ed. Sir W. A. Craigie, vol. i, STS, n.s. No. 7 (1919) and continued in vol. ii, STS, n.s. No. 20 (1927) pp. 65 et seq.

[Dunbar, William]. *My guddame wes ane gay wyfe bot scho wes rycht gend*; in *The Bannatyne MS* (*qv*), iii, STS, n.s., 23 (1928).

Dürers Niederländische Reise, Albrecht. von Dr. J. Veth und Dr. S. Muller Fz. (2 Bänder, Berlin und Utrecht, 1918), ii.

Elfin-Knight, The. in *The English and Scottish Popular Ballads*; ed. F. J. Child (*qv*), i.

Elyot, Sir Thomas. *The defence of good women* (in aed. T. Bertheleti, 1545).

────── *The Boke named The Gouernour* (T. Bertheleti, 1531); ed. E. Rhys, Everyman's Library (1907).

Engel, K. *Zusammenstellung der Faustschriften* (Oldenburgh, 1885).

Enikel, Jansen. *Die Weltchronik*; hg. von Philipp Strauch in *Monumenta Germaniae Historica. Deutsche Chroniken und andere Geschichtsbücher des Mittelalters*, iii (Hannover und Leipzig, 1900).

Entwistle, W. J. *European Balladry* (Oxford, 1939).

Epistola Luciferi ad regentes ecclesiasticos Parisiis primum impressa. Una cū tractatu poessus Sathane infernalis contra genus humanum; in *Controversial Tracts*, etc., No. 2. [1520?]. [British Museum: 3907 aa 17].

Erasmus, D. *A dialoge intituled yᵉ pylgremage of pure deuotyon. newly trāslatyd into Englishe* (Iohn Byddele, [1540]). [Translation of *Peregrinatio*].

────── *A mery Dialogue, declaringe the propertyes of shrowde shrewes, and honest wyues*. (Antony Kytson, 1557). [Translation of *Coniugium*].

Etmüller, L. *Theophilus, der Faust des Mittelalters* (Leipzig, 1849).

Eschenbach, Wolfram von. *Parzival und Titurel*, hg. Karl Bartsch. (Leipzig, 1875); in *Deutsche Classiker des Mittelalters*, Bd. ix.

Ewen, C. H. L.'Estrange. *Witch Hunting and Witch Trials* (1929).

Examination and Confession of certaine Wytches at Chensforde [Chelmsford] in the Countie of Essex before the Quenes Maiesties Judges, the XXVI daye of July Anno 1556, The. (Willyam Powell, for Wyllyam Pickeringe, 1566); ed. Herman Beigel, in Miscellanies of the Philobiblon Society, VIII (1863-4).

Exodus, The Booke of. Bible (*qv*).

Farmer's Curst Wife, The; in *The English and Scottish Popular Ballads*, ed. F. J. Child (*q.v.*), v.

Fausten, Historia von D. Johañ. (Frankfurt am Mayn, Johann Spies, 1587). [Referred to as *Faustbuch*].

Faustus, John. *The Historie of the damnable life and deserued death of Doctor Iohn Faustus*. Tr. P. F. Gent. (Thomas Orwin, sold by Edward White, 1592). [Referred to as *Faust Book*].

Fiorentino, Giovanni. *Il Pecorone* (In Milano, appresso di Giouann' Antonio de gli Antonij, 1558). [Although written in 1378, the story was not printed until the 16th century.]

────── *Il Pecorone*; in *Sources of The Merchant of Venice*, Shakesp. Libr, ii; ed. J. Payne Collier (1843), pp. 65 *et seq*. [the editor gives an English translation].

Firth, Sir Charles Harding. *The Ballad History of The Reigns of the Later Tudors*; reprint from *The Transactions of the Royal Historical Society*, iii, pp. 51-124 (1909).

Flemyng, *Ane Ballat of evill wyffis*; in *Ancient Scottish Poems* published from the MS. of George Bannatyne (1568), for John Balfour (Edinburgh, 1770).

Fort, Gertrud von le. *Die ewige Frau* (München, 1955), [1st edn. 1934].

Fulwell, Ulpian. *A pleasant Enterlude, intituled, Like will to Like quoth the Deuill to the Collier* (Edward Allde, 1587); ed. J. S. Farmer, The Tudor Facsimile Texts 1909). [1st edn. 1568.]

Gascoigne, Thomas. *Kalendre of the Newe Legende of Englande* (Richard Pynson, 1506).

Gayley, C. M. *Representative English Comedies* (2 vols. 1903-36).

—— *Plays of Our Forefathers* (New York, 2nd edn. 1907).

Genesis, The Booke of. Bible (*qv*).

George and the Dragon, St. (Anon), in Th. Percy (*qv*) *Reliques of Ancient English Poetry* (3 vols. 4th edn. 1794) iii.

Gesta Romanorum, ed. Sir F. Madden (1838).

Gifford, George. *A Dialogue concerning Witches and Witchcraftes* (Iohn Windet for Tobie Cooke and Mihil Hart, 1593); ed. Beatrice White, Shakesp. Ass. Facs. I (OUP, 1931).

—— *A Discourse of the subtill Practises of Deuilles by Witches and Sorcerers.* ([F. Kingston] for Toby Cooke, 1587).

Golden Legende, The. Jacobus de Voragine (*qv*) (1512).

Gosson, Stephen. *Pleasant Quippes for vpstart new-fangled Gentlewomen* (Richard Iohnes, 1596) [1st edn. 1595] in *Remains of the Early Popular Poetry of England*, ed. W. C. Hazlitt (*qv*), iv.

Gowans sae gay, The; in *the English and Scottish Popular Ballads*; ed. F. J. Child (*qv*), i.

Gowghter, Syr; in *Select Pieces of Early Popular Poetry*, ed. E. V. Utterson (*qv*) (2 vols., 1817), i.

Greene, Robert. *The Plays and Poems of*; ed. J. Churton Collins (*qv*) (OCP, 2 vols. 1905).

Greene, Robert. 'Against enticing curtizans' (*The Groatesworth of Wit*), in *The Plays and Poems*, ii.

[Greene, Robert] *The Historie of Orlando Furioso, One of the twelve Pieres of France* (collated edns. Iohn Danter for Cuthbert Burbie, 1594; and S. Stafford for Cuthbert Burby, 1599); in *The Plays and Poems*, i.

G[reene]., R[obert]. *The Comicall Historie of Alphonsus, King of Aragon.* (T. Creede, 1599); in *The Plays and Poems*, i.

Greg, W. W. 'The Damnation of Faustus', *MLR*, xli (1946).

Grim the Collier of Croydon by I[ohn]. T[atham]. (*qv*) in *Gratiae Theatrales* (R.D., 1662).

Guiney, L. I. *Recusant poets* (2 vols., 1938).

Gybson, Leonarde. *A very proper Dittie: to the tune of Lightie Loue* (Richard Jhones); in the *Henry Huth Collection* reprinted for J. Lilly (*qv*).

Halewijn. Uitgave F. van Duyse, *Het oude Nederlandsche Lied*, ('s Gravenhage, 4 delen, 1903-8), i.

Hall, F. T. *The Pedigree of the Devil* (1883).

Harbage, Alfred. *Annals of English Drama*, A.D. 975-1700. (Philadelphia, 1940).

Harrison, G. B. *Elizabethan Plays and Players* (1940).

—— *An Elizabethan Journal* (1928).

—— *The Trial of the Lancaster Witches AD MDCXII*, (1929).

Harrison, William. *Description of England* in R. Holinshed (*qv*) *The Chronicles* (1587).

H[arsnet]., S[amuel]. *A Declaration of egregious Popish Impostures* (Iames Roberts, 1603).

Hase, K., *Das geistliche Schauspiel* (Leipzig, 1858).

Hazlitt, W. Carew. *Remains of the Early Popular Poetry of England* (4 vols., 1864-6).

—— *A Manual for the Collector and Amateur of Old English Plays* (1892).

———— *A Select Collection of Old English Plays, originally published by Robert Dodsley in 1744* (4th edn. in 14 vols., 1875), xiv.

H[ead], R[ichard]. *The Life and Death of Mother Shipton* (for Benj. Harris, 1684.) [1st edn. 1677]

Heine, Heinrich. 'Shakspeare's Mädchen und Frauen' (1838) in *Sämtliche Werke*, Bibliothek Ausgabe, 13 Bde. (Hoffman und Campe, Hamburg 1885). Bd. iv.

Heisterbach, Caesarius von. *Illustrivm Miraculorum, et Historiarum Memorabilium* (Lib. xii In Officina Birckmannica, sumptibus Arnoldi Mylij, Coloniae Agrippinae 1591). [There is an earlier edn. [1475?], Brit. Mus., I B 2988].

———— *The Dialogue on Miracles* (2 vols., 1929). [This is a translation by H. von E. Scott and C. C. Swinton Bland of *Dialogus miraculorum*].

Heltzel, Virgil B. 'Traces of a Wildfrau Story in Erasmus', *PQ*, viii (Iowa, 1929).

Henslowe's Diary, P. ed. W. W. Greg (2 parts, 1904-8).

Herford, C. H. *Studies in the Literary Relations of England and Germany* (CUP, 1886).

Heuser, W. 'Eine Neue Mittelenglische version der Theophilus-sage' in *Englische Studien* (Leipzig, 1903).

Heywood, John. *A dialogue conteynyng the number of the effectuall prouerbes in the Englishe tounge, compact in a matter concernynge two maner of maryages. etc.* (1562); ed. John S. Farmer in *Early English Dramatists, iv* (1906).

Heywood, John. *The playe called the foure PP.* (Wyllyam Myddylton, [1545?]; ed. J. S. Farmer, The Tudor facsimile Texts (1908).

Heywood, Thomas. *The first and second partes of King Edward the fourth* (F. K[ingston]., for Humfrey Lownes and Iohn Oxenbridge, 1600). [1st. edn. 1599].

————, *The Hierarchie of the Blessed Angells* (Adam Islip 1635).

Hodgart, M. J. C. *The Ballads*, Hutchinson's University Library, English Literature, No. 38 (1950).

Holinshed, Raphael. *The first and second volumes of Chronicles.* (for Iohn Harison, George Bishop, Ra[l]fe Newberie, Henrie Denham, and Thomas Woodcocke, 1587).

Holland, Henr[y]. *A Treatise against Witchcraft.* (Cambridge, John Legatt, 1590).

Huth. *The Henry Huth Collection* [of broadsides] [Brit. Mus. Huth 50], mostly reprinted in J. Lilly (*qv*).

I., A. *A godly ballad declaring by the Scriptures the plagues that haue insued whordome* (1566); in the *Henry Huth Collection* reprinted for Joseph Lilly (*qv*).

Innocent VIII. *Summis Desiderantes affectibus* (Romae, 1484).

Iob, The Booke of. Bible (*qv*).

Iohn, The Gospel of S.; Bible (*qv*).

Isaiah, The Booke of. Bible (*qv*).

Iudicium. The Towneley Plays (*qv*); ed. A. W. Pollard.

James I. *Daemonologie, in forme of a Dialogue, Diuided into Three Bookes.* (Edinburgh, Robert Walde-graue, 1597); ed. G. B. Harrison, ix (Bodley Head Quartos, 1924).

Jewel, John. *Certaine Sermons preached before the Queenes Maiestie, and at Paules crosse.* (Christopher Barker, 1583).

Johnson, Richard. *The most famous history of the seauen champions of christendome* (for Elizabeth Burbie, 1608). [First edn. 1596].

Jonson, Ben. *The Divell is an Asse. A Comedie acted in the yeare, 1616 by His Maiesties Seruants.* (I. B. for Robert Allot, 1631); in *The Works of Benjamin Jonson,* ed. C. H. Herford Percy and Evelyn Simpson, (OCP. 1938) vi.

Joseph's trouble about Mary, York Plays (*qv*) ed. L. Toulmin Smith.

Kemp, William. *Kemps nine daies wonder. Performed in daunce from London to Norwich.* (E. A[llde]. for Nicholas Ling, 1600); ed. A. Dyce, and printed for the Camden Society (1840).

Knox, John. *The first Blast of the Trumpet against the Monstruous Regiment of Women* ([J. Crespin] Geneva, 1558); ed. E. Arber (1878).

Ker, W. P. 'On the History of Ballads', *Proceedings Brit. Ac.*, iv (1910).

Knuvelder, G. P. M. *Handboek tot de Geschiedenis der Nederlandse Letterkunde*, ('s Hertogenbosch, 2 delen 1970-1) i.

Kronenberg, M. E. 'Het mirakelspel van Mariken van Nieumeghen en het Engelsche volksboek', in *De Nieuwe Taalgids*, xxiii (Groningen, 1929).

Kühne, A. *Ueber die Faustsage* (Zerbst, 1860).

Lady Isabel and the Elf-Knight; in *The English and Scottish Popular Ballads*, ed. F. J. Child (*qv*), i.

Lavater, Lewes. *Of Ghostes and Spirites walking by nyght* (Henry Bennyman for Richard Watkyns, 1572); ed. J. Dover Wilson and May Yardley (OUP, 1929). [This is a translation by R[obert]. H[arrison]. of *De Spectris*, 1570.]

Lee, Sidney. 'The Original of Shylock', *Gentleman's Magazine*, n.s. ccxlvi (1880).

Leendertz jr, P. *Middelnederlandsche Dramatische Poëzie* (Leiden, 1907).

Lépée, Marcel. 'Sainte Thérèse de Jésus et le Démon'; in *Satan* (*qv*).

Levin, H. *The Overreacher* (1953).

Lewis, C. S. *The Allegory of Love* (Oxford, 1936).

—— *English Literature in the 16th Century excluding Drama* (Oxford, 1954).

Lewis, Matthew Gregory. *Tales of Wonder* (2 vols., 1801) i.

Lilly, Joseph. *A Collection of Seventy-Nine Black-Letter Ballads and Broadsides, printed in the reign of Queen Elizabeth, between the years 1559 and 1597*; (1867).

Lindblom, Andreas. 'Den Apokryfa Noahsagan i medeltidens konst och litterature'; in *Nordisk Tidskrift för vetenskap konst & industri*, Femte Haftet (Stockholm, 1917).

Lodge, Thomas. *The Complete Works*, ed. Sir E. Gosse (Hunterian Club, 4 vols. 1883 etc.)

L[odge]., T[homas]. *The diuel coniured* (Adam Islip for William Mats, 1596); in *The Complete Works*, iii.

Lodge, Thomas. *Wits miserie and the worlds madnesse. Discouering the Deuils Incarnat of this Age.* (Adam Islip, sold by Cuthbert Burby, 1596); in *The Complete Works*, iv.

Lodge, *Gentleman*, Thomas. and Robert Greene. *A Looking Glasse for London and England* (Thomas Creede, sold by William Barley, 1594); in *The Plays and Poems of Robert Greene*, ed. J. Churton Collins (OCP, 2 vols., 1905) i.

Luke, The Gospel of S.; Bible (*qv*).

Lupton, D. *London and the Countrey Carbonadoed and Quartred into Seuerall Characters* (Nicholas Okes, 1632); Aungervyle Society Reprints, XV (second series, 1884).

Machiavelli, N. *Belfagor*; in *Tutte le Opere di Nicolo Machiavelli.* (In Geneva, presso Pietro Alberto, 1550, divise in v parti.)

Maerlant, Jacob van. *Merlijn* (1261), uitg. J. van Vloten (Leiden, 1880). [from the Steinfort MS].

Maitland Folio MS, The. [1555-85] ed. Sir W. A. Craigie, STS, n.s., 2 vols. No. 7 (1919) and No. 20 (1927).

Mantuan, Baptist. *The Lyfe of Saynt George,* tr. Alexander Barclay [Richard Pynson, 1515]; ed. William Nelson, EETS, o.s., No. 230 (1955).

Marikē van nieumeghen. (Antwerpen, Willem Vorsterman, c. 1518) facs. uitgave A. L. Verhofstede (De Vlijt N. V., Antwerpen, 1951).

Marlowe's Doctor Faustus. 1604-1616, Parallel Texts, ed. W. W. Greg (OCP, 1950).

Marl[owe], Ch[ristopher]. *The Tragicall history of D. Faustus* (V. S[immes]. for T. Bushell, 1604); Tudor Facs. Texts (Oxford, 1914).

—— *The Tragical History of Doctor Faustus*, in Marlowe's *Doctor Faustus*; Greene's *Friar Bacon and Friar Bungay*; ed. A. W. Ward (*qv*).

—— *Tamburlaine the Great*; in *The Works*, ed. A. Dyce (3 vols., 1850) i.

—— *Lusts Dominion; or the Lascivious Queen. A Tragedie. Written by Christofer*

166

Marloe, Gent. (for F[francis]. K[irkman, Jun.]. and are to be sold by Robert Pollard, 1657).

Marlowe, Christopher. *Lust's Dominion;* in *A Select Collection of Old English Plays,* ed. W. Carew Hazlitt (*qv*) xiv.

Mary Magdalene. (M. B., for Miles Blomefylde); in *The Digby Plays* (*qv*) ed. F. J. Furnival, EETS, e.s. lxx (1896).

Mary of Nēmegen (J. van Doesborch, Antwerp. c. 1518); facs. edn. H. Morgan Ayres and A. J. Barnouw, *Mary of Nimmegen* (Harvard, U.P. 1932).

Mary of Nimmegen, A Marvelous History of. translated from the Middle Dutch by Harry Morgan Ayres, and introduced by Adriaan J. Barnouw (Columbia University; printed by Nijhoff, 's Gravenhage, 1924).

May Colven; in *The English and Scottish Popular Ballads,* ed. F. J. Child (*qv*), i.

Melville, Sir James. *Memorialis . . . specefeing of matters wherintill he hes bene employed be sindrie princes or has seen and vnderstand being in ther courtis or contrees, . . . 1549-93;* ed. George Scott, *Gent.* (E. H., for Robert Boulter, 1683), Bannatyne Club (Edinburgh, 1827).

Merline; in *Bishop Percy's Folio MS* (*qv*) i, *Ballads and Romances.*

Meteren, Emanuel van. *Commentarien ofte Memorien van den Nederlandtschen Staet/Handel/Oorloghen ende Gheschiedenissen van onsen tyden/ . . .* (Hermes van Loven, Schotland/buyten Danswijck, 1608).

Middleton, Thomas. *The Works,* ed. A. H. Bullen (8 vols. 1885-6) viii.

M[iddleton]., T[homas]. *The blacke booke* (T[homas]. C[reede]., for Ieffrey Chorlton, 1604).

Mierlo, J. van. *Anna Bijns en Mariken van Nieumeghen in Sprokkelingen op het gebied der Mnl. poezie,* 2ᵉ reeks (Gent, N. V. Drukkerij Erasmus, 1950); Koninklijke Vlaamse Academie voor Taal en Letterkunde.

Milite qui pactum fecit cum diabolo De; in *A Selection of Latin Stories,* ed. Thomas Wright (*qv*) (1842).

Mill, Anna Jean. 'Noah's Wife again' *PMLA,* lvi (1941).

Mirk's Festial, ed. T. Erbe, EETS (1905). [The text is that of the Oxford MS. and varies slightly from the 1502 Pynson edn.]. See Myrc.

Myrc [Mirk], John. *Liber Festiualis et Quatuor sermones* (R. Pynson, 1502). [The text is that of the Folio Westminster, 1st edn. Caxton, 1483].

Molina, Tirso de. [Gabriel Tellez], *El Burlador de Sevilla.* Teatro Español (Madrid, 1924).

———— *The Love-Rogue* (New York, 1923). [This is a free translation by Harry Kemp of Tirso de Molina (*qv*), *El Burlador de Sevilla.*]

Molitoris, Ulricus. *De Lamiis et Pythonicis Mulieribus* (Rutlingae, *ca.* 1489). [Title of copy in Univ. of London Library. *Cf.* note by G. W. Wolthuis (*qv*) p. 189, which argues in favour of the original title *De lanijs et Phito(n)icis* and differs regarding place of publication.]

Montgomerie, W. 'The Orkney Play of the Lady Odivere', *Scots Chronicle* (Glasgow, 1951).

Morus, Henricus. *Historia Provinciae Anglicanae Societatis Iesu,* collectore Henrico Moro (Audomari, Typis Thomae Gevbels, 1660).

Motherwell, William. *Minstrelsy Ancient and Modern* (Glasgow, 1873).

Murray, M. A. *The Witchcult in Western Europe* (OCP 2nd edn. 1952).

myracles of our lady, The. (Wynkyn de Worde, 1514) [1st edn. 1496].

Myrroure of Oure Lady, The. (Richard Fawkes, 1530); ed. J. H. Blunt, EETS, e.s. XIX (1873). [The editor believes Thomas Gascoign to be the author]

Nashe, Thomas. *The Works,* ed. R. B. McKerrow (5 vols. 1904-10).

———— *The Anatomie of Absurditie, contayning a confutation of the slender imputed prayses to feminine perfection.* (I. Charlewood for Thomas Hacket, 1589); in *The Works,* i.

—— *Pierce Penilesse His Supplication to the Diuell* (Abell Ieffes for I[ohn]. B[usby Sr.]. 1592); in *The Works,* i.

—— *Christs Teares ouer Ierusalem* (Iames Roberts, solde by Andrewe Wise, 1593); in *The Works,* ii.

—— *The Terrors of the Night, or a Discourse of Apparitions Post Tenebras Dies* (Iohn Danter for William Iones, 1594); in *The Works,* i.

Nettesheim, Agrippa von. *A Treatise of the Nobilitie and excellency of woman kynde* (Thomas Berthelet, 1542). [This is a translation by David Clapam of *De Foeminei sexus praecellentia*].

—— *Female Pre-eminence* (1670 [This is a translation by H. C[are]. of *De Foeminei sexus praecellentia*].

—— *Vermaakelijk Tractaat, waar in op een Satyrische en aangenaame wyse ondersogt en aangetoond werd, dat het Vrouwelijk Geslagt. In agting en waarde, vry meer in Luister en aansien gehouden moet werden, als dat van de Mannen* (Amsterdam, 1773). [This is a translation by J. d. V. of *De Foeminei sexus praecellentia* which has been placed in a humorous light by the translator].

Newcastle Play, The. Noah's Ark; or, The Shipwrights' Ancient Play or Dirge, in O. Waterhouse (*qv*), *The Non-Cycle Mystery Plays.*

Newes from Scotland, Declaring the Damnable life and death of Doctor Fian (for William Wright, 1591); ed. G. B. Harrison, ix (Bodley Head Quartos, 1924).

Noah and his wife, The Flood and its waning; York Plays (*qv*), ed. L. Toulmin Smith.

Noe, De Deluvio; The Chester Plays (*qv*) Pt. I, ed. H. Deimling (1892).

Norwich Play, The. The Story of þe Creacion of Eve with þe expellyng of Adam & Eve out of Paradyce; in O. Waterhouse (*qv*), *The Non-Cycle Mystery Plays.*

Noss, John B. *Man's Religions* (1969).

Notestein, Wallace. *A History of Witchcraft in England from 1558-1718* (OUP., 1911).

Oliva, Palmerin de. *The honourable Historie of Palmerin d'Oliua,* 2 parts. (Thomas Creede, 1597) This is a translation by A. M[unday] [1st edn. 1588].

Owst, G. R. *Literature and Pulpit in Medieval England* (CUP., 1933).

Pagina Seconda Pastorum, The Towneley Plays (*qv*), ed. A. W. Pollard.

Palmer, P. Mason and R. Pattison-More, *The sources of the Faust Tradition* (New York, 1936).

Plyament of deuylles, The. (Wynkyn de Worde, 1509); reprinted for R. Heber, Roxburghe Club ([1820?]). [not circulated]

Paul, S. *Epistle to the Corinthians. Bible* (*qv*).

P[eele]., G[eorge]. *The Old Wiues Tale. A pleasant conceited Comedie, played by the Queenes Maiesties players.* (Iohn Danter, sold by Ralph Hancocke, and Iohn Hardie, 1595); ed. W. W. Greg, The Malone Society Reprints (1908).

Percy, Bishop Thomas. *The Bishop Percy Folio MS,* ed. J. W. Hales and F. J. Furnivall (4 vols., 1868)iii.

—— *Reliques of Ancient English Poetry: consisting of Old Heroic Ballads, Songs and other Pieces of our earlier Poets, together with some few of later Date* [1555-1586] 4th edn. ed. Th. Percy (nephew of Bishop Percy) (3 vols. 1794).

—— *Reliques;* ed. H. B. Wheatley, (3 vols. 1876-77) iii.

Pitcairn, Esq., Robert. *Criminal Trials in Scotland from A.D. 1488-A.D.1624 compiled from the original records and MSS. with historical notes and illustrations.* (3 vols., Edinburgh and London, 1833).

Play of de Lathie Odiuere, The. Scottish Antiquary, viii (1894). See also Montgomerie, W.

Plönnies, L. v. *Reise-Erinnerungen* (Berlin, 1845).

Pollen, J. H. 'William Weston', *Catholic Encyclopedia* (*qv*).

P[orter]. *Gent.*, H[enry]. *The Pleasant Historie of the two angrie women of Abington*. (for Ioseph Hunt, and William *Ferbrand*, 1599); ed W. W. Greg, The Malone Society Reprints (1912).

Potts, *Esquier*, Thomas. *The Wonderfull Discouerie of Witches in the Countie of Lancaster with the Arraignment and Triall of Nineteen Notorious Witches. A.D. MDCXII* (W. Stansby for Iohn Barnes, 1613); ed. G. B. Harrison (*qv*).

Processus Noe. The Towneley Plays (*qv*); ed. A. W. Pollard.

Processus Noe. The Towneley Mysteries, ed. Surtees Society, iii (1836).

Proclamations, Tudor Royal. Vol. ii (1553-1587), ed. P. L. Hughes and J. F. Larkin (1969).

Prouerbes, The Booke of. Bible (*qv*).

Radermacher, L. 'Griechische Quellen', *Akademie der Wissenschaften in Wien, Sitzungsberichte* Bd. 206, 4 Abh. (Wien und Leipzig, 1927).

Raemond, F. de. *Erreur populaire de la Papesse Jeanne* (1588). [no place of publication is mentioned – possibly Lyons?]

Ranking, B. M. *Streams from Hidden Sources* (1872).

[Rathgeb, Jacob]. *Kurtze vnd Warhaffte Beschreibung der Badenfahrt: Welche der Durchleuchtig Hochgeborn Fürst vnd Herr/ Herr Friderich/ Herzog zu Württemberg . . . in 1592. Jahr/ . . In das weit berümbte Königreich Engellandt/ . . verrichtet hat dero mitraisendem Cammer – Secretarien* (Tübingen, Erhardus Cellins, 1602).

Rea, John D. 'Shylock and the Processus Belial', *PQ* viii (Iowa, 1929).

Revelation, the Book of. Bible (*qv*).

R[ich], B[arnabe]. *Greenes Newes both from Heauen and Hell* (1593); ed. R. B. McKerrow (1911), commended by B. R[ich].

Rich, Barnabe. *Riche his Farewell to Militarie profession* (Robert Walley, 1581), facs. edn. Thomas Mabry Cranfill (Austin, Univ. of Texas Press, 1959).

Rinne, Karl Friedrich. *Speculation und Glauben* (Zeitz, 1859).

Robert the deuyll (Wynkyn de Worde, [1502?]).

Robert the deuyll (Wynkyn de Worde, [1502?] in *Early English Prose Romances*; ed. W. J. Thoms (*qv*) i.

Rolland, Iohne. *The Seuin Seages* (*qv*) *Translatit out of prois in Scottis meter*. (Edinburgh, Iohne Ros, for Henrie Charteris, 1578); ed. G. F. Black, iii STS, 3rd series (Edinb, 1932).

Rollins, Hyder E. 'An Analytical Index to the Ballad-Entries in The Registers of The Company of Stationers of London', *SP*, xxi (Chapel Hill, 1924).

———— *Old English Ballads 1553-1625* (Cambridge, 1920).

Rombouts, Ph. and Th. van Lerius. *De Liggeren en andere Historische Archieven der Antwerpsche Sint Lucasgilde.* (Antwerpen, 2 delen, 1872) i.

Rossiter, A. P. *English Drama from Early Times to the Elizabethans* (1950).

Rothe, Johann. *Chronik von Thüringen*, hg. E. Fritsche (Eisenach 1888).

Roxburghe Ballads, The; ed. W. Chappell, etc., for the Ballad Society (9 vols. 1869-1899).

Rudwin, M. *The Devil in Legend and Literature* (Chicago, 1931).

Rvsh, The Historie of Frier. (Edw. All-de, 1620); facs. reprint (1810).

Rush, The Historie of Frier. (Edw. All-de, 1620) in *Early English Prose Romances* ed. W. J. Thoms (*qv*) i.

Rye, W. B. *England as seen by Foreigners in the Days of Elizabeth and James the First* (1865).

Sachs, Hans. *Sämtliche Fastnachtspiele*, hg. Edmund Goetze (Halle a/s, 1880-87).

———— *Der dewffel nam ain alt weib* (1557); in *Sämmtliche Fastnachtspiele*, Bändchen vii.

———— *Der Teüffel mit dem alten Weyb*; in *Sammtliche Fastnachtspiele*, Bändchen ii.

Salomon, Louis B. *The Devil Take Her, A Study of the Rebellious Lover in English Poetry* (Univ. of Pennsylvania, 1931).

Satan. 'Les Études Carmélitaines', éd. Père Bruno de Jesus-Marie, OCD. ([Paris], chez Desclée De Brouwer, 1948).

Saxoferrato, Bartolus, de. *Tractatus Quaestionis ventilatae coram domino nostro iesv christo*; in *Opera omnia extanta* (Basileae, v libri 1588-89) v.

———— *Tractatus iudiciorum Processus Sathane contra gems humanum* (Heinrich Mayer, Tolosae, [1485?].)

Schernberk, Theodorich. *Ein schön spil von Fraw Jutten* (1565); in *Fastnachtspiele aus dem fünfzehnten Jahrhundert*, Bibliothek des Litt. Vereins, xxix, Bd. ii (Stuttgart, 1853).

Scholem, G. G. *Major Trends in Jewish Mysticism* (Schocken Books, 1946).

Scot, Reginald. *The discouerie of witchcraft* (William Brome, 1584).

———— *The Discoverie of Witchcraft* (William Brome, 1584); ed. B. Nicholson (1886).

———— *The Discoverie of Witchcraft* (William Brome, 1584); ed. M. Summers (1930).

Scotland, Criminal Trials in. ed. Robert Pitcairn, Esq., (*qv*).

Scotland, *Acts of the Parliaments of Scotland 1424-1567* (1814).

Scott, Alexander. *Quha is perfyte*; in *The Bannatyne Manuscript* (*qv*) (1568) ed. W. T. Ritchie, iii STS., n.s. 23 (1928).

———— *Of Wemenkynd*; in *The Poems*, ed. James Cranstoun, STS., No. 36 (1896).

Scottish Antiquary, The. viii (Edinburgh, 1894).

Sevenste Bliscap van Onser Vrouwen, Die. (1447); bewerkt door W. Smulders; inleiding van Dr H. Moller ('s Hertogenbosch, 1913).

Seuin Seages, The. *Translatit out of prois in Scottis meter be Iohne Rolland* (*qv*) (Edinburgh, Iohne Ros, for Henrie Charteris 1578); ed. G. F. Black, iii STS, 3rd series (Edinburgh, 1932).

Shakespeare, Mr. William. Comedies, histories & tragedies. (Isaac Iaggard and Ed. Blount 1623); 1st Folio facs. edn. ed. Methuen & Co. Ltd. (1910).

Shakespeare, William. *A New Variorum edition*, ed. H. Howard Furness (Philadelphia, 1871-   ).

———— *The Complete Works*, ed. Peter Alexander (1951).

Shakespeare Jest Books; ed. W. Carew Hazlitt (3 vols., 1864), i.

Shirburn Ballads 1585-1616, The. ed. from the MS. by Andrew Clark (OCP. 1907).

Sidney, Sir Philip. *An Apologie for Poetrie* (for Henry Olney, 1595); ed. J. Churton Collins (OCP., 1907).

Skelton, John. *The Poetical Works*, ed. Alexander Dyce (2 vols., 1843), i.

———— *The Tunnyng of Elynour Rummynge*; in *The Poetical Works*, i.

———— *Womanhood, wanton, ye want*; in *The Poetical Works*, i.

Snellaert, F. A. *Nederlandsche Gedichten uit de 14e eeuw van Jan Boendale, (qv) Hein van Aken en anderen.* (Brussel, 1869).

———— *Schets eener Geschiedenis der Nederlandsche Letterkunde* (Gent, 1855).

Southwell, Robert. *Marie Magdalens Funerall Teares.* (A. I. for G. C[awood]., 1594). Both dedicatory epistle and preface to the Reader are signed 'S. W. to Mistresse D.A.' [1st edn. 1591].

———— *Marie Magdalen's Funerall Teares* (J. W[olfe]. for G. C[awood]., 1591); (reprinted for John Bumpus, 1827).

Spalding, T. A. *Elizabethan Demonology* (1880).

spel van de V vroede ende van de V dwaeze maegden, Het; in P. Leendertz, Jr (*qv*) *Middelnederlandsche Dramatische Poëzie* (Leiden, 1907).

Spenser, Edmund. *The Faerie Queene* (for William Ponsonbie, 1596); in *The Works*, A Variorum Edition, ed. Edwin Greenlaw, Charles Grosvenor Osgood, Frederick Morgan Padelford. (Baltimore, 1932-8).

Spenser, Edmund. *Poetical Works*, ed. J. C. Smith and E. de Selincourt (OUP, 1935).

Sprenger, Jacob, and Hendrich Kramer. *Malleorum Quorundam Maleficarum, tam veterum quam recentiorum authorum* (tomi duo, Francofurti, 1582), [First published in 1487].

——— *Malleus Maleficarum* (Frankfurt, 1582); tr. and ed. A. Montague Summers (1928). [This is the 1st. English translation of *Malleorum Quorundam Maleficarum.*]

State Papers, Calender of. Domestic Series of the Reign of Elizabeth 1581-1590 (1865).

Stationers of London, Registers of the Company of. 1554-1640 A.D., A Transcript, ed. E. Arber (5 vols., 1875-94) iii.

Statutes of the Realm, The. (1817), vols. iii-iv.

S[tevenson, William]. Mr. of Art. *A ryght pithy, pleasaunt and merie comedie; intytuled Gammer Gurtons nedle.* (Thomas Colwell, 1575); ed. J. S. Farmer, The Tudor Facsimile Texts (1910).

Stintzing, Roderich. *Geschichte der populären Literatur des römisch-kanonischen Rechts in Deutschland am Ende des fünfzehnten und im Anfang des sechszehnten Jahrhunderts* (Leipzig, 1867).

Stockum, T. C. van. 'Friedrich von Spee en de Heksen-processen', *Mededelingen der Koninklijke Akademie van Wetenschappen*, nieuwe reeks, xii (Amsterdam, 1949).

Stoll, Elmer Edgar. *Shakespeare Studies* (New York, 1927).

Stow, John. *The Annales of England* (Ralfe Newbery, 1600).

Stubbes, Philip. *The Anatomie of Abuses* (Richarde Jones, 1583); ed. F. J. Furnival (New Shakspeare Soc. 2 parts 1877-9).

S[tubbes]. Gent, P[hilip]. *A Christal Glasse for Christian Women* (Richard Ihones, 1591), in *The Anatomie of Abuses*; ed. F. J. Furnivall (New Shakspeare Society, 2 parts 1877-9) i.

Summers, A. M. *The History of Witchcraft and Demonology* (1926).

Tacitus, C. Cornelius. *Historiarum et Annalium Libri* (Antverpiae, 1574).

Tale of the Knight and His Wife, The. [from The Porkington MS.] in *The Life of St. Katharine*, etc. ed. J. Orchard Halliwell (Brixton Hill, 1848).

Talys, A. C. Mery. (Johannes Rastell, 1526), in *Shakespeare Jest Books* (qv) i. [From the unique copy at Göttingen.] [1st edn. 1525?].

Tamlane; in *The English and Scottish Popular Ballads*, ed. F. J. Child (qv), i.

T[arlton]. R[ichard]. *A prettie newe Ballad, intytuled: The Crowe sits vpon the wall, Please one and please all* (for Henry Kyrkham); in the *Huth Collection*, reprinted for J. Lilly (qv).

T[atham]. I[ohn]. *Grim The Collier of Croyden* (qv); or *The Devil and his Dame: with The Devil and Saint Dunstan*; in *Gratiae Theatrales or A choice Ternary of English Plays* (R.D., 1662).

Teresa [de Cepeda], Santa. *Los Libros de la Madre Teresa de Iesvs* (Al Salamanca, Por Guillelmo Foquel, 1588).

Theophilus. Niederdeutsches Schauspiel; hg. Hoffman von Fallersleben, Helmstädter MS (Hannover, 1854).

Thomas, Keith. *Religion and the Decline of Magic* (1971).

Thoms, W. J. *Early English Prose Romances* (3 vols., revised edn. 1858).

Thurston, H. 'Witchcaft', *Catholic Encyclopedia* (qv).

Towneley Mysteries, The; ed. Surtees Society, iii (1836).

Towneley Plays, The; ed. A. W. Pollard, EETS, e.s. lxxi (1897).

Traver, Hope. *The Four Daughters of God, Bryn Mawr College Monographs*, vi. (Bryn Mawr, Pennsylvania, 1907).

Troye, The wandring Prince of; in *Shirburn Ballads* (qv).

Unco Knicht's Wowing, The; in *The English and Scottish Popular Ballads*; ed. F. J. Child (qv), i.

Utley, F. L. 'The One hundred and Three Names of Noah's Wife', *Speculum,* xvi (Cambridge, Massachusetts, 1941).

Utterson, Edward Vernon. *Select Pieces of Early Popular Poetry* (2 vols. 1817).

Vann, Gerald. *Eve and the Gryphon* (1952).

Viret, P. *The worlde possessed with deuils* (Thomas Dawson for Ihon Perin, 1583).

Vives, Juan Luis. *Satellitium siue Symbola* (Brugis, 1524); in *Opuscula aliquot vere Catholica, ac imprimis erudita,* [1530?].

―――― *A very frutefull and pleasant boke called the Instructiō of a Christen womā.* (Thomas Berthelet [1529?]. [This is a translation by Richarde Hyrd of *De Institutione Foeminae Christianae,* Brugis, 1523].

―――― *The Instruction of a Christian Woman;* in *Vives and the Renascence Education of Women* ed. Foster Watson (1912).

―――― *The office and duetie of an husband* [1555?]. [This is a translation by Thomas Paynell of *de Officio Mariti,* Brugis, 1529].

Vocht, Henry de. *The Earliest English Translations of Erasmus' Colloquia 1536-1566.* (Louvain, 1928). [This contains two dialogues – *A Mery Dialogue Yᵉ Pylgremage of pure deuotyon,* and *Diuersoria*].

Vooys, C. G. N. de. *Middelnederlandsche Maria legenden* (2 delen, Leiden, 1903), i.

Vooys, C. G. N. de. *Middelnederlandsche Legenden en Exempelen* ('s Gravenhage, 1900).

Voragine, Jacobus de. *The Golden Legende* (Wynkyn de Worde, 1512). [First edn. W. Caxton, 1483. This is a translation by W. Caxton of the *Legenda Aurea,* 1470].

―――― *The Golden Legende* (W. Caxton, 1483), ed. F. S. Ellis (7 vols., 1900).

W., W. *A true and iust Recorde, of the Information Examination and Confession of all the Witches, taken at S. Oses in the countie of Essex* (Thomas Dawson, 1582).

Wager, Lewis, *A new Enterlude, The Life and Repentaunce of Marie Magdalene* (Iohn Charlewood, 1567); ed. J. Farmer, Tudor Facsimile Texts (1908). [First edn. 1566].

Wanton Wife of Bath, The; in T. Percy, *Reliques of Ancient English Poetry,* (3 vols., 1876-77), iii, [The poem does not occur in the earlier edition of 1794].

Warboys. *The most strange and admirable discouerie of the three Witches of Warboys* (Widdowe Orwin, for Thomas Man, and Iohn Winnington, 1593).

Ward, A. W. ed., *Marlowe's Doctor Faustus; Green's Friar Bacon and Friar Bungay.* (OCP., 4th edn., 1901).

Warton, Thomas. *The History of English Poetry;* revised edn. W. Carew Hazlitt, (4 vols., 1871).

Water-King, The. in M. G. Lewis, *(qv) Tales of Wonder,* i [The ballad is a translation from the Danish version in the Kiampe Viiser].

Waterhouse, O. *The Non-Cycle Mystery Plays,* EETS, e.s. CIV (1909).

Water o'Wearie's Well, The; in *The English and Scottish Popular Ballads,* ed. F. J. Child (qv), i.

Weston, William. The Autobiography of an Elizabethan. Translated from the Latin by Philip Caraman (qv) (1955).

Wier, Johannes. *De Praestigiis Daemonum et incantationibus ac ueneficijs,* Libri V. (Tertia Editione aucti, Basileae, per Ioannem Oporinum 1566). [1st. Latin edn. 1563; German translation by Fuglius, 1565; revised German translation by the author himself 1567].

―――― *De Praestigiis Daemonum, & incantationibus ac ueneficiis;* Libri sex (Basileae, 1583).

Wife wrapt in wether's skin, The; in *The English and Scottish Popular Ballads,* ed. F. J. Child (qv) v.

Wife lapped in Morels skin, The; in *Select Pieces of Early Popular Poetry* ed. E. V. Utterson (qv); ii.

Wildridge, T. Tindall. *The Grotesque in Church Art* (1899).

Wolthuis, G. W. *Duivelskunsten en Sprookjesgestalten* (Amsterdam, 1952).
Wright, Thomas. *A Selection of Latin Stories*; in *Early English Poetry, Ballads, and popular literature of the Middle Ages*, Percy Society, xxix (1842).
────── *Womankind in Western Europe* (1869).
York Civic Records, The House Books, ed. A. Raine, Y. A. S. Record Series. CVIII (1945); CX (1946).
York Diocesan Registry. Borthwick Institute, York, H[igh] C[ommission]. A[ct] B[ook]. 9 f. 20.
York Plays, The. ed. L. Toulmin Smith (OCP., 1885).

Manuscripts

Forrest, William. 'Of Theophilus'; in MS 'Harley 1703', 1572 [Brit. Mus.]
────── 'Of ladies foure'; in MS 'Harley 1703' 1572.
'Leendertz jr., Aantekeningen van Dr. P.' MS Verzameling L 16–30, doos XX B8 [Faustbronnen afgesloten 1923]. Universiteits Bibliotheek, Amsterdam.
'Ward, Vie de Mary'. Bar Convent MS 1650-57, Bar Convent, York. [This is a French translation of the English Life 'Brief Relation' written in Paris soon after 1645 by Mary Poyntz, probably assisted by W. Wigmore, Mary Ward's companions.]
Weston, William. 'Stonyhurst MSS Anglia A. 1, No 28', Anno circiter 1586 [contemp. endorsement]. [This is a letter by William Weston to Father Persons and signed E[dmund]. H[unt].]

Notes on illustrations

1 *Marikē van nieumeghen* (Willem Vorsterman, Antwerpen *ca.* 1518-19) Bayer. Staatsbibliothek München. Sig. Rar. 518 an.
Facs. uitgave A. L. Verhofstede (De Vlijt N .V., Antwerpen, 1951).

2 *Marikē van nieumeghen* (Willem Vorsterman, Antwerpen *ca.* 1518-19) Bayer. Staatsbibliothek München. Sig. Rar. 518 an.
Facs. uitgave A. L. Verhofstede (De Vlijt N. V., Antwerpen, 1951).

3 Günther Zainer [1471?] in Albert Schramm, *Der Bilderschmuck der Frühdrucke*, vol. ii (1920) no. 83.
By permission of Anton Hiersemann Verlag, Stuttgart.

4 Johannes Koelhoff, d. j., 'Sent Margareten Passie' (Darmstadt, 1495) in Albert Schramm's Collection, vol. viii (1924) no. 835.
By permission of Anton Hiersemann Verlag, Stuttgart.

5 Gotardo da ponto, *Una legenda molto bella Duna sanctissima ponzella (Margarita), etc.* (Milano, 1510) woodcut 28.
By courtesy of the British Museum.

6 From Johannes de Montevilla, *Itinerarius* (Bernhard Richel, 1474-82) in Albert Schramm's Collection, vol. xxi (1930) no. 443.
By permission of Anton Hiersemann Verlag, Stuttgart.

7 James I, *Daemonologie* (Edinb., Robert Walde-graue, 1597).
By courtesy of the University of London Library.

8 Sebastian Brant, *Stultifera Nauis*; tr. Alex. Barclay, *The Ship of Fooles* (John Cawood, 1570).
By courtesy of the University of London Library.

9 Ulricus Molitoris, *De Lamiis et Pythonicis Mulieribus* (Rutlingae *ca.* 1489).
By courtesy of the University of London Library.

10 Günther Zainer (Augsburg, 1475) in Albert Schramm's Collection, vol. ii (1920) no. 528.
By permission of Anton Hiersemann Verlag, Stuttgart.

11 Günther Zainer, in Albert Schramm's Collection, vol. ii (1920) no. 353 [1468-1478].
By permission of Anton Hiersemann Verlag, Stuttgart.

12 Diagram to illustrate the fall of the angels according to their guilt, based on Psellus, *de operatione daemonum*, cap. 8.

Index

For titles of works by authors in index see bibliography.
The letter 'n' after page numbers refers to footnotes only.